RECLAIMING LIBERTY

RECLAIMING LIBERTY

James Ronald Kennedy

Foreword by Walter Donald Kennedy

PELICAN PUBLISHING COMPANY

GRETNA 2005

The word "Pelican" and the depiction of a pelican are
trademarks of Pelican Publishing Company, Inc., and
are registered in the U.S. Patent and Trademark Office.

Library of Congress Cataloging-in-Publication Data

Kennedy, James Ronald.
  Reclaiming liberty / James Ronald Kennedy ; foreword by Walter
Donald Kennedy.
      p. cm.
  Includes bibliographical references and index.
  ISBN 9781589802759 (hardcover : alk. paper)
  1. Federal government—United States. 2. United States—Politics
and government—2001- 3. Libertarianism—United States. I. Title.

JK325.K397 2005
320.51'2—dc22   2004022432

Printed in the United States of America
Published by Pelican Publishing Company, Inc.
1000 Burmaster Street, Gretna, Louisiana 70053

This book is dedicated to two men whose writings and lives provide great inspiration to the author. The great vista of liberty and constitutional government that I see before all of us was not gained by my abilities but by studying the works of men such as Murray N. Rothbard and M. E. Bradford. They are two of the intellectual giants on whose shoulders I stand to see before us a day of liberty. This book is dedicated to the memory of these two great men.

Clearly the chances of converting those who are waxing fat by means of State exploitation are negligible, to say the least. Our hope is to convert the mass of the people who are being victimized by State power, not those who are gaining by it.

—Murray N. Rothbard
For a New Liberty: The Libertarian Manifesto
1978

Once Southern legislatures and courts have "dwindled down to the confined powers of a corporation," all complaints against the operations of an unlimited Northern power will be answered with something like, "Go; you are totally incapable of managing for yourselves. Go; mind your private affairs; trouble not yourselves with public concerns—Mind your business!"   —M. E. Bradford
Against the Barbarians and Other Reflections on Familiar Themes
1992

Contents

Foreword

In early 2003 *Dixie Daily News*[1] ran an article advocating that I challenge George Bush in the 2004 presidential primary. I had no knowledge of the article until I began getting e-mails from all across the country offering assistance and otherwise encouraging me to challenge the president. There is no doubt that many people are looking for some way to effect a change in America's leftist national character. In light of the positive response to a presidential bid, Ron and I sought to answer the following questions: (1) Could a presidential campaign be used as an educational effort to inform people about the need for and possibility of restoring the original constitutionally limited Republic of Republics? (2) Would the average Southerner and eventually all Americans rally to a nontraditional political campaign? (3) What solutions would we offer to resolve the problems of an out-of-control federal government?

The answer to the first question seemed rather simple. What better way to promote political and social ideas than during a political campaign? Generally the average person is too busy trying to make a living and tending to family matters to spend time contemplating politics. Other than a few short months during a political campaign, as citizens, our attention seldom turns to politics. Therefore, the best time to introduce new concepts is during these brief periods of political campaigning.

The second question required a little more contemplation. Would Southerners rally to a nontraditional campaign? Historically Southerners respond well to nontraditional campaigns, such as the States' Rights Democrats in the late 1940s and George Wallace's campaign in the late 1960s. It should be noted that Wallace's campaign was based in the South but made astounding inroads in the North. More recently, Ross Perot's campaign was one of the most successful nontraditional political campaigns of the twentieth century. The historical evidence certainly indicated that not only Southerners but also Americans in general have responded to a nontraditional presidential campaign.

The last question is the most vexing of all. It is always easy, and

---

1. www.southerncaucus.org.

part of our human nature, to be critical. To criticize is one thing, but it is much harder to offer well-thought-out solutions to difficult problems. The vast majority of conservatives are unhappy with the record of federal interventionism (regulations, guidelines, court orders, taxes, etc.), but how do we prevent these egregious federal intrusions? Most conservatives are unhappy with the federal government trampling upon (negating) the reserved rights of *we the people* of the states. Most conservatives believe that it is the right of the people of the states to legislate on such matters as (1) pornography, (2) abortion, (3) affirmative action, and (4) displaying of the Ten Commandments on state property. Also, most conservatives are enraged by unconstitutional federal actions such as (1) antigun laws that violate the Second Amendment, (2) environmental laws that violate a citizen's property rights, (3) hate-crime laws that deny equal protection under the law, and (4) inflation that robs working people of the value of their earned income. Obviously, we could go down an almost endless list of unconstitutional federal intrusions into the reserved rights of the people and the states. There is plenty to complain about, but the question remained—what plan could we offer to correct these problems?

The answer to this last question led to the writing of this book. Ron and I are convinced that no solution is acceptable unless it provides a remedy for all problems arising from an out-of-control federal government. We see our current political situation as one in which *we the people* have become the captives and pawns of a liberal/socialist political system. As we see it, no solution is acceptable if it leaves the current system in place! Our aim is to overthrow—in a peaceful and political manner—the current liberal/socialist political system and replace it with a Liberty-Based Society. Anything less would be tantamount to treating the symptoms while ignoring the underlying pathology—the real cause of the disease. Endlessly treating the symptoms and not the underlying pathology is a sure formula for disaster. What good would a physician be if you came to him with an irritating rash caused by a virulent infection and he only gave you medicine to make the rash feel better? The visible symptom, the rash, is a clinical clue to the physician that there is an underlying disease process (pathology) that must be treated in order to effect a *permanent* cure. During the past century, conservative "leaders" have calmed the rage of rank-and-file conservatives against big government by offering to treat the symptoms, but never have they offered to solve the real problem, that is, the malignant growth of big government. By establishing a Liberty-Based Society as described in this book, we will cure the disease and save the patient.

This book is the opening salvo in a historical movement to regain our lost rights. The overthrow of the current liberal/socialist political system will not be accomplished by one political campaign. The initial political campaign will be a precursor of or catalyst for future campaigns by advocates of liberty all across the country.

A political campaign contesting the next Republican presidential primary will be the *starting point* of this political revolution. Who our candidate will be is yet to be decided. That decision will be made by those individuals who, over the next several years, provide the human and financial resources necessary to promote the idea of a Liberty-Based Society. It must be made clear from the outset that if this movement is to be a success it must be based upon individuals who put aside their differences and work together to actualize their vision of a better country. A movement based on a charismatic leader is doomed to ultimate failure. Wallace and Perot are examples of men leading what appeared to be a successful and growing movement, yet when they left the scene, "their" movements collapsed. As explained in the last chapter of this book, the ultimate political goal is to establish a political movement that will support the election of men and women in offices all across the South and beyond. A single charismatic leader or even several leaders will not create a successful liberty movement. But when people are excited about the possibility of creating a *new* and *better* society, they can and will establish a successful liberty movement.

This book advocates radical changes in our society. Special-interest groups and those who profit from their close connections with big government will not go away without a fight. Big financial houses in New York that have profited for generations stand to lose if we are successful. In a Liberty-Based Society, friends of the Federal Reserve and proponents of fiat money will no longer be able to foist inflation and a perpetual boom-bust economy on *we the people.* Our gain will be their loss. You can expect no quarter from these enemies of working men and women. Those who profit by engaging in racial politics will scream "racism" with a passion. The liberal media will pick up the chant of racism and carry it forth to America as if it had come from the mouth of God. Those who enlist in the liberty movement will be taking on the entire liberal/socialist establishment plus the business-as-usual conservative "leaders." These so-called "leaders" have proven to be more concerned with reelecting incumbents than with defending *and* reclaiming our lost rights. The legion of liberty will find very few friends on the left or right.

Contemporary conservatives are faced with a dilemma. They have elected the president, witnessed a Supreme Court mostly appointed by conservative presidents, and elected majorities in both houses of Congress; yet, even under these circumstances, we see a federal government expanding at a faster rate than any time since the days of LBJ's Great Society. If conservatives continue doing business the same way they always have, then we will go on traveling the road toward less freedom. If you like the current left-of-center political system, if you like having government extort between 40 and 60 percent of your income—in essence, if you like more government and less freedom—then keep doing what is already being done. But if you want to change our political system to one based on liberty, then read this book and join the liberty movement.

Deo Vindice

WALTER DONALD KENNEDY[2]

---

2. Walter Donald Kennedy is coauthor of *The South Was Right!, Why Not Freedom! America's Revolt Against Big Government,* and *Was Jefferson Davis Right?* He is the author of *Myths of American Slavery.* www.kennedytwins.com.

RECLAIMING LIBERTY

Rush Limbaugh Meets Uncle Seth[1]

Uncle Seth, a long-departed Confederate veteran, would occasionally obtain a pass from St. Gabriel to come down to check on his Southern kinsmen. The old vet fought more battles with the South's enemies after the War for Southern Independence than he did during the "shooting" war. Today he decided to appear (impolite people would call it "haunt") at the Federal Empire's Capitol. With a little help from "upstairs," he managed a private conversation with the leading federal supremacist of the day—none other than Rush Limbaugh, who just happened to be waiting to confer with some of his political supporters.

Rush stood in amazement as the old Confederate veteran materialized before his eyes. Uncle Seth calmly studied the famous pundit. "Just wanted to know how the Constitution is faring," he said.

"Things are great," Rush replied. "We have a Republican president, we control both houses of Congress, and the Supreme Court is mostly full of Republican appointments. It's a great day for the party of Lincoln!" Rush had quickly regained his composure and could not resist an opportunity to remind the old man of just who had won the war.

"Well, then, young man," Uncle Seth spoke slowly as he sized up his opponent, "I guess you all have rolled back all of FDR's socialist legislation."

"Well, no," Rush responded in a tone that was almost apologetic. "But we've got the liberals on the run."

"Appears to me like they are making a run on what's left of your liberties," Uncle Seth replied. "What about the war tax your man Lincoln started—you know, that there income tax? Word is that you all got that one back. Done anything about it lately?"

Rush stared coldly at the old veteran. Uncle Seth could tell that Rush was becoming agitated with his inquiries, but he was determined to find out why this guy was so popular down South.

"What's the word on states' rights these days, young man?" Uncle Seth bore in with his questioning. "You all still respect the limitations imposed by the Ninth and Tenth amendments? Seems to me like just about everything you complain about could be corrected if the people were allowed to nullify all of those intrusive federal laws, court orders, and bureaucratic guidelines."

"You Southern people are crazy! You're a nut, one of those crackpot conservatives that give good loyal Republicans a bad name," complained Rush. "You guys want to take us back to the days of moonlight and magnolias, to a time when you could own people." Rush was getting red-faced and his voice strident. "You all are traitors. You want to break up the country and destroy our great nation!"

Uncle Seth slowly faded away. He was anxious to return to a better place, where evil was not excused and good always triumphs over evil.

"'States' rights'!" muttered Rush. "The very idea—this is the twenty-first century." Then a brilliant thought came to him. "Perhaps I should give it a little lip service every now and then."

1. James Ronald Kennedy, "Uncle Seth Fought the Yankees" (www.kennedytwins.com).

CHAPTER 1

Conservatism: A Century of Failure

The twentieth century in America witnessed glorious victories for those who believe in extreme federalism, big government, central control, liberalism, and socialism. Conservatives, on the other hand, can look back with shame at one humiliating defeat after another. At best, conservatives have had moments of brilliant but vain rhetoric; at worst, they have been reduced to serving as the guardians of the status quo, i.e., the keepers of yesterday's liberal/socialist victories. Freed from the necessity of protecting their prior successes, liberals/socialists busied themselves with even more onerous intrusions into the once sacred arena of individual liberty.

We Southerners tend to identify ourselves as politically conservative, and the South's voting record in the presidential elections of the last fifty years demonstrates a definite conservative leaning. The South's transformation from solidly Democratic to solidly Republican shows its adherence to traditional conservative values. In the late 1940s, the Democratic party renounced its traditional support of limited federalism and states' rights. Over the next twenty years liberals slowly seized control of the Democratic party and ejected conservative Southern delegates. The entire South was forced to choose between party loyalty (with all the perks and power attached to said party) and loyalty to its traditional conservative values of limited federalism, states' rights, and individual liberty. By 1970 it had become apparent that these traditional values were no longer shared by the majority of Americans. The conservative (primarily white) South had become America's only unrepresentative, and therefore, disposable minority! Current history demonstrates that the South's adherence to its traditional values transcends party loyalty. The South has stood firm in her allegiance to constitutional principles even though no major political party has seriously championed these values for over 150 years. Like a soldier who holds his position in the face of overwhelming force, the South has remained committed to the principles of the original constitutional Republic of Republics as handed down to us from the Founding Fathers.

But this raises a very interesting question. Are Southerners really conservatives, as defined in the contemporary political environment? If so, what are we trying to conserve? At the very core of conservative values is the belief in a Jeffersonian republic. States' rights and a constitutionally limited federal government are the hallmarks of Southern conservative political values. The writings of the Founding Fathers, both the Federalist and especially the anti-Federalist,[1] serve as the basis for Southern political philosophy. These writings were followed by the Resolves of 1798, penned by Thomas Jefferson and James Madison. In these famous (but almost unknown today) documents, Jefferson and Madison proclaimed the states' rights view that dominated the American political landscape until 1860. This view asserted that, within the original constitutional system, *we the people* of the Sovereign States have a right to use any method necessary to prevent an abusive Federal government from infringing upon those rights reserved to the states and the people thereof.[2]

During the 1840s, John C. Calhoun, as vice-president and then as senator from South Carolina, proclaimed the right, nay, the duty of the states to interpose their sovereign authority between an abusive Federal government and *we the people* of the states. Indeed, Calhoun demonstrated that the Founding Fathers were right when they promised Americans that the states would always be able to defend themselves against an abusive Federal government, provided we were armed with the defensive powers of Sovereign States within a limited Federal republic. Writing in *The Federalist Papers,* Alexander Hamilton declared, "We may safely rely on the disposition of the State legislatures to erect barriers against the encroachments of the national authority."[3]

From this short outline of our Southern political history, one can see that the South has been traditionally conservative—that is, we have used our political influence to conserve, preserve, and maintain a strong Constitution that sought to limit the powers of the federal government and preserve the vital and necessary right of the Sovereign States to protect its citizens from any encroachments upon their reserved rights.

1. James Ronald Kennedy and Walter Donald Kennedy, *Why Not Freedom!: America's Revolt Against Big Government* (Gretna, La.: Pelican, 1995), 23-32.

2. For a discussion of the Resolves of 1798, see James Ronald Kennedy and Walter Donald Kennedy, *Was Jefferson Davis Right?* (Gretna, La.: Pelican, 1998), 281-85.

3. Alexander Hamilton, as cited in Kennedy and Kennedy, *Why Not Freedom!,* 37.

"But what happened to states' rights?" one may ask. The sad fact of American history is that as U.S. Supreme Court chief justice Salmon P. Chase declared in 1868, "State Sovereignty died at Appomattox."[4] Even more telling are the words of the governor of Illinois in 1865, who declared that the War for Southern Independence had "tended, more than any other event in the history of the country, to militate against the Jeffersonian idea that the best government is that which governs least."[5] Why is it that today *we the people* of the states are powerless when confronted with costly, unfunded federal mandates? Why is it that *we the people* of the states no longer have the liberty to decide how we will manage our local public schools? Why is it that private real estate owned by a citizen of a state cannot be developed without first gaining permission from the federal "Wetlands Gestapo"? The answer is simple and sad. In America's contemporary political system, ideas such as states' rights, a constitutionally limited federal government, local control, and individual liberty are dead! Southern conservatives have spent the last century trying to preserve a political system that no longer exists. To make matters worse, liberals have known this all along, while our contemporary conservative leaders are either too foolish to recognize it or are too cowardly to admit it! How did we get to this point? How did we become the keepers of an extinguished flame? This mystery must be resolved before we begin our campaign to rekindle the flame of liberty.

American conservatism entered the twentieth century with a political philosophy so fatally flawed that it had no real means to defend itself from the attacks of those wanting to expand the powers of the federal government. The failure of conservatives to recognize their inherent vulnerability set the stage for a century of conservative defeat, retreat, and retrenchment. By the end of the twentieth century, no "right thinking" conservative could be found advocating a return to the original constitutional federalism, where the federal government was secondary and state and local control of limited government was primary. Today, neoconservatives focus their efforts on political schemes to regain control of the Federal Empire, with no concern about restoring the original constitutionally limited Republic of Republics as created by the Founding Fathers. Too often in history the new century is held captive by the mistakes of the prior century. Today, as we peer into the possibilities of a new century, we

4. As cited in James Ronald Kennedy and Walter Donald Kennedy, *The South Was Right!* (Gretna, La.: Pelican, 1994), 219.

5. Gov. Richard Yates, as cited in Kennedy and Kennedy, *Was Jefferson Right?*, 238.

need to understand the errors of the last century and take those steps necessary to make sure we do not repeat those errors. Therefore, it is imperative that we understand the origins of conservatism's twentieth-century fatal flaw.

1900: NEW CENTURY—OLD FALLACIES

Conservatives carried into the twentieth century the mistaken belief that, under our system of constitutional government, an agency of the federal government, specifically the federal Supreme Court, was the final arbiter of the extent of federal power. This anti-states' rights fallacy in effect disarmed the common man and placed him defenseless before an all-powerful federal government. Today, even conservatives in the South are shocked to hear that the federal Supreme Court was *not* established by the Founding Fathers as the final arbiter of the constitutional prerogatives of the federal government![6] The rapid growth and total dominance of the federal government that occurred during the twentieth century were made possible due to the following "conservative"[7] defeats brought forward from the nineteenth century.

Controlling the Money, Controlling the People

By 1900 the concept of a centrally controlled bank or a federally sponsored national banking system had become generally accepted. During Pres. George Washington's first term, a controversy arose between commercial interests (principally New York, Philadelphia, and the New England states) and the agrarian states of the South as to whether or not the Constitution allowed the federal government to establish a national bank. Alexander Hamilton championed the commercial interests and argued in favor of a national bank, while Thomas Jefferson championed the agrarian interests, which opposed a government-controlled banking system. Hamilton used a constitutional argument that became known as "loose construction" to rationalize the use of federal money and prestige to establish the bank. Jefferson, on the other hand, using "strict construction," argued that if the Constitution did not specifically provide authority for the establishing of a national bank, then it would be unconstitutional for the federal government to assign such powers unto

---

6. This principle is too extensive to cover here, but it is covered extensively in Kennedy and Kennedy, *Why Not Freedom!*, *Was Jefferson Davis Right?*, and *The South Was Right!*

7. The term *conservative* as applied to pre-twentieth-century statesmen would include those who in their time were known as anti-Federalists, Jeffersonian Republicans, Andy Jackson Democrats, strict constructionists, or Confederates.

itself.[8] Jefferson knew that the monied interests would use their political influence to benefit themselves at the expense of yeoman farmers and common laborers. (The technique used by central bankers to enrich themselves at our expense will be discussed in chapter 8.) The Northern commercial interests won the argument and "loose construction" of the Constitution ushered in the Bank of the United States, demonstrating its effectiveness in undermining constitutional restraints on the expansion of federal powers.

Murray N. Rothbard (1926-95), a well-known twentieth-century economist, described the efforts of central banking proponents:

> Throughout the first century of the Republic, the party favoring a Central Bank, first the Hamiltonian High Federalists, then the Whigs and then the Republicans, was the party of Big Central Government, of a large public debt, of high protective tariffs, of large-scale public works, and of subsidies to large businesses in that early version of "partnership between government and industry." Protective tariffs were to subsidize domestic manufactures, while paper money, fractional reserve banking, and Central Banking were all advocated by the nationalists as part of a comprehensive policy of inflation and cheap credit in order to benefit favored businesses. These favorites were firms and industries that were part of the financial elite, centered from the beginning through the Civil War in Philadelphia and New York, with New York assuming the first place after the end of that war.[9]

By 1900 the proponents of unlimited federal power had in place a federalized central banking system that would allow them to finance favored government programs via the indirect tax of inflation—thereby avoiding the messy process of passing new taxes—while enriching their favored banking clientele by allowing them to issue unsupported credit. With inflation, the politicians could vote for expenditures without having to answer to the public. As inflation gradually worked itself through the economy, the last people in the inflation/unsupported-credit pyramid scheme would eventually pay the price—but the last people, though great in numbers, had no one in Washington dedicated to protecting their rights! So it was and so it remains, at least until we do something about it.

8. Forrest McDonald, *A Constitutional History of the United States* (Malabar, Fla.: Kriger, 1982), 42.

9. Murray N. Rothbard, *The Case Against the Fed* (Auburn, Ala.: Ludwig von Mises Institute, 1994), 72-73.

The Fraudulent Fourteenth and Fifteenth Amendments

After the tragic conclusion of the War for Southern Independence in 1865, the Northern power elite used their control of the newly established Federal Empire to pass several onerous amendments. The Fourteenth and Fifteenth amendments were passed while the Southern states were under military rule. The assent of the Southern states to these amendments was gained at the point of federal bayonets! There is no provision in the Constitution that would allow Congress to use military force to gain a state's ratification of a proposed amendment. Therefore these amendments were enacted via unconstitutional compulsion, and even though they were declared ratified, they remain a perversion of our original Constitution. (See Addendum XII for more information regarding the fraudulent Fourteenth Amendment.)

The federal government forced the South to accept a radical change in the nature of the government as the price for "readmission" into the "Union" from which she had formerly been denied the right to secede. The Radical Republicans in control of the federal government at the time never had the needed votes to constitutionally submit these amendments to the states nor the influence to gain the requisite number of ratifications from the states. Despite this handicap, these amendments were declared to be a part of the Constitution.[10] Aside from the fact that constitutional and parliamentary procedures were trampled upon and the free and unfettered consent of the people of the South was destroyed, the most important result of the unconstitutional enactment of these amendments was that, for the first time in American history, the federal government was given the authority to enforce its mandates upon *we the people* of the states. Furthermore, the people of once Sovereign States (both North and South) were denied any alternative to unconstitutional actions of the federal government but to accept and obey the will of the federal government. The Federal Empire is now established; the emperor speaks and his subjects dutifully obey!

The Fifteenth Amendment destroyed the right of the people of the states to establish reasonable qualifications for voting. Thus, in our day we have motor voter laws and laws allowing people to register to vote when they sign up for welfare. The franchise is now used as a means of legalized looting. The more numerous class of tax consumers flock to the polls to vote for professional politicians who promise to redistribute wealth from the productive members of society via tax-and-spend federalism. Incumbency has been assured for

10. Kennedy and Kennedy, *The South Was Right!*, 167-76.

the politician who promises the most to the most—paid for of course by middle-class taxpayers.[11] (Legitimate, nonarbitrary voting qualifications will be dealt with in detail in chapter 7.)

In the meantime an activist federal judiciary has used the judicial theory of incorporation to turn the limitations imposed on the federal government by the Founding Fathers in the so-called Bill of Rights into a grant of unlimited federal power over *we the people* of the states. Even though the right of secession and implicitly nullification/interposition and other rights originally reserved by the states were suppressed by overwhelming military force during the War for Southern Independence, these rights in theory still remained and were protected by the U.S. Constitution as late as 1866. The Northern power elite who controlled the federal government recognized this and used these two fraudulent amendments to remove states' rights from the American political system.

By the time Reconstruction rule was overturned and legitimate Southern representatives were seated, the harm had already been accomplished. The Southern members of Congress were forced to tacitly accept the radical and unconstitutional alterations in exchange for an unspoken détente with the Northern power elite. Through this unspoken agreement, the South was allowed to nominally control their states and the North agreed that it would not reinstate Reconstruction upon the South. The South, prior to the war, had been America's champion of limited federalism and states' rights, but now she is forced to accept the new centralized governmental order imposed on her from Washington, D.C.[12] Conservatives at the beginning of the twentieth century blindly held to their faith that the mode of American government was essentially the same as that handed down by the Founding Fathers. Conservatives' refusal to recognize and react to the paradigm shift that had occurred during the nineteenth century set the stage for a liberal/socialist takeover of America's political vision in the following century.

Jim Crow and Racial Antagonism

When the thirteen American colonies seceded from their union with Great Britain[13] in 1776, the British attempted to incite slave revolts in the colonies by offering to emancipate all slaves who left their masters and joined the British. To the dismay of the British, most slaves

---

11. Kennedy and Kennedy, *Why Not Freedom!*, 181-93.
12. Kennedy and Kennedy, *The South Was Right!*, 241.
13. Kennedy and Kennedy, *Was Jefferson Davis Right?*, 258.

rejected the offer. Lincoln attempted the same thing during the War for Southern Independence, but with no more success. The relationship between white and black Southerners has mystified observers from the beginning of the Republic. This relationship held for the most part even in the harsh years of invasion and occupation during both wars (1776 and 1861). But it could not withstand the assaults of Reconstruction imposed by the federal government.

During Reconstruction the government managed to do what the British and Lincoln could not—turn race into a political issue. The Radical Republicans promised the newly freed slaves "forty acres and a mule" if they voted against their former masters. Unfortunately for the former slaves, the promise (like thousands of promises to follow) was never kept! But Reconstruction did drive a wedge of mistrust between two peoples who had more in common with each other than either had with the Radical Republican power elite who controlled an all-powerful federal government. Jim Crow (white supremacy) laws enacted after the end of Reconstruction reinforced this racial mistrust.

Most people think of segregation laws as something imposed upon blacks by evil Southern legislatures. But these laws were based upon Black Codes established by Union general Ben ("Beast") Butler after he invaded and occupied New Orleans during the war. Indeed, by the early 1900s racial segregation was a fact by law (*de jure*) or by socially enforced tradition (*de facto*). White society in the North as well as the South believed in and practiced racial segregation. The infamous *Plessy* v. *Ferguson* case, in which the United States Supreme Court codified racial segregation laws (Jim Crow laws), was based upon precedent set by a Massachusetts law passed in the 1840s. The federal judges who approved Jim Crow were, with only one exception, Northerners. The chief justice who presided over the deliberation was from Michigan. The only Southerner on the court came from a family that formerly owned slaves and for a short while he had owned slaves. This Southerner was the only dissenting vote in the now infamous Jim Crow decision.[14] But despite these little-known and ironic facts, the South has been forced to bear the cross for the "sin" of racial segregation.

This racial divide played into the hands of those who wanted to keep the South politically weak and on the defensive. Liberals of the twentieth century saw the South as their greatest enemy, the one foe who would not accept their socializing schemes to enlarge the role of the federal government. The more the South fought such schemes as

14. Kermit L. Hall, ed., *The Oxford Companion to the Supreme Court of the United States* (New York: Oxford University Press, 1992), 361.

Social Security, the more determined the liberals were to use black voters just as the Radical Republicans had during Reconstruction to neutralize Southern conservative resistance to liberal federal social-welfare programs. And so the South, which was a major part of the twentieth-century conservative movement, entered that century with a racial vulnerability that begged for liberal exploitation. By the end of the century, Southern conservative political power was not even a shadow of what it had been at the beginning. Jim Crow was a two-edged sword—it cut all Southerners, black and white.

1913—The Federal Income Tax Reappears

The reappearance of the federal income tax at the beginning of the twentieth century is an excellent example of how the failure of one generation of conservatives can have an enormous negative impact on the property rights and liberty of successive generations. In 1910, total federal revenues as a percent of gross domestic product (GDP) were only 1.9 percent. Today, after almost a century of liberal-sponsored "progressive" income tax, total federal revenues amount to 18.2 percent of GDP.[15] In 1913, when the income tax was adopted, there were only 400 pages of federal tax rules. During the twentieth century, one conservative defeat after another allowed those rules to grow to 45,000 pages. If that rate continues, by 2099 the American tax slave will have to comply with more than five million pages of rules![16] It's long past time to do something about the federal tax monster.

The income tax was first introduced in America during the Lincoln administration as a way to finance his war against the Southern people. This tax and inflationary paper money (green-backs) were used to fleece Northern citizens during the war. As more paper money, unsupported by gold, is issued, inflation drives up prices, and eventually wages will make some adjustments upward. Because the income tax is not indexed to inflation, workers who are paid at inflated wages are pushed "progressively" into higher tax brackets even though their real earnings have not improved. This "invisible inflation tax" results in a revenue windfall for politicians. They collect more revenue but can go home and brag to their constituents that they never voted for a tax increase. Some politicians claim they have indexed the income-tax system, but what they have done is index the deductions, which, as we all know, are not a dollar-for-dollar deduction for taxpayers. A real index would reduce the

15. "Total Federal Revenues, 1900-2003 (Percent of GDP)" (www.cato.org, 2002).
16. Ibid.

income that is subject to taxation by the rate of inflation *before* deductions are applied. Best of all would be just to get rid of the entire system!

At the beginning of the last century, the U.S. Supreme Court ruled the income tax to be unconstitutional. Conservatives celebrated while liberals and other self-anointed "progressives" plotted. Congress soon asked the states to overrule the Supreme Court by ratifying the Sixteenth Amendment, establishing constitutional authority for the present income tax. Conservatives railed against it but quickly forgot about it and moved on to other issues. This would become an all-too-common pattern. Advocates of big government, centralized federalism, and socialist social policy would advance a selected cause; conservatives would protest; populist propaganda and "learned elites" would insist that it was very "progressive" and would only cost the rich; conservatives would eventually "compromise" enough to allow the legislation to pass; and thereafter conservatives would attempt to incorporate the legislation into their party platform. The liberals/progressives won and were then free from any concern of a conservative counterattack. Even after 100 years, the pattern continues to repeat itself. Liberals push the envelope of progressive taxation, socialist social programs, and conservative compromises, i.e., surrender by degrees. *Conservatives never regain rights once they are lost.* How many times must it be said? The last century has been one of conservative failure. Our current income tax is an excellent case in point.

1913—America Welcomes Central Banking with the Creation of the Fed

The theory of "loose construction" of the Constitution was first used by Federalist Hamilton during President Washington's first term. Hamilton used it to read into the Constitution powers not specifically granted to the government. His efforts were directed at the establishment of the Bank of the United States. Jefferson opposed a central bank because he knew that it would be used by the favored few and its excesses would eventually be paid for by taxpayers. Andrew Jackson's Democrats opposed it for similar reasons.[17] However, Lincoln and his fellow Republicans used their control of the government to push through various monetary policies during the War for Southern Independence. Federal control of monetary and banking policy was an accepted fact by the time legitimate Southern representatives and senators returned to Washington after

17. McDonald, *A Constitutional History*, 72-74.

Reconstruction. The primary financial argument was between a gold standard and an inflationary silver standard. The monied interests in New York, primarily the Morgan and Rockefeller families,[18] were vocal proponents of federal control of money and banking. They were close to the source of power and could logically expect to, and in fact did, benefit from such governmental policies.

In 1913 Congress created the Federal Reserve. It was established due to assurances that it would be able to control disruptive business cycles, panics, and bank runs. Conservatives accepted the Fed and today can be counted on as its main "business" defenders. The Fed has evolved into America's answer to central banking. Conservatives have ignored the warnings by sound-money economists that government-sponsored, monopolistic banks are inflationary. Conservatives should know that central banks that are allowed, even encouraged, to create money out of thin air (fiat money) and expand the money supply via unsupported credit are inflationary. The Fed's monetary policies will stimulate the economy for a while, but eventually the boom turns into a bust and someone has to pay for the preceding bad investment. As with any Ponzi or pyramid scheme, those close to the source will benefit while those farther away will end up "holding the bag." The failure of conservatives to stand up for the "little man" is the result of a century of conservative fatal flaws. The only economic theory that would provide protection to the taxpayer happens to be the only one rejected by liberals and conservatives. The Austrian[19] theory as espoused by Rothbard stands for sound money and liberty. Unfortunately, by the end of the twentieth century, mainstream conservatives had rejected sound money as well as liberty.

The Twentieth Century—100 Years Away from the Gold Standard

Economist Murray N. Rothbard divides America's monetary breakdown into nine phases.[20] Phase I is the Classical Gold Standard, which lasted from 1815 until 1914. The gold standard was important because it helped keep in check the inflationary tendency of all governments. As we have already seen, inflationary economic policies can be used as an indirect tax upon citizens. Phase II occurred during World War I, when European nations went off the gold standard in order to finance their war efforts. Because the United States entered the war much later, it did not drop the gold standard. The

18. Rothbard, *The Case Against the Fed,* 90-101.
19. See www.mises.org for more information on Austrian economic principles.
20. Murray N. Rothbard, *What Has Government Done to Our Money?* (Auburn, Ala.: Ludwig von Mises Institute, 1963), 90-111.

important point for conservatives to remember is that a *warfare* state is just as dangerous to liberty as is a *welfare* state. Rothbard noted, "It was not gold that failed; it was the folly of trusting government to keep its promises."[21] Phase II was the beginning of international disaster as nations began to abandon the gold standard. Rothbard wrote, "The grave political flaw is to hand total control of the money supply to the Nation-State, and then to hope and expect that the State will refrain from using that power."[22]

The problem that conservatives refused to deal with was that "the dollar was artificially undervalued and most other currencies overvalued by 1945, the dollar was made scarce, and the world suffered from a so-called dollar shortage, which the American taxpayer was supposed to be obligated to make up by foreign aid."[23] In 1971 Republican president Richard M. Nixon took the U.S. completely off the gold standard and converted the dollar into fiat money—with nothing to back it up except a government promise.

Conservatives have been handmaidens to the destruction of our money. Both political parties have engaged in, encouraged, and politically benefited from the move from sound money backed by gold to fiat currency backed by nothing. This artificially created economic system sets the stage for severe and sometimes catastrophic boom-bust cycles. In an economy of fiat currency and unsupported credit, those bankers and special-interest groups close to government benefit during the boom phase. Those of us who have no connections to the Fed or the power brokers in government will ultimately pay the price during the bust phase. From a monetary-policy point of view, it is evident that over the last century conservatives have abandoned the middle-class taxpayers.

1933—Social Security Is Socialism by Any Other Name

The classic twentieth-century example of conservative failure is their enfeebled protest against and eventual embracing of FDR's socializing program of Social Security. On August 14, 1935, with very little public or congressional debate, FDR signed into law the Social Security Act. FDR, in a masterstroke of political savvy, introduced socialism to America and assured its acceptance by calling it "insurance" instead of social welfare payments. In prior decades, the American Socialist Party had called for the passage of a social pension plan. Democrat Al Smith

21. Ibid., 94.
22. Ibid., 99.
23. Ibid., 100.

declared that FDR and company had "caught the Socialists swimming and ran away with their clothes."[24] FDR assured the public that the law would control the wide economic swings of the business cycle and tame the evils of deflation and inflation.

The ardent socialists who had spent their lives pushing for a nationalized economy were disappointed because the law did not go far enough! FDR allayed their complaints by promising that much more was coming.[25] (Indeed, conservatives got a hint of just how much more was coming when, toward the end of World War II, FDR proposed a 100 percent tax on all income above $25,000.)[26]

For the first time in American history, massive social programs were being concocted by "experts" in faraway Washington, D.C. and forced upon citizens. The sufferings caused by the Great Depression made it easier to convince the public to accept this socialist scheme. The liberal/socialist power elites claimed that big government could use fiscal policies to inject inflation into a depressed economy, thereby jumpstarting it. Social Security would introduce fiat money into the economy and make a huge portion of the population dependent on political elites in Washington. For the socialists, it was a great way to move the United States away from a free-market economy, establish Washington's control over the economy, and make serfs out of American citizens, who until then had been ardent individualists. (It is not lost on contemporary politicians that 43 million Americans get monthly Social Security checks, and they all vote.)

Social Security introduced the idea to Americans that they were not competent to take care of themselves and therefore required elites and experts working out of an enormous bureaucracy in Washington to take care of the average—and presumably incompetent—person. Gone were the concepts of thrift, self-help, and community that the pioneers had used to build America. In fact, one of the many unforeseen consequences of government intervention via Social Security is the continuing erosion of family ties, as government bureaucrats take over where once family stood. As Gregory Bresiger wrote:

> Prior to 1935, social insurance for Americans was not a government responsibility. It was entirely private. One got help through the community, fraternal groups, and above all, the family.[27]

24. Gregory Bresiger, *The Revolution of 1935: The Secret History of Social Security* (Auburn, Ala.: Ludwig von Mises Institute, 2002), 8.
   25. Ibid., 1.
   26. Ibid., 51.
   27. Ibid., 18.

Before the Social Security Act passed, the best remedy for and prevention of social sufferings was considered to be a strong economy. However, the promise of taming and controlling the swings of the business cycles made by those central planners who pushed through the Federal Reserve Act in 1913 had obviously not materialized by the time of the Great Depression. Yet, despite their failure to prevent the depression, here they were a mere twenty-two years later attempting to use the medicine of greater central control to cure the disease that their programs had caused![28]

By 1935 many social scientists and self-proclaimed political experts had given up on America's political system of liberty and free-market capitalism. One of these experts, Abraham Epstein, declared that "our modern system of industrial production has rendered our lives insecure to the point of despair." He blamed the depression on "the blind greed and stupidity of our business leaders."[29] He thought that the only way to end the Great Depression was with the strong control of a centralized government. These liberals/socialists blamed the depression on the failure of the market, but in reality it was a result of government's intrusive and perverting influence in the market.[30]

FDR, along with other liberals and socialists, believed that the American free-enterprise system would slowly evolve into a quasi-socialist system. It is hard to believe today, but in the mid-1930s many looked longingly toward Hitler's National Socialist Germany and wanted America to adopt some of Stalin's Marxist socialist and Hitler's National Socialist programs.[31] The gallant liberty warrior, Llewellyn H. Rockwell, Jr., noted the connection between fascist socialism and its 1930s American socialist counterpart:

> The links among socialism, fascism, and political developments in the United States were not lost on the intelligentsia. In 1933, the same year that Franklin Delano Roosevelt abolished the gold standard, created the Tennessee Valley Authority, established the Civil Conservation Corps, and regimented industry under the National Industrial Recovery Act, that same year, the *New York Times Magazine* published glowing reports on the brilliance and vision of Professor Mussolini, even as academic treatises heralded the advances made by the central planning

28. See Murray N. Rothbard, *America's Great Depression* (Auburn, Ala.: Ludwig von Mises Institute).

29. Bresiger, *The Revolution of 1935*, 40-41.

30. See Rothbard, *America's Great Depression*.

31. Bresiger, *The Revolution of 1935*, 22, 68.

movement from Moscow, to Berlin, to Washington.

We must not flatter ourselves into thinking that the poison of totalitarian ideology infected only Russia and European states. What has happened in the United States differs in degree, not in kind. New Deal planners looked to Russia as a model for organizing the agricultural sector, and were inspired by an Italian fascist theoretician in imposing the NIRA and the Blue Eagle. And by way of further illustration, consider that in 1936 the economic treatise by English economist John Maynard Keynes that provided the economic rationale for the New Deal appeared in Germany, with an introduction by Keynes himself.[32]

FDR and his vice-president Henry Wallace believed in and worked for the "convergence" theory, which held that the United States' and Russia's economic and political policies would eventually converge into one system. For example, Wallace advocated the New Deal idea that the government "balance" the economy—i.e., control production and consumption—which is after all the very essence of socialism.[33] And no doubt Stalin smiled approvingly upon these tentative steps toward total central control. Thus we see in a nutshell the transition of American free-market individualism to our present quasi-socialist economy, in which almost 60 percent of our economy is controlled by the bureaucratic planners in Washington, D.C.

The corruption of both political parties by the lure of easy votes via Social Security payments can be seen by looking at the party platform of the Democratic party. It previously had been the traditional champion of states' rights and sound money (i.e., gold standard). Even as late as 1932 the Democratic party platform called for a balanced budget, sound money, and a 25 percent reduction in federal spending.[34] During the 1920s, Republicans won numerous elections by running on their record of reducing federal spending, cutting taxes, and dismantling government regulatory bureaucracies that had been developed to control the economy during World War I.[35] By 1935 FDR and his gang of liberals/socialists had seized control of the former states' rights Democratic party.

The Republicans were a little more timid as they approached socialist programs, their erstwhile mortal enemy, but they quickly overcame their reserve. In 1944 Frances Perkins, a member of

32. Llewellyn H. Rockwell, Jr., "The Mises Institute: The Next 20 Years" (www.mises.org, 2002).

33. Bresiger, *The Revolution of 1935*, 68.

34. Ibid., 6.

35. Ibid., 17.

FDR's cabinet, observed that the era of "modern government" had become a permanent fixture in America because by that time the GOP's platform had adopted essentially all of FDR's social programs. He mused that the GOP had become a "me-too" party.[36] Indeed, by the time the Republicans captured political power in 1952, they had lost the courage and desire to attack FDR's socialist programs. As Bresiger wrote:

> When the GOP recaptured power in 1952, party members learned to embrace FDR's welfare-state polices and play the vote buying game as well as the Democrats. Republicans increased Social Security benefits in election years. Republican administrations signed expansions of the Social Security program into law and wanted credit for doing so. The GOP claimed to be opposed to welfare state measures, but by the 1950s *Life* magazine wrote, "Both major political parties maintain a pleasant fiction about the American welfare state."[37]

Never in American history have "me-too" conservatives initiated a campaign to reclaim lost rights. Mediocre, business-as-usual politicians, and party hacks who are concerned with gaining and holding on to political power, are the mortal enemies of liberty in any free republic. The United States is not an exception to this rule.

Can you imagine if the Founding Fathers had learned that one day their government would tell the private citizen when he must retire? Or how much money he may earn each year or where he may invest his income? Or that he would only be allowed to earn 1.5 percent on his (Social Security) "investment," even though in the private market average investments were earning three to four times that? Such a socialist system would have been unthinkable and unacceptable to the likes of Thomas Jefferson and Patrick Henry. But after a century of conservative defeats, it is now not only acceptable to Americans, but most citizens cannot even imagine a world without their socialist security blanket!

News accounts today are full of examples of politicians promoting Social Security without telling the public that it is socialism that they are being asked to support. One pro-liberty author related the following:

> The process of selling socialism under another name has been a success. At the time of this writing, presidential candidate

36. Ibid., 7.
37. Ibid., 47.

George Bush was confused regarding whether Social Security was a federal program or not. My congressman, Anthony Weiner (D-N.Y.), at a recent town hall in Kew Gardens, New York, insisted that, "Social Security is not socialism." But of course he also insists that payroll taxes are "only 7.65 percent." He conveniently excludes the employer part of the tax, which [makes it a total of] 15.30 percent![38]

By this time it should come as no surprise that the single greatest expansion of the Social Security program came not under a liberal Democrat president but when a Republican, Nixon, was in the White House. Whether it was Nixon, Reagan, Bush I, or Bush II, it matters little—Social Security not only was safe; it flourished. And with each tax increase to fund the bankrupt program, our liberties were reduced. With each tax dollar taken away from the private sector, an undeterminable opportunity cost is incurred. In other words, as private-sector money is drained away to fund socialist programs, the opportunity to invest that money in new businesses and new jobs is lost. As the economy begins to stagnate, due to tax burdens imposed by the government, liberals/socialists mount the cry for more social programs to remedy "market" failure. The failure is not in the free market. It belongs to the conservative movement that for 100 years has allowed liberals/socialists to use government force to corrupt the marketplace and steal working citizens' income.

What has been the conservative approach to this vast scheme to force socialism upon us? Since the establishment of Social Security, conservatives have ardently supported the effort! They have not submitted a single piece of legislation to roll back this socialist law. Indeed, they have sought at every opportunity to expand its reach and use its vote-buying power in upcoming elections.

As far back as 1912, Theodore Roosevelt, the idol of modern-day neoconservatives, was advocating his expansionist scheme called "New Nationalism," which forced the "conservative" Woodrow Wilson to move his social programs to the left in order to win election. After all, as all good neoconservatives will tell you, winning elections is more important than defending ideas. It should come as no surprise that Theodore Roosevelt, who loved social welfare, expressed contempt for Thomas Jefferson[39] and Jefferson Davis.[40] As I noted previously, liberals/socialists always cause conservatives to

38. Ibid., 28.
39. Ibid., 13, 15.
40. Kennedy and Kennedy, *Was Jefferson Davis Right?*, 41.

move to the left, but seldom has the opposite occurred! In 1952, when the conservative Republicans captured control of Congress, they did not roll back or attempt to curtail any of FDR's welfare-state, socialist programs. In 1972, again under a Republican president, conservatives and liberals were in a bidding contest to see who would get credit for increasing Social Security, and therefore who would receive votes from Social Security recipients. This competition ended in a bipartisan compromise that assured the reelection of politicians from both parties. Incumbency rules! The eventual cost to taxpayers would border upon the unbearable. The conservative failure of 1972 is summed up by free-market economist Bresiger: "In fact there was no philosophical disagreement over expanding the program, merely a disagreement over who was going to get the political credit. The 1972 deal meant American politics' two major parties were the Big Government party and the Bigger Government party."[41]

Mr. Conservative, Ronald Reagan, who was at one time a strident critic of Social Security, declared that "Social Security has proven to be one of the most successful and popular [federal] programs."[42] America's leading neoconservative, Jack Kemp, proclaimed the holy nature of the program when he warned that any presidential candidate who opposed Social Security was "a candidate for a frontal lobotomy."[43] Thus we have witnessed in our lifetime the movement of conservatives from opposing socializing schemes to adopting them, *provided* this would help them win political office. In the twentieth century, conservatives exchanged principles for the idea that the end justifies the means. *In so doing, conservative leaders have become willing collaborators of the liberals, as together they move America away from the principles of liberty and toward the enslaving ideas of socialism.* The political history of the twentieth century in America was written in the language of failure—conservative failure! In chapter 13 we will discuss how we can roll back Social Security, thereby freeing younger workers and future generations without harming those who have for generations been forced to pay into the federal old-age pension plan.

The 1960s—The Conservative Death March Begins

The mid-1960s marked the beginning of the end of even the pretense of conservative loyalty to the original constitutional Republic of Republics. Up to that time, at least in the South, politicians gave lip

41. Gregory Bresiger, "The Disastrous Deal of 1972" (www.mises.org, 1999), 4.
42. Ibid., 39 n. 9.
43. Ibid.

service to the idea of states' rights and constitutional limits on the powers of the federal government. After the passage of the 1964 Civil Rights Act, followed by the passage of the 1965 Voting Rights Acts, all such pretenses even in the South were discarded. Both of these acts had their constitutional justification in the fraudulent Fourteenth and Fifteenth amendments, highlighting the disaster created by the conservatives' failure to continually challenge these illegal acts during the previous 100 years. Both acts gained their social authority from the failure of conservatives to appropriately respond to the anti-liberty Jim Crow laws. Thus, it can be said that conservatives brought this disaster upon themselves. This is usually the case when people abandon their principles in favor of political utility.

1964—The Great Society

In May 1964 Lyndon Baines Johnson declared the beginning of his Great Society. In his socialized society, poverty would be removed, equality assured, those left behind would be brought forward, and presumably problematic individuals, programs, or social traditions would be corrected, converted, or convicted and punished. The pernicious failure of conservatives to defeat LBJ's Great Society programs dealt a mortal blow to any hope of restoring constitutionally limited federalism to America in the twentieth century. Its political effect is surpassed only by the moral effect of the cowardly manner in which conservative politicians adopted, defended, and in many cases expanded these socialist programs in an effort to win elections. By the end of the twentieth century, no national conservative leader would question the federal government's power to issue unfunded mandates to the states, tell small-business owners where their customers could park, or force states to provide for illegal immigrants even though the federal government was encouraging their flow by refusing to protect our borders.

As part of the Great Society, Congress enacted into law—in addition to the Civil Rights Act of 1964 and the Voting Rights Act of 1965—Medicare, Medicaid, the Economic Opportunity Act, the Appalachian Regional Development Act, the Elementary and Secondary Education Act, the Higher Education Act, and the National Foundation for the Arts and Humanities. LBJ, just like FDR before him, was determined to use the police power of government to take property from those who earned it and distribute it to those who otherwise had no right to it. He would use government force to redistribute wealth and create his vision of a better society (how else would you describe a socialist?).

Writing on the twenty-fifth anniversary of the Great Society, William Murchison noted:

> The Great Society fell flat. Education declined instead of advancing; racial tensions rose instead of falling. The welfare culture of the '60s created a whole new stratum of government dependents—the "underclass," unmotivated, uneducated, ridden with AIDS and cocaine. Intact black families . . . sundered and shriveled, especially as moral forces. Yet the conventional wisdom still commends the Great Society for its idealism.[44]

The onerous interference caused just by the war on poverty programs resulted in "6,000 pages of federal rules and regulations governing welfare [and] 59 major poverty programs, with a 1985 cost of $132 billion, compared with $21 billion for all poverty programs in 1960," noted Murchison. "Poverty likewise still is with us."[45] The cost of the Great Society is indicated by the fact that in 1968, after four years of increased spending, the total social welfare spending was $226 billion; by 1990 the total expenditures had reached $614 billion![46]

This cost is borne not only by the Bill Gates "rich" class but also by middle-class taxpayers. This is yet another example of the negative effect that conservative failure has had upon the very people that conservative politicians claim to represent. The poor, especially poor blacks, have fared even worse. LBJ claimed that his programs would elevate them from poverty to affluence, from dependence to independence. Anyone even remotely conversant with free-market reality would have known better. A racist desiring to use government force to destroy black families, communities, and even hope itself could not have designed a more effective program than what the socialist bleeding hearts foisted upon blacks in America. As Charles Murray wrote:

> The racial gap between the median income for full-time, year round male workers declined from 1980 to 1990, but only because the real median wage for whites declined more than the median for blacks. . . . The black-white gap in median family income increased, largely reflecting the continued decline in

44. William Murchison, "The Great Society and 25 Years of Decline," in *The Economics of Liberty,* ed. Llewellyn H. Rockwell (Auburn, Ala.: Ludwig von Mises Institute, 1990), 179.

45. Ibid.

46. Charles Murray, *Losing Ground: American Social Policy 1950-1980* (1984; reprint, New York: Basic Books, 1994), xviii.

two-parent families among blacks. . . . By 1990, 65.2 percent of black births were to unmarried women.[47]

Conservative political leaders were too cowardly to point out the disastrous results of these programs within black communities, because to do so would make them vulnerable to liberal media attacks and charges of racism. The media and self-appointed black leaders were used to keep conservatives in line. Here again we see the disastrous effect of conservative failure. The elites who control the GOP determined long ago that it was more important to win elections than to defend core principles. Thus they made no efforts to roll back the essential elements of either FDR's or LBJ's socialist programs. Holding office became an end unto itself. Any compromise was permissible if it held the promise of future electoral victories. Liberals reaped the benefit of promising more payments to a huge bloc of welfare voters. Add to this the even larger group of Social Security recipients. The elderly were also easy to mobilize against conservative candidates because the liberal media would assure them that the conservatives were going to cut out Social Security payments. With these two blocs of voters, liberals became the key power in the now predominantly socialized American economy. A cynical observer would conclude that the liberal establishment did not want to resolve the issue of black poverty. To do so would cause black voters to leave a federal dependence class, which assured their liberal voting, and move to the middle class, where they might get the crazy idea that government has no more right to divest them of their income than slave masters had prior to the black man's so-called freedom!

By the end of the twentieth century, it had become evident that the promises of the Great Society—just like all socialist promises— were empty ones that worked primarily for the benefit of social workers, government bureaucrats, and liberal academics and politicians. And to add insult to injury for black Americans, the vast majority of those who truly gained from these programs were white. The question must be asked: After all of these socialist interventions, had the poverty levels in America changed? When LBJ left office in 1968, the poverty rate, according to the government, was around 16 percent. Twelve years and billions of tax dollars (read as "your income inappropriately seized by the government") later, in 1980 the poverty level was 16 percent![48] Socialists will never admit their

47. Ibid., xviii-xix.
48. Ibid., 8.

failure. Therefore, each year they offer up a new scheme to tax the "rich," which includes everyone with an annual family income of $30,000, to help the "oppressed masses" created by this "cruel" capitalist system. Conservative political leaders, on the other hand, cannot find the courage to attack social programs for the miserable moral and social failures that they are, nor defend the free market as the only way to increase wealth and provide an opportunity for raising everyone's standard of living.

1968—Busing

In *Green v. County School Board of New Kent County*, the U.S. Supreme Court overturned a freedom-of-choice school-desegregation plan and ordered the public-school district to bus students so as to achieve "racial balance," whatever that is. Thus began the American odyssey of busing for the sake of face counters (the number of white faces must equal the number of black faces—if it sounds absurd that's because it is!), as opposed to allowing parents to freely choose what school they (not a social worker, liberal expert, or federal judge) think will best equip their children for a successful future. Busing quickly became liberalism's Vietnam. Early on, liberals knew they were losing the battle. Parents moved, sent their children to private school, or opted for the increasingly popular concept of home schooling. After a few years, schools that were formerly almost all white (liberals' definition of segregation) had become almost all black (using liberals' definition—the school had become segregated again). In addition, in some school districts, federal judges had assumed the authority to raise local taxes in order to pay for busing! What happened to the idea of "no taxation without representation"? And to distress the liberals even more, opinion polls demonstrated that black Americans opposed busing almost as much as did their white counterparts.

Conservative leaders attempted to hide from the issue, until a vocal anti-busing leader emerged in the 1968 presidential primaries by the name of George Wallace. He forced Nixon to change his rhetoric so much that Nixon at least sounded as if he understood the anger busing evoked from the middle class. But when civil rights leaders expressed concern, Nixon quietly sent them the message, "Look at what we do, not at what we say!"[49] Once again, middle-class issues would be sacrificed in order to assure "conservative" electoral victory. Had conservative leaders had any foresight, they could have turned this issue into a debacle for liberal social schemes.

49. Kennedy and Kennedy, *Why Not Freedom!*, 91.

Unfortunately for the middle class of all races, by this time conservatism had lost its tentative connection to the original constitutional Republic of Republics and therefore could see no value in an essentially ideological fight that might expose them to electoral defeat.

1971—Affirmative Action, Minority Set-Asides, and Quotas

Affirmative action, minority set-asides, and quotas came to us via Republican presidents and an unbridled, activist federal Supreme Court.[50] In *Griggs* v. *Duke Power Company* (1971), the Supreme Court adopted the theory of disparate impact. Essentially it means that if an employer does not have the right ratio of black-to-white employees, then he is presumed to be guilty of illegal discrimination. Notice that the employer's intent or non-intent to discriminate has no bearing on the case—it's simply justice by the numbers. Count the number of white faces, count the number of black faces, and if the numbers do not reflect the white and black percentages in the general population, then go straight to jail. Well, not really—it's worse. Go straight to the Equal Employment Opportunities Commission (EEOC), and be sure to bring your checkbook.

In *Albemarle Paper Company* v. *Moody* (1975), our black-robed masters affirmed the disparate impact theory. It provided a strong incentive for those under Title VII of the 1964 Civil Rights Act (virtually everyone) to engage in race counting in hiring to avoid entanglement with the federal "Race Gestapo," formerly known as the EEOC. (Granted, that's not the exact dicta used by the Supreme Court, but the message is essentially the same.)

The June 6, 2002, issue of the *Wall Street Journal* carried an editorial, "The Conundrum of Quotas," in which they ask, "Most of the public doesn't like racial preferences—but President Bush I is afraid to attack them. Why is that?" The paper criticized a recent Supreme Court (a Reagan court at that) decision that affirmed a lower federal court ruling allowing universities to use racial quotas in admissions. The *Journal* described this Supreme Court decision as a "blow to conservatives." The writer was very insightful in declaring that "conservatives will always be at an inherent disadvantage in American political life until the timeless principles they believe in—merit, accountability, competition, the pursuit of excellence, etc.—win moral authority by proving their effectiveness against those

50. Recall that I had previously discussed the dangers inherent in a federal republic in which a branch of the government is given exclusive authority to determine the limits on its own powers. Affirmative action is yet another example of this danger.

great enemies of the nation's promise; racism and poverty." The writer continued, "But moral authority is the fruit of moral risk." Michelle Malkin's column "Next: Get Rid of Racial Boxes"[51] calls Bush II's eventual criticism of quotas as "only a teeny-tiny step in the right direction." She points out that the Bush administration, "not the Clinton-Gore administration, backed the Federal government's payment of cash bonuses to highway construction firms that accept bids from companies owned by members of certain minority groups." The potential of negative polls will send elected neoconservatives running from principles in order to worship at the ideological idols of liberalism. And as I have previously noted, modern-day conservatives always count the cost first and then decide whether or not to engage our mortal ideological enemies. Here we see yet another example of conservative failure.

1982—The Reagan Nonrevolution

Most conservatives like to point to the Reagan era as an example of victorious conservatism. But alas, there were no real victories on the domestic scene. The best that can be said is that Reagan reduced the rate of growth of government. However, he did not reduce its size, and it still continued to grow during the Reagan years. So government got bigger than before but not as big as it could have gotten! Robert Higgs, a pro-liberty writer, described Reagan's failure to reduce the size of government:

> As a check, one can secure an organization chart of the Federal government for, say, 1979 and a corresponding chart for 1989. Comparing the two, can one see any evidence that the government's scope has been diminished? The Civil Aeronautics Board has disappeared, but the Department of Veterans Affairs has appeared. Bad test? Too simple? Then peruse the *Federal Register* for recent years to see whether the government has taken itself off someone's back.
>
> But surely the vaunted tax cuts signify a blow against big government? No. There has been no tax cut, properly speaking. The best simple measure of the nation's tax rate is the proportion of the national product commanded by government spending. Total government expenditures for final goods and services (transfer payments are *not* included in this total) relative to gross national product averaged 29.9% for 1970-80 and 31.8% for 1980-88; the federal spending portion alone rose from 20.5% to 23.2% of GNP. No shrinking government here. Nor will any

51. www.jewishworldreview.com, Jan. 17, 2003.

shrinkage be found when one examines the mushrooming totals from federal direct loan obligation or guaranteed loan commitments.[52]

Southerners should be twice as outraged by the inability of the Reagan Revolution to reduce the size and scope of the federal government. We had the supreme stroke of luck to have the required renewal of the 1965 Voting Rights Act during the Reagan administration. But once again, conservative fear of liberal press precluded any hope that Reagan would refuse to sign its renewal. So Mr. Conservative gleefully signed the renewal of the 1965 Voting Rights Act (which was based on the unconstitutional Fifteenth Amendment and other Reconstruction legislation). No doubt his advisors thought this would help "conservatives" in the black community, and after all, even if the renewal upsets a few Southern conservatives, what are these poor Southerners going to do about it? Where would they go? Even under the most "conservative" president in modern history, conservatism was a failure when measured against the test of restoring the original constitutional Republic of Republics.

1992—Read My Lips

The modern-day retreat of conservative ideology became a rout during Bush I's administration. As most of us know, whether we will admit it or not, by this time conservative leaders had no ideology other than doing whatever was necessary to win office. Bush came to office with the firm promise not to increase taxes, yet when confronted by determined liberals armed with their socialist ideology, he caved. His choice was to reduce the size of government, always a good option, or risk the wrath of the liberal establishment, especially the media. A vicious media campaign would certainly harm his and other "conservative" elected officials' chance of winning reelection. Once again, the neoconservatives were faced with a choice—principles or politics—and guess which one they chose! Added to this disgrace was Bush's signing of the 1991 Civil Rights Bill, which he had previously characterized as a "quota bill." We must remember that the conservative leadership failed in the twentieth century, not conservative individuals.

52. Robert Higgs, "Triumph of Liberty? Not in the U.S.A." in *The Economics of Liberty*, ed. Llewellyn H. Rockwell (Auburn, Ala.: Ludwig von Mises Institute, 1990), 188-89.

CENTRALIZED FEDERALIZED TYRANNY
—AND THE BEAT GOES ON

It would be impractical to make an exhaustive list of the past and ongoing conservative failures. Below is a short list of some of the most notable ones. They all represent rights lost due to conservative failure to control an unconstitutional federal government.

Federal Supreme Court bans prayer and Bible from school
With *Roe* v. *Wade*, Federal Supreme Court denies sovereign state the right to establish when life begins
Unfunded federal mandates (another invisible federal tax)
Gun control—Brady I and II
Federal seizure of private property via wetlands legislation
Congress ignores illegal immigration
Anti-white reverse discrimination
Crime and the breakdown of law and order
Busing (yes, it's still going on)
Failure to establish merit-based voting qualifications

The point is that for the past century, conservative ideas have been crushed by the onslaught of liberalism and socialism. At first it was slow to manifest itself, but in the last decade of the twentieth century it was a given that the government can do anything it decides to do in the name of public policy. Indeed, three years before the close of the century, the United States solicitor general was asked by a Supreme Court justice to name just one activity that he felt would fall outside of the government's constitutional authority. The solicitor general stood before the court dumbfounded—he was unable to think of anything his government could not do if it so desired![53] In his world of practical politics, states' rights and a constitutionally limited federal government no longer existed. What better demonstration do we need of a century of conservative failure?

WHAT DOES THE FUTURE HOLD?

After 100 years of disappearing liberty, it is time to stop and take stock of the rights we have lost and the inability of current conservative leaders to defeat liberalism/socialism and restore the original

53. Kennedy and Kennedy, *Was Jefferson Davis Right?*, 279.

constitutionally limited system of federalism and states' rights. One would almost conclude that modern Americans do not want to live free in a constitutional Republic of Republics. One would be tempted to think that Americans no longer desire a land of low taxes and individual responsibility. But before we make that conclusion, we need to recall that, for over a century, no viable political party or conservative spokesman has had the vision or nerve to challenge the gains of liberalism and big government special-interest groups. I say that the day has come and *we the people* of the South are the people to lead that challenge!

QUESTIONS AND ANSWERS

Q. The Civil War is almost ancient history. Why do you attach so much importance to that war when most of our rights have been lost in recent history?

A. First of all, the Civil War was not a "civil war" any more than the American Revolution of 1776 was a "civil war." To be precise, this conflict was the War for Southern Independence. But you do raise a point here that needs to be explained.

Can our past affect us today? Definitely! It can and does! By waging an aggressive war against the people of the South, the federal government assumed dictatorial powers and compelled the Southern people to live under a government against our consent. The original Constitution, which was designed to limit the powers of government, was discarded in favor of political pragmatism. Those who controlled the government would no longer be held to a strict interpretation of the Constitution but would be able to use subterfuge and sophistry to read into it powers that the Sovereign States never intended to grant to the federal government. After the unfortunate conclusion of the war, no state (North or South) would be allowed to interpose its sovereign authority between an aggressive federal government and the people of that state. All the limitations of the Constitution, but especially those contained in the Ninth and Tenth amendments, became tokens of the past. Those who control the government would pay lip service to "states' rights" when it was politically convenient, but they would never allow the people of a state to stand in the way of federal expansion. If history has taught Southerners anything, it is that the federal union, originally designed to be a Republic of Republics, cannot exist without states' rights. A federal union held together by the moral persuasion of bloody bayonets becomes an empire controlled by the numerical majority to the detriment of the numerical minority. All of this arose as a result of the victory of the Northern industrial, commercial, and political powers in the War for Southern Independence.

Q. You are very critical of conservative efforts during the twentieth century. But what about the fact that we elected Ronald Reagan, won the Cold War, and won back Congress?

A. My point of criticism is not that we have not won some interesting local or tactical victories. My point is that, despite many opportunities, conservatives have never met and defeated liberalism/socialism. We have never rolled back their victories. We have been an effective army at times, but our leaders have never figured out what to do with our victories. They have never followed up by pursuing the enemy and destroying his strong positions. Once our leaders get elected, their primary goal is to stay in office. Fear of losing the next election prevents them from doing what we elected them to do.

Yes, we won the Cold War. But while we were fighting the Cold War, what happened to our liberty/rights here at home? Would you prefer to pay the income-tax rate of 1946 (around the beginning of the Cold War) or what you have to pay today? Do you think you get more value for the money you are forced to hand over to the federal government than you could have purchased for yourself and your family had you been allowed to keep your income? Do you think that unconstitutional government intrusion is less today than it was at the beginning of the Cold War? Do you think that the men who died in World War I, World War II, Korea, Vietnam, and numerous other conflicts died so that the government could order busing and affirmative action, begin the campaign to enforce "gay" rights, federalize a limited definition of pornography, and on and on? Our very few conservative victories are overwhelmed by our leaders' failure to envision a strategic plan to destroy the liberal/socialist political system that has been foisted upon the people of the United States and to return us to a land of liberty.

It is easy to understand why our leaders react as they have for the past century. Conservatives have been playing the role assigned to them by the proponents of federal supremacy ever since 1865. As long as we play their game, by their rules and refereed by their agents, we will always end up losing the contest. The time has come for *we the people* of the Sovereign States to change the game!

Q. The powers that are arrayed against conservatives are so great that it seems unlikely that we could ever prevail against them. How could we win?

A. We are really in an enviable position when compared to many people who have won back their liberty in the past 100 years. Look at the Baltic States. They were compelled to join the Soviet Union. At one time there were as many Russians living in these states as there were native citizens. The cruel Soviet army occupied their countries. Yet, in our lifetime we have seen how these brave people used nonviolent methods to awaken first their own people and then the world to the cause of liberty for the Baltic States. The Baltic States seceded from the Soviet Union because their people looked to the future and not at the enormous enemy arrayed against them.

The people of Quebec were militarily forced into the Canadian union. For generations they suffered discrimination against their culture at the hands of the English majority. But even though they are outnumbered and with no friend in the community of nations willing to support them, they have used political strategy to force significant concessions from the majority. The mere threat of Quebec secession has been the primary tool expertly used to gain these victories.

Are *we the people* of the Sovereign States of the South and the rest of America less in talent or heart than these peoples? I think not! Both the possibility and probability of the establishment of a Liberty-Based Society are very good. All that is needed are the men and women who will look beyond temporary difficulties and begin the struggle for liberty.

Q. Can't we do this without an appeal to the right of secession? The very word makes me nervous.

A. If it makes you nervous, just imagine how nervous our enemies will be when they see a massive movement of Americans demanding that government restore to *we the people* our inherent right to judge the extent of federal powers. The ultimate check on any government is the right of *we the people* to withdraw our consent. For a more detailed discussion of secession as a tool to preserve and protect individual liberty, see Addendum XIII of this book.

Q. I like what you are saying, but how can it be done?

A. The explanation of how we can establish a Liberty-Based Society will be developed in the remainder of this book. The main point to remember is that we intend to use the South as the base from which to offer to all of the United States the opportunity to regain their lost rights and establish a Liberty-Based Society.

The Marriage of Brother Jonathan and Virginia

Virginia's husband of royal descent had abandoned her and their children. She knew that evil people would attempt to take advantage of her and her children. Her royal husband had promised to be a good protector of the family and to assure that the children would grow up as free and self-reliant people. But as so often occurs, from royal blood springs insistent demands. After much pleading on Virginia's part, it became evident that she could do nothing to salvage the marriage. She took her children out of the marriage and, after fighting off royal rage, she and her children were free. She then had to determine the best way for them to survive in this world fraught with great dangers.

One day Brother Jonathan called on Virginia. He was a cunning and thrifty Yankee. He too was looking for some way to increase his security and wealth in this cruel world. He had a proposition to make. If Virginia would marry him, then the resources of the two families would be so great that cruel people would not be able to invade their interest. In addition, Brother Jonathan, who was engaged in numerous commercial enterprises, saw an excellent opportunity to use the enlarged family to increase his personal wealth. Virginia and her children, on the other hand, were contented with their rural lifestyle. Virginia's eldest son, Patrick, was most alarmed about the potential union. He argued that if his mother married Brother Jonathan, then Brother Jonathan and his children would eventually be able to plunder all of Virginia's wealth, leaving nothing for Virginia or her children. But Virginia was swayed by Brother Jonathan's assurances of fidelity to their marriage and his written promise to respect her rights and the interests of her children.

Within a very short time after their union, Brother Jonathan began seizing more and more of Virginia's wealth and converting it for his own use. When she protested and demanded that he abide by their solemn marriage agreement, he replied that the agreement allowed him to do everything necessary and proper to assure the success and security of their union. As far as Virginia was concerned, her new husband was just as bad as her royal husband had been. Seeing her own and her children's condition gradually deteriorating, she determined to do the same thing with the second bad husband as she had done with the first. But Brother Jonathan and his children were determined to keep the source of their newfound wealth. They used their overwhelming numbers to seize Virginia and her children. Her beautiful home was put to the torch and many of her children slaughtered as they rose to defend their mother. Virginia appealed to the world for help, but fearing Brother Jonathan's wrath, no one dared to answer. With her home destroyed, most of her children killed or wounded, and her honor stained by a cruel husband, Virginia had no choice but to return to the marriage. Her children would grow up to be employed by and serve Brother Jonathan's children. Her heart would break and her eyes would fill with tears whenever she thought on such matters. But what could she do? It seemed to her that her children would never be free again. She sobbed as she watched over her surviving but impoverished children and wondered, "Was the flaw in the contract of the union or in the character of the person I married?"

CHAPTER 2

The Anti-Federalists Were Right

The vast majority of American conservatives accepted the notion that the system of government we live under today is the same one the Founding Fathers established—with only a few minor modifications, such as the abolishment of slavery and granting women the right to vote. If you ask most of the voters in the "red" states (those states that voted for Bush instead of Kerry in the 2004 election) to identify the origin of liberal dominance in America today, if they provided any answer at all, they would point to FDR's packing of the federal Supreme Court and his subsequent liberal social programs. Some may include LBJ's Great Society, with its huge growth in federal social spending and federal enforcement agencies. They would be correct, but they fail to realize that none of these liberal successes could have occurred in the original system of constitutionally limited federalism. These successes were merely the symptom of a far greater disease— unbridled federalism!

From the birth of the United States in 1776 up to 1865, there was an unrelenting struggle between the forces of the commercial North and the agricultural South regarding the proper role of their mutual federal government.[1] Popular history—that is, history as written by the victors in the War for Southern Independence—informs us that the struggle was really one over human dignity, brotherly love, and freedom as advocated by those virtuous people living up North, who were opposed by supporters of slavery and racism down South. But history is written by the victor to mask his crimes and to assure the prosperous continuation of his regime. What does the truth of history really tell us?

---

1. This is a general statement—actually there were forces contending for their respective views on both sides of the great North/South divide. But generally speaking, the forces favoring consolidated federalism were in the majority in the North, and the forces favoring a constitutionally limited federal government and states' rights were in the majority in the South.

The Founding Fathers established a federal government with limited and specific duties. Those duties were delegated to the Federal government by the individual Sovereign States. The federal government does not possess original sovereignty—sovereignty arises from *we the people,* who reside in our local communities within our Sovereign States. Each Sovereign State, acting on behalf of and with the free and voluntary consent of its citizens, delegated (as opposed to surrendered) a very limited portion of its sovereign authority to the federal government to be used only for those specific tasks enumerated in the Constitution. Any act of the agent (the federal government) outside or incongruent with the limited specifications in the contract that empowered the federal government (the original Constitution) would be an illegitimate exercise of political force. Therefore, the Sovereign States reserved the right to take whatever steps were necessary to protect their citizens from the potential of oppressive and onerous use of federal force. The Ninth and Tenth amendments make it clear that all powers whatsoever not delegated to the federal government nor prohibited to the states remain with the states to be exercised as they see fit. Included in the innumerable rights reserved to the states is the right to nullify unconstitutional acts of the federal government or secede if necessary to protect their citizens from an abusive federal government. Absent these rights, *we the people* stand before the federal government not as free citizens but as supplicants begging their master not to harm his subjects.

Nullification and secession provide a means to escape oppression. The mere presence of these weapons produces the same effect on tyrants as an armed citizen has on criminals. Their presence is generally enough to prevent oppression from the central government. This is the beauty of these weapons. *You don't have to use them if you have them*—but if you don't have them, then you find yourself at the cruel mercy of tyrants, with no means of escape. The Founding Fathers knew this because they too were secessionists. They knew by experience what happens when a tyrant refuses to recognize the right of *we the people* to live under a government ordered upon the free and voluntary consent of the governed.

THE AMERICAN COLONIES SECEDE FROM GREAT BRITAIN

The United States of America was born by an act of secession! The colonies removed themselves from the authority of Great Britain, severing the union that had previously existed. In May of 1776, more than a month before the famous July Fourth joint Declaration of

Independence, the colony of Virginia seceded from the union with Great Britain, making the following statement in its secession document: "Resolve, That the union that has hitherto subsisted between Great Britain and the American colonies is thereby totally dissolved, that the inhabitants of this colony are discharged from any allegiance to the crown of Great Britain."[2]

Many conservatives are surprised by the similarity between the language used in 1776 when the American colonies seceded from the union with Great Britain and the language used by the Southern states when they seceded from the federal union. Among the many similarities is the fact that the British attempted to use slaves to help them defeat the secessionists, by offering freedom to any slave who would leave his master and fight for the British—a precursor to Abe Lincoln's tactics! The British also tried to dehumanize the American secessionists by calling them "rebels" and encouraging the destruction of rebel property and death to all rebels who refused to obey the will of the central government—a precursor to General Sherman's tactics![3] So we see that the United States was born via secession. Furthermore, slavery was a distinct aspect of all American colonies at that time, not just Southern colonies.[4]

THE NORTH AND THE SOUTH—
ADVERSARIES FROM THE BEGINNING

Important economic reasons compelled each side, North and South, to want to control the federal government. This was evident even as early as the Articles of Confederation and Perpetual Union, which existed prior to the adoption of the Constitution. Even then it was clear that the North and the South would be forever locked in a struggle for political control. Note that this was the issue, not slavery!

Whichever side controlled the federal government could use that power to protect and/or expand its wealth. The South wanted free access to the Mississippi River to allow it an inexpensive channel to move its goods to market. The North on the other hand wanted to prevent this, because it would mean less business for their ships. Cotton leaving America via the port of New Orleans would be carried in foreign ships, because New Orleans at that time belonged to Spain. In addition, the New England states were "landlocked." There was no way for them to bring more New England states into the Union, but if the

2. Kennedy and Kennedy, *Was Jefferson Davis Right?*, 258.
3. Kennedy and Kennedy, *The South Was Right!*, 271-303.
4. Walter D. Kennedy, *Myths of American Slavery* (Gretna, La.: Pelican, 2003), 21-67.

South moved toward the Mississippi River, then many new Southern states would be brought in. If this happened, the South would have a majority in Congress and would therefore control the government. From the very beginning of the republic, the Northern states held a slight majority, and they were determined not to relinquish their nominal control of the government!

In a letter dated August 12, 1786, Gov. Patrick Henry of Virginia noted the intent of the Northern states to use whatever means necessary to obtain a treaty with Spain that would give the Northern commercial states special trading privileges in exchange for the United States surrendering navigation rights on the Mississippi. This arrangement would be a windfall for the North but an economic (not to mention political) disaster for the South. Note Henry's own words:

> [John Jay of New York] had engaged the eastern states in the intrigue, especially Mass.; that New York, Jersey and Penn. were in favor of it, and either absolutely decided, or so much so to promise little prospect of change. . . . It appears that they [Northern states] have seven states, and we [Southern states] five, Maryland included with the southern states. . . . It appears that they will go on under seven states in the business, and risqué the preservation of the confederacy on it. . . . Certain it is that committees are held in this town of eastern men, and other of this state [New York] upon the subject of a dismemberment of the states east of the Hudson from the union, and the erection of them into a separate government. . . . The measure is talked of in Mass. . . . and is supposed to have originated there.[5]

Again note that it was a struggle between the Northern and Southern states over the control of the government, and the motivations were sparked by economics.

MASSACHUSETTS THREATENS TO SECEDE FROM THE UNION

In the debate over the Louisiana Purchase, the Sovereign State of Massachusetts, seeing that the addition of this vast landmass might upset the North's hold over Congress, argued against it. This fine Yankee state even threatened to secede if this large territory was added to the United States! Later, when Louisiana petitioned for admission to the Union, Massachusetts congressman Josiah Quincy

5. Kennedy and Kennedy, *Was Jefferson Davis Right?*, 206.

declared, "If this bill passes, it is my deliberate opinion that it is virtually a dissolution of this Union; that it will free the States from their moral obligation, and as it will be the right of all, so it will be the duty of some, definitely to prepare for a separation, amicably if they can, violently if they must."[6] The same threat of secession from the "Glorious Union" (i.e., glorious only when it serves your economic purposes!) was again heard from Massachusetts when Texas petitioned for admission to the Union.

NEW ENGLAND'S SECESSION CONVENTION—1815

During the War of 1812, when the United States was facing British invasion, the New England states met in solemn convention to discuss their forthcoming secession from the United States. Amazingly, this occurred while we had a powerful invader with a powerful invasion fleet poised just off our shores, ready to strike! The issue once again was New England commercial profits—or lack thereof as a result of the War of 1812. The war had brought New England's shipping commerce to a standstill. No doubt they were suffering, and to relieve their suffering they decided to pull out of the Union and form their own nation. Fortunately (or unfortunately depending on your perspective) the War of 1812 ended before the decisions of the Hartford Secession Conventions could be put to the test. But note the two facts that have become the central themes of early American political history: (1) the economic division between the North and the South and (2) the appeal to the right of secession as a means to settle these disputes. In other words, the federal government was seen as having no authority to prevent the people of Sovereign States from using their reserved rights to redress their grievances.

TARIFF OF ABOMINATION

After Virginia graciously gave its Northwest Territory to the United States, the Northern states found that overnight they were no longer "landlocked," and soon new Northern states such as Ohio, Indiana, and Illinois were admitted to the Union. With this new territory, Northern dominance of Congress was assured. The North used its greater numbers in Congress to pass protective tariffs that favored its industry and commerce. This forced the South to pay higher prices for its trade goods (which enriched Northern commerce) and the South received less for its goods on the foreign market because part of its "profits" were reduced by foreigners in order

6. Ibid., 260-61.

to pay American tariffs. In other words, the South paid the tariffs with lower profits.

In 1828 the Northern-dominated Congress passed the Tariff of Abomination. It had been only forty-one years since the anti-Federalists, led by men such as Patrick Henry, had warned the South about the danger inherent in the proposed Constitution. Henry had predicted what would happen if the South placed power to tax Southern agriculture in the hands of Northern commercial powers, who would have a vested interest in taxing Southern wealth. The Tariff of Abomination produced the first threat of secession from a Southern state. Again note that the issue revolved around economics, not slavery. Southern wealth and resources were being forcefully extracted by the Northern numerical majority who controlled the government and who used the government to benefit their section.

Southern congressmen complained that almost 75 percent of the revenues used to run the government were obtained from Southern agriculture. In the words of Missouri senator Thomas H. Benton, the South had become the milch cow of the Union.

> Before the Revolution [the South] was the seat of wealth; . . . wealth has fled from the South, and settled in regions north of the Potomac. . . . Under Federal legislation, the exports of the South have been the basis of the Federal Revenue. . . . Virginia, the two Carolinas, and Georgia, may be said to defray three-fourths, of the annual expense of supporting the Federal Government; and of this great sum, annually furnished by them, nothing or next to nothing is returned to them, in the shape of Government expenditures. That expenditure flows in an opposite direction—it flows northwardly, in one uniform, uninterrupted, and perennial stream. This is the reason why wealth disappears from the South and rises up in the North. Federal legislation does all this.[7]

LINCOLN AND SOUTHERN REVENUES

The election of Lincoln is unique in American history because for the first time a purely sectional political party had seized control of the government. The South had little choice—stay in the Union and see its wealth completely confiscated by the "legal" technique of tariffs or pull out of a sectional Union that favored commerce at the expense of agriculture and form their own independent nation. As we have seen, the fate of the Union between these two distinct peoples was not difficult to predict. Their struggle had continued from

7. Thomas H. Benton, as cited in Kennedy and Kennedy, *The South Was Right!*, 49.

the inception of the United States under the Continental Congress, through the federal government formed by the Articles of Confederation, and into the federal government under the Constitution. Peaceful secession was now the best solution, but would the North allow its "milch cow" to peacefully walk away?

The commercial leaders and their political leaders realized what would happen if they allowed the South to escape their tariff nets. On March 30, 1861, the *New York Times* made very clear why they were supporting the invasion, conquest, and eventual occupation of the South:

> The predicament in which both the Government and the commerce of the country are placed, through the non-enforcement of our revenue laws, is now thoroughly understood the world over. . . . If the manufacturer at Manchester [England] can send his goods into the Western States through New Orleans at a less cost than through New York, he is a fool for not availing himself of his advantage. . . . The products of the West, instead of coming to our own port by millions of tons, to be transported abroad by the same ships through which we receive our importations, will seek other routes and other outlets. With the loss of our foreign trade, what is to become of our public works, constructed at the cost of many hundred millions of dollars, to turn into our harbor the products of the interior? . . . The commercial bearing of the question has acted upon the North. . . . We now see clearly whither we are tending, and the policy we must adopt. With us it is no longer an abstract question—one of Constitutional construction, or of the reserved or delegated power of the State or Federal Government, but of material existence. . . . We were divided and confused till our pockets were touched.[8]

An editorial in the *Manchester (N.H.) Union Democrat* had a similar tone when it declared:

> The Southern Confederacy will not employ our ships or buy our goods. . . . It is very clear that the South gains by this process, and we lose. No—we MUST NOT "let the South go."[9]

The *New York Evening Post* in an editorial titled "What Shall Be Done for a Revenue?" warned Northerners about the loss of Southern revenues if the North allowed the South to go in peace.[10] When Abe

8. Kennedy and Kennedy, *The South Was Right!*, 52.
9. Ibid.
10. Ibid.

Lincoln was asked why he did not just let the South go, he exclaimed, "Let the South go. Let the South go? Where then shall we gain our revenue?"

And so we see the sad consequences of forming a Republic of Republics and not making it expressly clear that the Sovereign States retained the right to nullify any act of the federal government that they felt was not authorized by the Constitution, as well as the right to secede if their fellow states did not agree with the nullifying state. From the very beginning of the United States commercial interests have struggled to control the government and use its taxing authority (originally via tariffs—that was before Abe Lincoln's introduction of the income tax) to confiscate other people's money (OPM) for the enrichment of special interest groups, businesses with close connections with the government, and incumbent politicians. The clear and acknowledged right of nullification and secession could have prevented the distortion of the original Republic of Republics.

QUESTIONS AND ANSWERS

Q. All my life I have been taught by very patriotic men and women that the Constitution is the perfect instrument to organize a democracy. Are you saying that this beautiful document is flawed?

A. Not so much the document as the people. All people are flawed in that we are fallen creatures (if you believe in orthodox Christianity), or at least as a general rule, people tend to choose things that will help them personally even if it may not be the best for society. Therefore, any government that can use force to compel people to surrender their income, and other rights/liberties, will eventually find itself controlled by people who use that government for their own benefit. The Founding Fathers knew this and attempted to give us a Republic of Republics in which the federal government could be limited. Among the many techniques left to *we the people* of the Sovereign States to control an abusive federal government was the right of nullification and/or secession. Even though these rights are not prohibited to the states, and even though states had appealed for nullification and secession in the past, when the South tried to secede in 1861, the North rose en masse and denied the Southern people one basic right—the right to live under a government ordered on the free and unfettered consent of the governed. This throttling of freedom could have been prevented if the original Constitution had clearly and precisely acknowledged these rights.

Q. Even if the original Constitution had recognized the right of nullification and secession, would it not still be possible for the numerical majority to use force to compel the numerical minority to accept a government detrimental to the minority's interests?

A. Absolutely, and it happens very often in history. The Soviet Union's constitution claimed to acknowledge the right of self-determination by the people. Yet up to the very end of their union, the Soviets denied the right of the Baltic States to secede. But by acknowledging the right, the Soviets were forever branded as international criminals for refusing to allow the exercise of a right that their constitution recognized. It also gave the occupied people moral support to know that they were struggling for their rights as acknowledged by the very people who were oppressing them.

Because the original Constitution did not explicitly acknowledge the right of secession and nullification, it allowed those desiring the establishment of a strong all-powerful federal government to use various propaganda tricks to convince the world (as well as the average person in the North) that Southerners had no right to secede. It allowed Northern propagandists to slander the good name of the people of the South by accusing them of fighting for slavery. It would have made it a lot more difficult for the Federalists to consolidate power if the Constitution itself had acknowledged that *we the people* of the Sovereign States are the final arbiters of our liberties under the Constitution.

Measuring a Society's Civility

How do you measure a society's civility? What is that makes a society worthy of our respect and emulation? Let us begin the inquiry by defining the opposite. What are the things that you would not want to have in your neighborhood? Crime would be high on the list. Every minute of every day in America, three people die due to violent crime, two people are robbed, twelve homes are burglarized, and twelve women are raped—every minute of every day! Put high crime rates on the list of things that mark a society as lacking civility. Most of us would not want to live in a society where immoral acts of public figures (elected or non-elected leaders) are met with silence and indifference—a society so desensitized to unethical, immoral, or illegal behavior that it loses its capacity for righteous indignation. We would not want our neighborhood to turn into a place where agnosticism is the majority's attitude toward Eternal Truths. We would not want to live in a society where people refuse to help each other. All of these things that we do not want in our society are symptomatic of a sick society, a dumbed-down society where common courtesy and human kindness are used as a subterfuge to gain an advantage over other human beings.

A friend recently returned from a trip to Ireland. The countryside was beautiful and the people friendly. The Sunday before he left, he decided to get up early, rent a car, and take a private drive through the beautiful countryside. He began shortly after sunrise. Everywhere, he noticed young children and mothers walking about. Some of the mothers carried infants in their arms. They were all dressed in what Southerners would call "their Sunday best." Occasionally, he would see a local drive by and the children and young women, using the universal hitchhiking sign, ask for a ride. Usually the driver would pull over and offer the child or young lady a ride. My friend asked a resident about what he had seen, but it took a while for the man to understand the question. As far as the resident was concerned, there was nothing strange in women and children hitchhiking. He explained that it was Sunday morning and they were going to church. Everyone knew each other and looked out for each other. If anyone were bold enough to try to harm someone, the villagers would ruthlessly, yet efficiently, make sure it would never happen again. My friend returned to America with a new benchmark for a civilized society—any society in which young women and children cannot hitchhike to church without concern for their safety fails the test of civility and civilization!

CHAPTER 3

The Dimensions of a Liberty-Based Society

The American political system spent the last half of the twentieth century fixated on "rights." Yet at no time in our history have we as a people had less civil liberty! When we measure our right to keep the product of our labor (our income), we can see the dramatic loss of this one right that separates free men from serfs and slaves.[1] As demonstrated in the graph below, at the beginning of the past century (1900), the average American's federal tax burden was 3 percent of Gross Domestic Product (GDP), but by the end of the century (2000) that burden had risen to 20.8 percent of GDP![2]

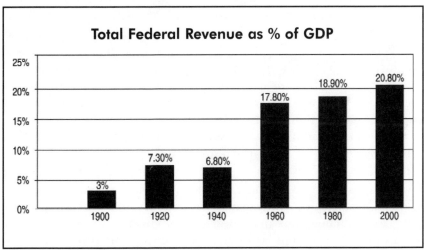

As the federal government takes more and more of your income, your resources available to live as you choose are severely limited. In fact, what is happening is the federal tax collector is limiting your

1. Kennedy, *Myths of American Slavery*, 236.
2. www.cato.org/research/fiscan_policy/2002/growth1, Dec. 2, 2002.

liberty. Federal politicians need to provide special interest and minority groups with large outlays of federal dollars in order to assure that these groups will help them maintain their incumbency. These groups have vocal and active organizations/corporations that ensure their "right" to your income, but average taxpayers have no such organization to protect their income. One would think that our conservative "leaders" would be the first in line to attack these groups and challenge their assertion that they have a "right" to your money. Yet the conservative movement has shied away from addressing this misspent fixation on group rights for fear of being labeled racist, homophobic, anti-feminist, etc. Their primary fear was and still is that by standing up for conservative principles they would increase the probability of losing the next election. Protecting liberty is impossible if, for political expediency, one abandons core principles that define liberty.

CIVILITY—THE FIRST REQUIREMENT FOR A FREE SOCIETY

Free people define their freedom within the context of their society. A socialized people use the force of national government to define their "freedom," which is in fact no freedom at all within the traditional American context. It is important to understand the distinction between these two concepts of "freedom." A free people, such as the American people at the founding of the nation, build, maintain, and nourish a free nation. The nation cannot produce or perfect free people, but a nation's government can be used by unscrupulous people to enrich themselves and pervert our liberty. The Founding Fathers understood the dangers to freedom posed by government and in fact knew that government is a free people's greatest potential enemy.

One of the essential elements of a free society is the traditional concept of civility, as it relates to the sense of social responsibility. This concept is different from the modern idea of using the correct fork at a formal dinner party. The Founding Fathers would have used the word to mean a deference or allegiance to the social order befitting a citizen. Unfortunately, this definition is now considered antiquated by modern dictionaries but it nonetheless describes the proper relationship between citizens and their society. Civility denotes the personal connection the individual has with his local community and society at large. This connection is internally motivated; it does not require the police force of the nation to compel allegiance. It does not require force to compel the obeying of commonly accepted rules of civil order. Civility compels individuals to respect other people's property rights and civil liberties. Many people living today can remember a time when people would never think of locking the front door of their homes or would leave their keys in their parked vehicles without so much as a second thought. This was the workings of civility within the community. This sense of civility limited the necessity of a public police force. A general rule for social liberty is that "the smaller the requirements of public police, the greater the degree of personal liberty in that society." The opposite is also true—the larger the requirements for public police to maintain order, the smaller the degree of personal liberty. Thus we see the vital role played by civility in maintaining our liberty.

The "plain folk" of the Old South provide an excellent example of this ancient civility in action. To assure social security, they would voluntarily exchange work when a member of the community was sick or injured. This was done out of a sense of community responsibility. No government coercion was needed to provide for the injured or sick.[3] New York City provides modern examples of the extremes, civility and the absence of civility, in action. During the attacks that occurred on 9/11/01, the citizens of that city gave the world a lesson in civility. They seemed to desire to help each other, without regard to status. There was no distinction made regarding where people worked, their financial status, or their ethnicity. All these factors were irrelevant. Citizens were determined to help each other through the crisis. There was no need of police to compel people to do what was right under the circumstances. People helped each other because it was the right thing to do—this is the hallmark of civility in a society. But to be effective, civility must be present during everyday life as well as during times of high crisis. Crime is the polar opposite of civility. The more crime a society has, the more it must depend on a government police force to maintain order and the less freedom the "law-abiding" citizens enjoy. Another extreme example from New York City is the vicious attacks that occurred during the disgusting "wilding" incident. Here we see a complete breakdown in respect for personal rights as a group of thugs stripped a young woman and subjected her to public humiliation. This vicious act of violence occurred with the encouragement of many in the crowd and within sight of public police—police who were powerless to compel respect for the rule of law.

A free society as envisioned by the Founding Fathers, and as once enjoyed by many of us living today, does not need extensive public rules and a government police force to compel its people to respect the civil liberties of their fellow citizens. A civilized people are naturally free and do not need to be tightly constrained by laws and

3. Kennedy and Kennedy, *The South Was Right!*, 20-21.

monitored by a Big Brother government in order to preserve "rights" within the community. Therefore, we can conclude that the first requirement of a free society is civility. This civility cannot be mandated by government. It must arise naturally from within the people of a society. It is nourished by the teachings of churches and other religious/ethical organizations within each community; it is taught within families and celebrated and rewarded within the local community. Government intervention distorts the normal relationships within communities and families. Eventually it hinders the work of the family, religious groups, and citizens as they labor to inculcate the principles of civility within the local community.

NONINTERFERENCE—THE SECOND
REQUIREMENT FOR A FREE SOCIETY

Civil liberties are a natural result of people who share similar social values seeking to protect each other's rights—as opposed to a group with the backing of political forces enacting laws to force people to give them "civil rights" above and beyond the general rights of society at large. A right is something that exists at the same time for all members of the community. My right to free speech does not lessen my neighbor's right to free speech. A right confers no obligation on others, other than the duty of others not to interfere with an individual's free exercise of his right. The rule of law must apply to all citizens, not one particular group. Laws passed to "legalize" the use of government police force to compel one group to submit to the demands of another group violate the principle of the rule of law. The most one person's "rights" should allow is to compel noninterference from others. For example, my right to publish these ideas extends to the public at large only to the extent that the public at large will not attempt to use illegal force (lynch mob, for example) or "legal" force (hate crime laws, for example) to prevent me from writing and publishing these ideas. Economist Walter Williams used the following example to describe the characteristics of laws in a free society.

> Let's think about baseball rules (laws) as a means to approach this question. Some players, through no fault of their own, hit fewer home runs than others. In order to create baseball justice, how about a rule requiring pitchers to throw easier pitches to poorer home-run hitters or simply rule what would be a double for anyone else a home run?[4]

4. Walter Williams, "American Contempt for Rule of Law" (www.jewishworldreview.com/cols/williams1.asp, July 5, 2001).

Professor Williams makes a succinct point that even a law passed for good purpose, i.e., to help the downtrodden or poor, must pass the noninterference test if it is to be considered an acceptable law. Another example is that, every year at the opening of Congress, lobbyists descend on Washington, D.C., pockets stuffed with money, to persuade "our" elected leaders to use the police power of government to grant and enforce special status/privilege to their group. Such grants enforced by government violate the principle of noninterference and therefore are an attack upon individual liberty. Unfortunately, individuals do not hire lobbyists to go to Congress every year to protect their liberty and property (especially income) rights; therefore, our rights are easy prey for the special interest groups, party politicians, and government bureaucrats.

Liberty is about the free exercise of choice by the individual within the context of a community of mutually accepted obligations— what we have described as civility. This choice must be free from interference, either private (mob violence, for example) or public (the use of government tax collectors to remove personal income, for example). The concept of rights is not just a philosophical abstraction pulled out of some dusty document. Rights arise out of the mutual obligations that we as a society accept and nourish in the local community. As Thomas Sowell wrote, "Today, when some people talk blithely about 'animal rights,' as if animals were part of some system of mutual obligations, even the obvious has to be explained to some of the products of our dumbed-down education. . . . Citizens are people who have a legal obligation to play by certain rules, and who are therefore protected by that same national system of rules."[5]

Thus we see that no law enacted to protect one group's rights should be considered fair if it violates the principle of noninterference. Laws designed to protect civil liberty should only compel individuals not to arbitrarily or capriciously interfere with another person's free exercise of his rights. To use a modern-day example, the right of an individual to attend a publicly financed school should limit another person only to the extent that the second person is compelled not to interfere with the first person's right to attend that school.[6] As a society we have mutual obligations, and from those we derive the mutual benefits enjoyed by members of society. Laws passed under the pretense of "protecting" or advancing the rights of a specific group will

5. Thomas Sowell, "Abstract People" (www.jewishworldreview.com/cols/sowell1.asp, Jan. 28, 2002).

6. Education in a Liberty-Based Society will be covered in chapter 9.

ultimately result in limiting the rights of individuals not associated with the "protected" group. As government enters into the social context, it corrupts the mutuality of benefits arising from and freely established by society and replaces it with force. This force is arbitrarily and capriciously applied by those who control or influence government. Society then begins to disintegrate into warring camps, each attempting to capture control of the government in order to advance its special claims at the expense of the "out-of-power" group.

SKEPTICISM OF GOVERNMENTAL POWER—THE THIRD REQUIREMENT OF A FREE SOCIETY

The protection of liberty requires a clear understanding of the danger posed to it by government. By the end of the twentieth century, most Americans looked upon government as the dispenser of rights and freedoms. A simple review of our founding document, the Declaration of Independence, will relieve Americans of that dangerous error. According to that document, liberty is ordained by God and therefore cannot be legally abridged, amended, or encumbered by government. If we accept the fallacy that our rights come from the government, then we must also accept the fallacy that the government may tell us what rights we have and how and when we may exercise them. What master gives, master can take away. Skepticism of government is the hallmark of the rugged American individualism that built this country.

Southerners came early to the conclusion that government is a dangerous, though necessary, force. John C. Calhoun, from South Carolina, in the mid-1800s declared, "Government has within itself the tendency to abuse its powers."[7] Even earlier, James Madison, from Virginia, stated, "Where there is power and an interest to use it, wrong will be done."[8]

While this healthy skepticism appeared early in American history, it is not limited to Americans. At the beginning of the twentieth century, Austrian economist Ludwig von Mises warned, "There is an inherent tendency in all governmental power to recognize no restraints on its operation and to extend the sphere of its dominance as much as possible. To control everything, to leave no room for anything to happen of its own accord without the interference of the authorities . . . this is the goal for which every ruler secretly strives."[9]

7. John C. Calhoun, as cited in Kennedy and Kennedy, *Why Not Freedom!*, 108.
8. James Madison, as cited in Kennedy and Kennedy, *Why Not Freedom!*, 108.
9. Ludwig von Mises, as cited in Llewellyn H. Rockwell, Jr., "Freedom Is Not 'Public Policy'" (www.mises.org, June 20, 2002).

In 1973, Murray N. Rothbard wrote a scorching denunciation of state (i.e., government) powers, declaring:

> • Libertarians regard the State as the supreme, the eternal, the best organized aggressor against the persons and property of the mass of the public. *All* States everywhere, whether democratic, dictatorial, or monarchical, whether red, white, blue or brown.
> • The State . . . has cloaked its criminal activity in high-sounding rhetoric.
> • Think of the State as a criminal band and the entire libertarian attitudes will logically fall into place.
> • The libertarian sees a crucial distinction between government, whether central, state, or local, and all other institutions in society.
> • *Only* the government obtains its income by coercion and violence. . . .
> • *Only* the government can use its funds to commit violence against its own or any other subjects. . . .
> • Historically, by far the overwhelming portion of all enslavement and murder in the history of the world have come from the hands of government.
> • There is another reason why State aggression has been far more important than private. . . . The reason is the absence of any check upon State depredations.[10]

In the opening years of the twenty-first century, there are still a few writers who recognize the potentially corrupting power that government has. Joseph Sobran declares:

> People are naturally cooperative, capable of loving each other and usually driven by loves of various kinds. Making allowances for Original Sin, their average level of humanity and honesty is far above the average for rulers of the force-systems we call states or governments. . . .
>
> But ordinary people aren't saints, either, and they too can be corrupted by power. They wouldn't rob their neighbors, but if the state will do it for them, they may accept a government check, without inquiring too closely into where it came from. They wouldn't murder people either, but if the state sends soldiers abroad to kill and conquer, calling it "defense" they won't usually object. The state spares them the pain and risk of committing crime, while sharing the profits thereof.
>
> Thus, dependence on the state corrupts millions of otherwise

---

10. Murray N. Rothbard, *For a New Liberty* (New York: Collier Books, 1973), 46-47.

decent people. If they hold government jobs, they may even flatter themselves that they are "contributing to society" when they
are, in fact, parasites on society—like the state itself.[11]

Americans of another era would proudly proclaim that the less
governed are the best governed. They knew what too many of us
today have forgotten. As long as a society embraces the traditional
concept of civility, its citizens insist on the principles of noninterference with regard to laws designed to protect liberty. And as long as
the citizens maintain a healthy distrust of government, then liberty
is safe. But one other concept must be clearly understood. The safety of liberty will not and indeed should not guarantee equality of
outcome. The free market will provide the best opportunity for
advancement, but it will not assure success—that depends upon
many factors, not the least of which is the determination of the individual involved. Seeing people "left behind" energizes bleeding-
heart liberals as well as fainthearted conservatives to begin insisting
that the government use its taxing power to take from those who
have (presumably too much) and give it to those who have too little.
Thus socialism creeps into our free society.

CAPACITY TO RECOGNIZE THE IMMORAL
NATURE OF SOCIALISM—THE FOURTH REQUIREMENT
FOR A FREE SOCIETY

The fact that I equate liberalism with socialism will anger no small
number of people. But the fact is that since the beginning of the
twentieth century, it has been liberals who have been the most successful in advancing the ideas of the former American Socialist movement. In the early 1900s, the American Socialist party had called for
a mandatory government pension system. Their call failed soundly.
But by 1935, liberals led by FDR had foisted a mandatory pension
plan upon America. Harry Hopkins, one of FDR's closest advisors, set
the stage for a new philosophy of socialism disguised as liberalism.
He borrowed many of the principles of the socialists, who heretofore
had been thoroughly defeated.[12] Soon liberal politicians would be
heard speaking at the Democratic party convention, declaring that
the party that had for so long championed states' rights (and therefore anti-federal socialism) would now leave the dark shadows of
states' rights and enter the glorious sunlight of human rights.

11. Joseph Sobran, "Why Wolves Rule" (www.sobran.com/columns/, July 25, 2002).
12. Bresiger, *The Revolution of 1935*, 17.

Liberalism clothed its socialist ideology in the most humane and compassionate verbiage available. Who could resist such progressive ideas as providing food to the needy or unemployment checks to those out of work through no fault of their own? Of course, there was no mention from the conservative camp that central banking, fiat money (government paper money with nothing of value to back it), and government taxation were largely responsible for the unsavory social conditions that liberals were now trying to solve—with more government! No matter how good a particular government program may sound (and it always sounds best when you receive the benefit but don't have to pay), it must be remembered that government has no money of its own. Government can give away only what it forcefully extorts from its citizens. Thus we see the fallacy of compassionate liberalism/socialism. It violates the principle of civility by interjecting government into the social setting that free citizens should be exclusively handling through their families, churches, and community groups. Compassionate liberalism/socialism violates the principle of noninterference by coercing private citizens to hand over part of their income for the benefit of programs and/or people they would otherwise not be inclined to fund. And it undermines our natural skepticism of government—we highly suspect that very little of the money will be spent for the stated purpose, but taxpayers have little control over this spending. Meanwhile, incumbent politicians use taxpayers' income to influence the voting patterns of those who receive our income. This is a very efficient scheme by which party hacks and other politicians use your money to buy votes for themselves!

Socialism and its twin, liberalism, rely on the government's police power to accomplish it goals. Force and liberty are at opposite ends of the political spectrum. Any system that relies on force will, by the very nature of force, degrade freedom. Ludwig von Mises, the economist who was forced to leave his native Austria when Hitler's National Socialists seized control of it, had personal knowledge of socialism's threat to freedom. He contrasted socialism and the free market. On socialism, he declared:

> Under the Fuhrer principle, under the kind of collaboration which we call socialism under an organized or "planned" society, under this system, there is one central will that determines everything and all the other people have to follow. They have to obey. . . .
>
> Socialism is a wonderful system; it is wonderful, very good, excellent, if we accept the ideas of the Fuhrer—if we only accept the ideas of the Fuhrer who leads the whole thing to the end. . . .

The ideal of socialism was always connected with the firm conviction that there is only one good plan possible and that only one plan ought to be put into practice, and that all the other plans for deciding affairs should be forbidden and considered as illegal, as unreal, as immoral, and so on.

And continuing, he discussed the advantages of a free market:

Over several thousand years, we have developed a practical system in which people can use their different qualities, their different knowledge, their different abilities and the various things which they find in their geographical environment, in order to receive from other people other things which they want to have or obtain. We have developed in this way a system of markets. . . .

What has made people better, what has given people better conditions and what has created all those things which we today consider as the pride of human accomplishment, was not due to some declamations, some talks, some dreams about a better world, or some attempts to realize a better world by the power of arms. What brought about all these things was the daily fine works of people, the attempts of people to improve their own conditions by working hard and by doing things which were unknown to previous ages, and even to themselves in their previous times. Therefore, we must say the market system—the system of producing something for the sake of giving it away, but only for giving it away to people who themselves are giving something away to us for our improvement, this market system may be considered a very common, but yet a very necessary system. . . .

It is the system that has converted people, whose ancestors were living on a scale of life which we now consider extremely unsatisfactory, into descendants who are continually committed to the idea of improving conditions by working more and more, by studying the conditions of nature more and more and by finding out better and better methods to fight all those things which we consider unsatisfactory. This is the right way for men to live.[13]

The right way for men to live is through voluntary exchange via the free market. Yet socialists would replace voluntary exchange with compulsion. Liberals usually deny they are socialists, while attempting to hide their collectivist schemes behind high-sounding verbiage declaring their affinity for the poor, the downtrodden, and those

---

13. Ludwig von Mises, "Socialism vs. Market Exchange" (www.mises.org, Aug. 16, 2002).

they claim the free market has left behind. But alas, their schemes are useless without your property, so liberals, like all good socialists, organize the police power of government to forcefully remove your property and turn it over to the self-anointed guardians of the poor. But since an individual liberal has no natural right to put his hand into your pocket and forcefully deprive you of your property, he cannot delegate that right to an entity called government—even if that government was blessed and sanctified by a majority vote in the last election.

Liberty is not license. It does not contemplate anarchy, but it does contemplate free and voluntary interaction between individuals. As the Founding Fathers understood, the role of government was to be very limited and the scope of its authority restricted to specific and enumerated sections of the political process. The primary role in our society was to be played by self-reliant individuals working within the context of their family and community.

Attributes that were taken for granted in 1776 must be rediscovered if we as Americans are to regain our lost rights. These attributes include the role of civility (a deference and allegiance to the society in which we live), accepting the principle of noninterference with regard to the rights of others (and not passing laws by the "compassionate" to protect the "rights" of the oppressed), and a healthy skepticism of government and those who seek to exercise governmental power. Added to this list in the twentieth century is the capacity to recognize the immoral nature of socialism in all its diverse forms, including contemporary liberalism.

Before we can achieve these high ends, we must prepare ourselves for the exciting and challenging political contest to come—one that *we the people* of the South will lead. This struggle will be a movement using peaceful and nonviolent political civil disobedience to overthrow the current liberal/socialist political system and replace it with a Liberty-Based Society. Liberty—it's worth the struggle!

QUESTIONS AND ANSWERS

Q. The social system that you are proposing would remove all the legal gains minorities have made. Are you really in favor of repealing the Civil Rights Acts and other similar legislation?

A. The legislation that you refer to was passed to correct defects in the liberal/socialist political system. No one can go back in history and determine what the evolution of the Republic of Republics would have been had it not been hijacked by special interest groups in the mid-1800s. Jim Crow laws and other means of segregation were established throughout America after the end of the War for Southern Independence. It is not our purpose or desire to defend the distortion that occurred in American politics and society (North and South) after the Federal government assumed its current position as the ultimate arbiter of American liberties. It is our intention to establish a society where individual liberty is the primary focus of politics and society.

In a Liberty-Based Society all rights will be respected but no special privileges will be "granted" to one group over others in society. In a society that respects the principle of noninterference, there will be no need for "civil rights" laws. The federal government will be prohibited from giving special privileges and *we the people* of the Sovereign States will assure that the state and local governments follow the same rule of law. But what would we do if a state decides to violate the principles of liberty? This could happen but *we the people* of the other states would have nonviolent means to convince our errant brothers and sisters to reform their ways. This will be discussed in some detail in chapter 4.

Q. You stress the importance of the community in nurturing children. Are you agreeing with Hillary Clinton's philosophy that "it takes a village to raise a child"?

A. The local community is composed of a collection of family units who share a common set of values. Raising children is the duty of the family but the family does not do this in a vacuum. The family's teachings and examples of civility must be reinforced by the community's teachings and examples (especially examples). A child's understanding of civility as taught by his parents should be supported by the actions of those who live around him. For example, the child should see that the teachings of honesty are useful because it is a common value that the child sees in operation daily.

Q. Your stress on the importance of community seems to hearken back to the days when people were born, lived, and died in the same locale. Most working professionals move every three to five years during their careers. Do you think we can make community important in such a mobile society?

A. The moral and social values by which people order their communities are important regardless of how temporary our residence in a particular community may be. Another thing you must keep in mind is that a lot of the moving around in contemporary society is due to the unstable boom-bust economy that the liberal/socialist political and economic system has foisted upon us. Also, in a Liberty-Based Society, the low tax structure will allow working people to keep more of their income and it will also provide for increased and sustainable economic growth. This will allow many families to find and keep jobs in their local area as opposed to "pulling up stakes" and moving across the country in search of employment. This is discussed in more detail in chapters 5 and 8.

Whenever you are thinking about how a Liberty-Based Society will work, you must not fall into the trap of thinking that it will work similar to the liberal/socialist model with which we are currently saddled. *We the people* have paid and are continuing to pay an enormous opportunity cost as a result of government's interventions in the economy (indirect taxation) and its heavy-handed tax-and-spend policy (direct taxation). Once this huge cost is lifted, we will begin to see a new world of social and economic opportunities that as of now most of us cannot even imagine.

We the people have a lot in common with the confused people of the former Soviet Union after the collapse of Communism. They had never lived without a socialist state, with all of its bureaucracy and central planning. The people had no idea how to manage without their commissars telling them where to work, how much to produce, and how much they would earn. They had no frame of reference with which to measure the future—their old socialist model had failed them and they had no experience in the free market. We are in a similar position. We have never lived in an economy where *we the people* decide how much to spend on retirement savings (Social Security), how to invest the full 90 percent of our income (currently the government takes around 40-50 percent in direct taxation alone), or how to order our local communities (currently the federal Supreme Court does that via busing court orders, affirmative action plans, federalizing the abortion issue, and numerous other social-engineering court orders). Initially people will have a difficult time judging the future because they too do not have a reliable frame of reference. Remember a Liberty-Based Society is not perfect, but it is one in which self-reliant individuals will be rewarded for their hard work and foresight. On the other hand, shiftless individuals who would like to live at the expense of others will find very little to comfort them in a Liberty-Based Society. They will not be allowed to spend other people's money because politicians in a Liberty-Based Society will not have the ability to extort our money!

Secession—Treason or Patriotism?

From the inception of the federal union under the Constitution of 1788 there has been a heated debate as to the proper relationship of *we the people* of the Sovereign States to the federal union. Do we as a people owe it our unqualified allegiance? Does the federal union have the authority to compel our allegiance? Did our Founding Fathers encumber our right to live under a government ordered on the consent of the governed, or do *we the people* still hold the right, as announced in the Declaration of Independence, "to alter or to abolish it, and to institute new Government" if our existing government becomes repressive and unresponsive?

John C. Calhoun condemned the argument that the federal government had the right to force our consent to its will.

> We are told that the Union must be preserved, without regard to the means. And how is it proposed to preserve the Union? By force! Does any man in his senses believe that this beautiful structure—this harmonious aggregate of States, produced by the joint consent of all—can be preserved by force? Its very introduction will be certain destruction to this Federal Union. No, no. You cannot keep the States united in their constitutional and federal bonds by force. Force may, indeed, hold the parts together, but such union would be the bond between master and slave: a union of exaction on one side, and of unqualified *obedience* on the other. . . . Disguise it as you may, the controversy is one between power and liberty.[1]

For those who view the federal union as divine, anyone who questions its authority or its edicts is guilty of heresy. But the same could have been said about anyone who questioned the divine right of kings, or who questioned the demand for total loyalty to the ayatollah, or who questioned the requirement of strict obedience to the party line of the Communist party. Occasionally men and women must summon up the courage to challenge anti-liberty acts, even if those acts come from those in control of the federal union.

John C. Calhoun's toast to the union should be every conservative's motto: "To the union, next to our liberties, most dear!" Who is the real traitor? He who blindly follows those in control of the federal union or he who demands a strict adherence to the original Constitution and asserts that *we the people* of the Sovereign States are the final arbiter of the limits imposed by the Constitution on the federal government?

---

1. Clyde N. Wilson, ed., *The Essential Calhoun* (New Brunswick, N.J.: Transaction Publishers, 1992), 371-72.

CHAPTER 4

Back to the Constitution

Should states be allowed to execute convicted murderers? This is a question that under the original Constitution would have never arisen. But as we noted in chapter 1, there are no effective limits on the meddling abilities of the current federal government. The question about capital punishment is only one of many examples of intrusive federalism. Recently a noted conservative columnist complained that the Supreme Court seemed ready to accept unsubstantiated data asserting that executions of convicted murderers do not deter other acts of murder. He pointed out that two more recent studies found that there is a correlation between executions and deterrence. The columnist closed his article with the following lament: "But neither facts nor the Constitution are likely to carry much weight among those wedded to fashionable dogmas. Unfortunately, that includes members of the Supreme Court."[1]

The implied conclusion is that there is not much anyone can do because the Supreme Court has ruled against conservative principles. And under the current liberal/socialist political system, this is true. If the Supreme Court issues a ruling contrary to the better notions of *we the people* of the states, then the best we can hope for is that one day these offending justices will retire and we will be lucky enough to have a conservative president in office at that particular time in history who will nominate a "right-thinking" justice and at the same time have a conservative Senate that will then confirm that "right-thinking" justice. This is not exactly the best system for defending individual liberty! It is certainly not the system contemplated and designed by the Founding Fathers. Most modern-day conservatives are shocked to hear that under the original system of a constitutionally limited Republic of Republics, *we the people* of the

1. Thomas Sowell, "Death Sentences" (www.jewishworldreview.com, July 1, 2002).

states reserved unto ourselves the right to decide if an act of the federal government was unconstitutional and therefore null and void. The right (indeed the duty) of the Sovereign State to interpose its sovereign authority between an oppressive federal government and the otherwise defenseless citizens of the state was seen as an indispensable counterbalance to the development of an all-powerful and abusive federal government.

Imagine what would happen today if *we the people* of the states still possessed this indispensable right. Abortion would no longer be a national political issue. Gun control would be settled within the greater community of the individual state. Busing, affirmative action, quotas, illegal immigration, violations of the Second Amendment right to keep and bear arms, and unfounded federal mandates would all be resolved by *we the people* within our respective Sovereign State. The role of the federal government in the daily life of our citizens would become almost invisible—which is the exact role envisioned by the Founding Fathers. The federal government would be responsible for protecting our borders (what a unique thought), dealing with foreign nations, and assuring a free trade zone within the union of Sovereign States.

Let us review the wisdom of the Founding Fathers as it pertains to this most essential right—i.e., the right and duty of the Sovereign State to defend constitutional liberty against the encroachments of an abusive federal government. Our Founding Fathers were confident that the Sovereign States would always be ready and able to defend our "dearest interest." James Madison stated: "I am unable to conceive that the State legislatures, which must feel so many motives to watch, and which possess so many means of counteracting, the federal legislature, would fail either to detect or to defeat a conspiracy of the latter against the liberties of their common constituents."[2]

Alexander Hamilton was a virulent Federalist who personally wanted to see a dominant federal government, with a president serving for life and the Senate appointed for life in a fashion similar to the British House of Lords. But even Hamilton soon realized that Americans would not easily surrender their hard-earned liberty to another centralized government—even if it were an American-made government. To convince those who were skeptical about the federal government proposed under the new Constitution, he adopted the language of the anti-Federalists by declaring: "We may safely rely on the disposition of the State legislatures to erect barriers against the encroachments of the

2. James Madison, as cited in Kennedy and Kennedy, *Why Not Freedom!*, 39.

national authority. It may safely be received as an axiom in our political system, that the State governments will, in all possible contingencies, afford complete security against invasions of the public liberty by the national authority."[3]

From these quotes it can be seen that the Founding Fathers looked to the Sovereign State as the final arbiter of the legitimate extent of federal power under the Constitution. To leave such an important question up to the Supreme Court or any other branch of the federal government would have been tantamount to asking the agent of the states, the federal government, to decide the limitations imposed on it by the Constitution! For a full examination of the history behind the ratification by the states of the Constitution, the acts of the principles, and the Sovereign States' creation of their agent, the federal government, see *Was Jefferson Davis Right?*[4]

After the adoption of the Constitution, the Federalist party gained control of the government and used their political power to pass laws that were clearly a violation of citizens' freedom of speech and press. Newspaper editors and numerous other Americans were arrested, tried, and convicted by the Supreme Court.[5] Thomas Jefferson and James Madison authored the famous Virginia and Kentucky Resolutions of 1798, in which they declared to the world that the Sovereign States had the authority to take whatever actions were necessary to protect their citizens' liberty.

> . . . and that whensoever the general government assumes undelegated powers, its acts are un-authoritative, void, and of no force: That to this compact [the Constitution] each state acceded as a state, and is an integral party, its co-states forming as to itself, the other party: That the government created by this compact was not made the exclusive or final *judge* of the extent of the powers delegated to itself; since that would have made its discretion, and not the Constitution, the measure of its powers; but that as in all other cases of compact among parties having no common judge, each party has an equal right to judge for itself, as well of infractions, as of the mode and measure of redress.[6]

3. Alexander Hamilton, as cited in Kennedy and Kennedy, *Why Not Freedom!*, 29.

4. Kennedy and Kennedy, *Was Jefferson Right?*

5. Early in American history, in addition to hearing cases, the federal Supreme Court justices rode "circuit" and carried out duties now discharged by district and circuit federal judges.

6. Kentucky Resolutions, Nov. 10, 1798, as cited in Kennedy and Kennedy, *Was Jefferson Right?*, 282.

Thus we see an early example of the Founding Fathers (Jefferson and Madison) looking to states' rights as a means of controlling the abuses of the federal government. The selection of the most appropriate "mode and measure of redress" as mentioned above is left to the discretion of the political leadership in the Sovereign State. It may be as simple as an appeal from one state legislature to her sister state legislatures, or nullification of the onerous and unconstitutional federal act, or maybe as extreme as the secession of the offended state from the union.

IF SECESSION IS POSSIBLE, HOW DO YOU KEEP THE COUNTRY TOGETHER?

The states' right of secession is the single most misunderstood principle of the original constitutional Republic of Republics. It should be recalled that the division of powers was not limited to the newly created federal government, but it included the counterbalance provided by the Sovereign States. Within their sphere each was primary, but it must be remembered that only the Sovereign States had original authority. The limited and specific authority exercised by the federal government was a secondary authority—authority received from the states in the form of a conditional grant. The union held together not due to the moral suasion of bloody bayonets but due to the mutual benefits each party received from the union. Mutual benefits, mutual respect, and anticipation of continued benefits and respect were the bonds that held the original union together. Liberty departs from a union as soon as force is used to compel a member to remain in the union. The union of a dove's breast and a hawk's talons is a union of sorts but hardly representative of the type of union contemplated by the Founding Fathers—though certainly representative of the one forced upon us by Abraham Lincoln.

From the adoption of the Constitution in 1788 until 1860, the union held firm while weathering several turbulent political crises. In 1815 the New England states met in convention and voted to begin the act of secession. They found this necessary because of the harm done to their commerce by the War of 1812. Fortunately, the war ended before their secession became necessary.

Again in 1828, Congress passed the Tariff of Abomination, which would have made the Southern states the primary source of federal revenues (this was in the good old days before Lincoln introduced America to the federal income tax), and South Carolina nullified the onerous tariff and then threatened to secede if the federal government attempted to collect said tax. The benefits of the union were still great and the other states did not want to see one of their own leave the union, so calm minds worked out a compromise acceptable to all parties.

Then again in the 1850s, numerous Northern states nullified the federal Fugitive Slave Act. Here we see an example of how Sovereign States of the North used their sovereign authority to prevent federal actions that they felt were immoral even though the Constitution allowed for the return of fugitive slaves.[7] The use of these rights did not cause the breakup of the union but assured its continuation. The union held together under the original Constitution, in spite of radical differences among the member states.

Contemporary world history provides examples of how the right of secession served to hold unions together even though the constituent parts held conflicting opinions. The province of Quebec has held several elections regarding secession from the federal union of Canada. But the mere threat of secession, coupled with Canada's acceptance, in theory at least, of the right of Quebec's secession, has had the positive effect of calming the political debate. As long as the principle of secession is accepted, then secession itself is not necessary. In such circumstances, the acknowledged right of secession serves as the catalyst for compromise. The parties to the union still see that the mutual benefits of their union outweigh the benefits of separation. This is the paradox of secession. As long as the right is recognized by all parties, then secession from the union is not necessary, and compromise is very likely to be found. But what happens when the right of secession is denied?

The Baltic States under the former Soviet Union provides an example of what happens when a union rejects the right of secession. Even though the former Soviet Union's constitution assured the right of self-determination for its various states, no one took this promise literally—least of all the power brokers in the Kremlin. But after nearly fifty years of Soviet domination, in the late 1980s the Baltic States began their open struggle for independence. The Soviet Union refused to allow such acts of disloyalty and sent in troops using their typical brutal oppression and secret police to keep the secessionists in line. Fortunately for the Baltic States, the Soviet Union imploded before it could crush their secession movement. But Mikhail Gorbachev had sounded very similar to Abraham Lincoln as he prepared to put down the movement. If secession had been honestly recognized, and the benefits of remaining in the Soviet Union

7. U.S. Constitution, art. 4, sec. 2.

mutually satisfactory, then no secession would have occurred. But as most of us understand, the Soviet Union was not a union for mutual benefits. It was an empire—one that used the resources of its member states to enrich its own power brokers. A union of *Sovereign* States is held together by the mutuality of benefits derived from the union. A union that is held together by the use of bloody bayonets forfeits its claim of being a free republic and becomes an evil empire.

If by some stroke of a luck or alchemy the federal government suddenly recognized the states' right of secession and nullification, would the U.S.A. break apart and drift away into fifty (more or less) insignificant, petty nations? If you listen to both neoconservatives and liberals, you would think this would happen. They each hate the concept of states' rights (which must include the right of secession and nullification, or else there is no way to enforce these so-called "states' rights"). Why do they hate it? Because they both want their turn at the controls of the empire! As was demonstrated in chapter 1, while the Democratic party is the party of bigger government, the Republican party has become the party of big government. Neoconservatives don't have a problem with big government. They do have a problem with liberals (as opposed to neoconservatives) controlling big government.

So back to our question: What would happen to the union if *we the people* of the now Sovereign States found ourselves armed with the power of states' rights? What major mutual benefits do we receive from the union? The fifty states, and territories, offer us a tremendous free trading zone that encourages commerce and investment; the union makes us collectively one of the major players in world commerce; and our size makes any potential aggressor think twice before he launches an attack against us. Would possessing the right of secession and nullification change any of these benefits? No. Then why would any state want to secede?

If states' rights were once again allowed to be exercised by the states, we most likely would see some changes in the size and scope of the federal government. For instance, I doubt that the people of Nevada would allow their fair state to become the federal nuclear-waste dumping ground. The people of Oregon most likely would negotiate a better deal with the federal government regarding water rights for their farmers. States along the Mexican border might nullify onerous federal unfunded mandates requiring welfare services and "free" public education for illegal aliens. Yes, there would be changes, but they would reflect the will of *we the people* of the Sovereign States and not the will of self-appointed experts, bureaucrats, and political hacks in Washington, D.C.

Just for fun, let's see what would happen if a state did something totally unacceptable as far as the other states are concerned. What recourse would *we the people* of the offended states have? Say the mythical state of Oklarado high up in the Rocky Mountains decided to nullify the Thirteenth Amendment and reinstitute slavery. Under the system of states' rights, as previously described, "those people"[8] would have the right to do exactly that—just as Northern states had the right to nullify the federal Fugitive Slave Act in the 1850s. But what could we do? The U.S.A. believes in liberty! We could not allow slavery to exist in our modern nation. And we would be correct. The difference is that instead of rousing armies to invade and occupy Oklarado, we would meet in a convention of states and give Oklarado an ultimatum—give up slavery or get out of the union. In addition, private citizens could decide for themselves if they wanted to do business with the people in Oklarado or allow citizens of Oklarado to visit within the U.S.A. In other words, the cost of maintaining their foolish and immoral attachment to modern-day slavery would force their political leadership to rethink this course and abandon it. All of this would be done without firing a single shot or spilling a single drop of blood. The enjoyment of mutual benefits and the acceptance of mutual obligations are what hold a union based on liberty together. Bloody bayonets belong to tyrants, dictators, and universal criminals who oppress people attempting to exercise their inalienable right of self-determination.

HOW DO WE RESTORE THE CONSTITUTIONAL PREROGATIVE OF STATES' RIGHTS?

As I noted in chapters 1 and 2, the federal government's attitude toward states' rights is that it "died at Appomattox." This being the case, *we the people* are left with the responsibility of resurrecting states' rights. In *The South Was Right!* my brother and I referred to this as a "radical restoration of the original constitutional Republic of Republics."

One of the failures of conservatives during the twentieth century—a failure that assured a century of conservative retreat before aggressive liberal/socialist factions—was the failure to recognize that constitutional liberties cannot be secured without states' rights. In

---

8. "Those people" is a term Gen. Robert E. Lee applied to the enemy during the War for Southern Independence. I use it to show contempt for the actions of the people of my imaginary state of Oklarado.

short, without states' rights, *we the people* are not free! The federal powers may from time to time allow us to exercise certain rights, but it is always the federal government's prerogative whether or not to allow its subjects to continue to enjoy those "rights." For example, it is the federal government's prerogative to decide via the Internal Revenue Service (IRS) how much income its subjects may enjoy. This anti-liberty situation could not have occurred if *we the people* of the states had at our disposal the states' right of nullification (anyone care to nullify the IRS?). Neoconservatives and liberals reject the notion of states' rights because it tends to limit the size and scope of their empire, but as private citizens *we the people* know who ultimately pays for this anti-liberty, big-government empire. Therefore, to protect our civil liberties and property rights, we must restore balance to the federal/state governmental arrangement. To do this, I offer a constitutional amendment—the State Sovereignty Amendment.

Some "conservatives" may ask why an amendment is needed to secure enforceable states' rights. They usually point to the Ninth and Tenth amendments and proudly proclaim that they are sufficient. But the important point that these conservatives miss is that under our current liberal/socialist political system, the federal courts are the final arbiters of the limitations imposed upon the federal government by these amendments. The federal courts usurped this authority, but with the passage of my amendment, *we the people* of the Sovereign States will return this authority to states and the people thereof. With the establishment of a Liberty-Based Society, the final authority as to the extent of federal powers will once again rest with *we the people.*

All political activity must now be directed toward the overthrow of the current liberal/socialist political system and the adoption of the State Sovereignty Amendment. *We the people* of the Sovereign States shall restore the original constitutional Republic of Republics and establish our Liberty-Based Society. In chapter 16, entitled "Political Reality," I will give an overview of the strategy we will use over the next several years to force this issue onto America's political stage. The amendment appears below.

THE STATE SOVEREIGNTY AMENDMENT[9]
These United States of America are a Republic of Republics deriving its authority from the consent of the governed residing within

9. A complete discussion of the State Sovereignty Amendment can be seen in Kennedy and Kennedy, *Why Not Freedom!,* 289-308. The general text of the amendment is taken from that book.

respective Sovereign States. Each Sovereign State is the agent of the people thereof. The federal government formed by the compact of the United States Constitution is the agent of the Sovereign States. Federal authority shall be supreme in all areas specifically delegated to it by the Constitution. All acts or legislation enacted pursuant to the Constitution shall be the supreme law of the land. The Sovereign State reserves an equal right to judge for itself as to the constitutionality of any act of the federal government.

Section I. The Sovereign State specifically reserves the right to interpose its sovereign authority between acts of the federal government and the liberties, property, and interests of the citizens of the state, thereby nullifying federal acts judged by the state to be an unwarranted infringement upon the reserved rights of the state and the people thereof.

1. State nullification of a federal act must be approved by a convention of the state.

2. Upon passage of an act of nullification, all federal authority for the enumerated and nullified act(s) shall be suspended.

3. Upon formal acceptance of nullification by three-fourths of the conventions of the states, including the original nullifying state, the enumerated federal act(s) shall be prohibited in the United States of America or its territories.

4. Upon formal rejection of nullification by three-fourths of the conventions of the states, the enumerated federal act(s) shall be presumed to be constitutional, notwithstanding any judgment of any federal or state court.

5. Until or unless there is a formal approval or rejection by the conventions of the states, the nullified federal act(s) shall remain non-operative as to the original and any additional nullifying states. A state that in its convention ratifies a particular act of nullification shall be construed to have nullified the same act as enumerated in the initiating state's nullification.

6. No federal elected official, agent, or any individual working within or associated with any branch of the federal government may or attempt to harass, intimidate, or threaten a Sovereign State or the people thereof for exercising their rights under this amendment. No federal elected official, agent, or any individual working within or associated with any branch of the federal government shall attempt to influence or use his office to attempt to influence the deliberations of the people regarding the nullification of a federal act, or the acceptance or rejection of a nullified federal act(s).

7. Any United States military officer, noncommissioned officer, or federal official or agent who carries out or attempts to carry out any order by a federal official, officer, or agent to deny or hinder the people of a Sovereign State from exercising their rights under this amendment shall be subject to the offended state's laws and may be tried accordingly. Jurisdiction in such cases is specifically denied to all federal courts, military courts, or any other court other than the courts of the offended state.

Section II. The government and people of these United States approve the principle that any people have a right to abolish the existing government and form a new one that suits them better. This principle illustrates the American idea that government rests on the consent of the governed and that it is the right of a people to alter or abolish it at will whenever it becomes destructive of the ends for which it was established. Therefore, the right of a Sovereign State to secede peacefully from the union created by the compact of the Constitution is hereby specifically reserved to each state.

1. An act of secession shall be executed by a convention of the people of the state.

2. The seceded state shall appoint representatives to negotiate settlement of all debts owed the federal government, the purchase of federal properties within the Sovereign State, and the removal of federal military installations and personnel.

3. Upon acceptable arrangement for the payment of sums owed the federal government, the representatives may negotiate treaties of friendship, common defense, and commercial relations. Said treaties are subject to the same constitutional ratification as other treaties.

4. Readmission of a seceded state shall follow the same constitutional requirements as for any new state.

5. No federal elected official, agent, or any individual working within or associated with any branch of the federal government shall attempt to influence the people of the Sovereign State regarding their decision to secede from, remain with, or join this union.

6. Any United States military officer, noncommissioned officer, or federal official or agent who carries out or attempts to carry out any order by a federal official, officer, or agent to deny or hinder the people of a Sovereign State from exercising their rights under this amendment shall be subject to the offended state's laws and may be tried accordingly. Jurisdiction in such cases is specifically denied to

all federal courts, military courts, or any other court other than the courts of the offended state.

7. The duty of the people of the Sovereign State to exercise their inalienable right to govern themselves is a right that existed before the formation of the federal government, and therefore nothing in this amendment shall be interpreted in such a manner as to deem the federal government to be the donor of the rights as exercised by the people of the states.

RECLAIMING LIBERTY

With the passage of the State Sovereignty Amendment to the federal Constitution, *we the people* of the Sovereign States will have the one sure means at our disposal to correct current abuses and to prevent future unconstitutional abuses of federal powers. No longer will issues near and dear to the people in their local communities be held hostage by self-anointed experts, special interest lobbyists, and governmental bureaucrats in Washington, D.C. With this right restored within the American political system, liberty at last will be secure and we can reverse over one hundred years of conservative failure. To pass such a bold and revolutionary amendment will require a dedicated cadre of Liberty Freedom Fighters. For the first time in over a century, we are in a position to win our struggle for liberty, but your help is necessary!

QUESTIONS AND ANSWERS

Q. I believe in states' rights and a constitutionally limited federal government. The amendment you propose would certainly give the people of the states a means to override onerous federal laws and court orders, but how can we ever expect to get such an amendment passed?

A. Your skepticism as to the possibility of passing such an amendment under the current business-as-usual, liberal/socialist political system is well founded. If we continue to play by the rules that they have established, then we will never win. That is why we must change the game! In chapter 16 I outline the political movement needed to accomplish our goal of establishing a Liberty-Based Society. Essentially, it is a grassroots effort based in the South that first educates Southern conservatives on the need and possibility of establishing a Liberty-Based Society. After the initial phase, we will contest the Republican presidential nomination in an effort to normalize the concept of a Liberty-Based Society, putting the business-as-usual crowd that controls the GOP on notice that they must adopt our platform and name our candidate on the GOP's presidential ticket or else we will run for president on a third-party ticket! The third-party run will amount to a plebiscite for independence. After the third-party run, we will then have a Liberty movement in every Southern and many non-Southern states. We will then begin a campaign to capture the governor's offices, legislatures, and other political offices in these states. With this base of political power we will initiate a campaign of political civil disobedience to convince the rest of the states to pass our amendment.

Q. You quoted Alexander Hamilton as declaring that the states would always be able to "erect barriers against the encroachments of the national authority." How can this be? I thought he was an ardent Federalist who wanted a supreme federal authority.

A. You are correct—Hamilton was an ardent Federalist. But when he wrote these words he was trying to counter the arguments of the anti-Federalists, who were warning Americans that even a central federal government limited by a written constitution posed a threat to our liberties. No one knows if he was being sincere, but he and the other Federalists did manage to convince a slight majority of Americans to accept the proposed federal government created by the ratification of the Constitution. It was not long before Hamilton began reading into the Constitution federal authority that had not been specifically granted to the government by the states via the Constitution. Americans were warned at the time of the ratification of the original Constitution that a constitution was merely a parchment barricade—it would never withstand the assaults of those who wanted to establish an American nation/state and commercial empire via a supreme federal government.

Q. If all that we need to correct over a century of lost rights is an amendment to the Constitution, why hasn't it been proposed before now?

A. This is a good question, but I should warn you that it will take more than an amendment to accomplish what needs to be done. It will require the re-education of our people so that they understand the essentials of liberty, such as self-reliance, civility, and the inherent dangers of liberalism/socialism. As far as why this has not been offered before—you need to ask those who have been leading (misleading) American conservatives for the past 140 years or more! The truth is that our business-as-usual party politicians have much to lose if *we the people* pass this amendment and establish a Liberty Based Society that would so severely limit their power to dispense other people's money.

This is why I stress the need to overthrow the current liberal/socialist political system and replace it with a Liberty-Based Society. This struggle will be different from anything we have done in the past. We will change the game and make our own rules! We will select the time, place, and battles that we will use to push our program forward. *We the people* of the Sovereign States do not need a king, a strongman dictator, or even a democratically elected conservative leader to restore our lost rights. We are competent to do the job ourselves. And when it is done, we will owe no human for our liberty, and *we the people* of the Sovereign States will know who will be responsible to be ever vigilant to assure that unhampered liberty is passed on to our children and their children for generations to come.

Q. What can I do to help advance the cause of establishing a Liberty-Based Society?

A. The first task is for all of us to think through the logic that justifies the need for a Liberty-Based Society. In chapter 1 I make the point that conservatives have been reactionaries—and poor ones at that—to the latest liberal/socialist incursion upon our reserved rights. We must first understand that we cannot win by doing the same things we have been doing for the past century. After that we must begin the task of informing our friends and neighbors and the mass of conservative voters. It will be our responsibility to introduce the concept of a Liberty-Based Society to our fellow conservatives. We must build working groups that will support our mass education efforts and slowly over the next several years build a grassroots network of dedicated men and women who are willing to sacrifice for the cause of liberty. When this has been accomplished, we will be ready to launch our political-action campaign. More detail will be provided in chapter 16.

The Free Market's Wealth Generator

1. Liberty-based government decreases payroll tax, increasing take-home pay

    1a. Liberty-based government decreases government spending by equal amount

2. Workers spend part of increased take-home pay

    2a. Workers save part of increased take-home pay

3. Increased spending raises demand for goods and services

    3a. Increased savings decreases interest rates for loans

4. Entrepreneurs read decreased interest rates as signal of future healthy economy

    4a. Entrepreneurs borrow at lower interest rate to increase output

5. Capital-goods industry expands to meet demand for more capital equipment

    5a. Significant number of new labor jobs opens in the expanding economy

6. More payroll-tax revenues flow into government treasury

    6a. Liberty-based government *lowers* payroll-tax rates and government spending

7. Decreased payroll tax increases take-home pay [cycle repeats, gaining more sustainable economic growth with each cycle]

This is the only way government can optimize the wealth-creating potential of the free market. The expansionary boom is sustainable because it is based on a healthy economy as signaled by increased savings and decreased loan interest rates. Capital expansion creates more jobs, but it also requires a long time before entrepreneurs can begin to reap a return on the initial investment. This is the fatal flaw in the current liberal/socialist economic system typified by the federal government's unsound monetary policies. Under the current federally imposed economic system, by the time the boom is at its zenith, it becomes apparent to entrepreneurs that there is no real savings to support the boom. This puts entrepreneurs on notice that a situation of poor investment exists. They realize that the market will eventually "adjust" in order to liquidate bad investments and restore a sound investment environment. This is when the average investor watches in horror as his 401K and other investments lose a large part of their value.

CHAPTER 5

The South from Poverty to Prosperity

Around the beginning of this century the per-capita income in the United States was around $30,472. The per-capita income for those living in Washington, D.C. is an astounding $40,150.00—your federal taxes at work![1]

Per Capita Income Southern States Comparison[2]

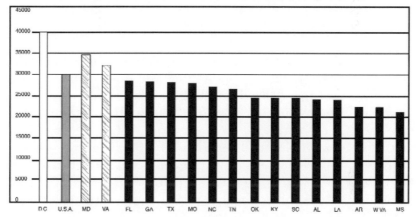

The per-capita income of the sixteen Southern states[3] was only $26,758. The only Southern states to rise above the national average were Maryland ($35,188) and Virginia ($32,431). It is more than mere coincidence that the only Southern states with per-capita income above the national average are the two adjacent to Washington, D.C. The per-capita income for the other Southern states ranges from $28,947 for Florida to $21,750 for Mississippi, America's lowest. Poverty has become the birthright of the South.

1. www.bea.gov/bea/regional/spi/drill.cfm.
2. Ibid., Jan. 20, 2003.
3. The eleven traditional Confederate states plus Kentucky, Maryland, Missouri, Oklahoma, and West Virginia.

Most Americans, indeed most Southerners, accept this as if it were the natural order of things. Most people equate poverty in the South with "other" naturally occurring things, like sand at the beach. One thing is certain. The people who live in those sections associated with the victor in the War for Southern Independence enjoy a much higher income level than those residents of areas traditionally associated with the defeated South.

Region	Per-Capita Income	Region	Per-Capita Income
New England	$37,115	Southeast	$27,246
Mideast	$34,968	Southwest	$27,439
Great Lakes	$30,103		
Plains	$29,313		
Far West	$32,047		

The above table[4] shows the regions that currently enjoy the highest incomes (the victors) as opposed to the vanquished in 1865.

The boom of the 1990s did little to fundamentally improve the Southern economy. From 1963 to 2000 the South *lost* ground in the important arena of research and development. Even though the South accounts for about 20 percent of the United States economy, as of 2000, only 7 percent of the research was performed in the South, and this was down from a paltry 8.5 percent in 1963![5] According to a spokesperson for the Southern Growth Policy Board:

> We have served as the tenant farmers. Somebody else owns the farm and we provide the labor . . . we created a branch plant economy. The home office, along with R&D (research and development) was not here [in the South].

One of the major social problems with the Southern "branch plant economy" is that when the inflated economy cools and the inevitable bust occurs, the first workers to get "laid off" are not those in the home office up North but those in the "overflow" branch

4. www.bea.gov/bea/regional/spi/drill.cfm.
5. Ed Anderson, "Southern Region Loses Ground in Industry-Performed Research," *New Orleans Times-Picayune*, Aug. 28, 2002, sec. A, p. 11.

plants—mostly down South where "cheap labor" can be found. But poverty is a part of our Southern condition, and the questions remain. Is poverty a naturally occurring event in Dixie? Are we victims of our own beloved environment? Could it be that instead of a naturally occurring condition, this poverty is the result of political decisions made by those who benefit from Southern impoverishment?

FORCED INTO POVERTY BY THE FEDERAL GOVERNMENT

Prior to the South's loss of the War for Southern Independence, its economic power contributed greatly to American prosperity. Before the 1860s, around 60 percent of federal revenues were obtained from the South! As one Southern political leader complained, the South had become America's "milch cow,"[6] providing the rest of the country with a painless way to finance all manner of federally sponsored internal improvements. For those who understand Southern history, it is not surprising to find out that when the South fired upon Ft. Sumter in 1861, they aimed their first shots at the hated Federal Customs House, where the despised tax on Southern commerce was collected by federal tax collectors. Lincoln knew the real reason for keeping the South in the Union and declared as much when he was asked why not just let the South go in peace. His response was that of a wounded tax collector: "Let the South go. Let the South go? Where then shall we gain our revenue?"[7] The South's impoverishment was required in order to assure the eventual international dominance of the North's financial/commercial empire.

The impoverishment of the South was a direct result of war, conquest, and the inability of Southerners after the war to control their own political, economic, and social destiny. The forces that inflicted this impoverishment had been determined from the very beginning of the republic to improve their economic standing at the expense of the South. The financial disaster that befell the South as a result of war and its aftermath lingers with Southerners today. Most Southerners find it uncomfortable even to think or talk in detail about it. Why? Because whenever we talk about anything regarding the war, we (or others in the conversation) feel obligated to mention the sad topic of slavery.

The powers that currently dominate the South have forced upon her people a sense of slave guilt. This "guilt" works as an efficient

6. Kennedy and Kennedy, *The South Was Right!*, 48.
7. Ibid., 50.

liberal tool to silence Southern dissent. If Southerners raise their voices in protest, they are immediately branded as advocates of slavery and racism!

Liberals, especially Northern liberals, are not constrained by such guilt. Most have forgotten or simply ignore the fact that slavery is a part of their history too. Prior to the war, the North had been very careful to liquidate its capital investments in slaves by selling them to the South (or even worse, selling them to the Caribbean sugar plantations, where life expectancy was much shorter). If they did not sell their slaves, Northerners would free them after a given point in time. This allowed the Northern slave owner to keep his slaves during their productive years, and then after the Northern slave owner had earned a handsome profit on his investment, he would free the slave when the slave was old and had become a liability. The system of Northern emancipation allowed them to liquidate their capital investment, remove a people from their society with whom they did not wish to associate, and then take that money and reinvest it in other profitable enterprises. This technique allowed Northern capitalists to effectively expand their economy. Unfortunately, the South was not allowed to liquidate its huge capital investment in slaves. The slaves in the South were emancipated without compensation to the owners. The loss of Southern capital (money invested in slaves) meant that both white and black Southerners would have less opportunity to work because there would be no newly created jobs. It meant that industry owned and financed by native Southerners would be less likely to develop in the South. It meant guaranteed poverty to all who resided in the South. It also meant that there would be no new Southern factories or industry competing against established Northern industrial interests—what a coincidence!

To get an idea of the capital loss in slaves alone, let us look at the capital assets loss suffered by just one Southern state after emancipation. Louisiana lost $170,000,000 of capital investment in slave property, and that was 1860s gold-backed dollars![8] (Slaves were less than a third of the total loss—remember the loss of human resources, infrastructure, emerging local industry, and political leadership that resulted from the war.) Recall that this is not about the loss that the plantation owners suffered. The problem is that the entire Southern society, black and white, suffered when this tremendous amount of investment capital suddenly

8. Ibid., 37.

disappeared—unlike what had happened up North. Is this ancient history still important and relevant to us today? Go back to the tables above and then answer this question. This is a sacrifice that no other section of America had been forced to make. The resulting impoverishment of the South fell on black Southerners even worse than it did on white Southerners. Black Southerners entered their freedom with even fewer material assets than their impoverished white neighbors. It is important to understand the origins of our poor Southern economy, but we must not dwell upon it. The question now facing us is, "How can we transform our current second-class economy into an expanding and prosperous economy?"

BEWARE OF THOSE WHO MEASURE POVERTY

How do you measure poverty? Usually this is done by taking measurements at a specific point in time. But thankfully, the economy is not static. It does not stand still; it is moving—it is a dynamic economy. This is important because if someone is making minimum wages today, he most likely will not be in a relatively short period of time—say five to ten years. This is demonstrated by the fact that most of the people in the bottom 20 percent (economically) in 1975 have been in the top 20 percent of income earners since then.[9] This fact gives us a good idea of what the free market can do, even one encumbered by government regulations and liberal/socialist taxes. Imagine what would happen in a true Liberty-Based Society with an unencumbered free market! But those who measure poverty do not take this into account. They measure as if the world is static and declare the free market to be a failure or at least an unfair (what's fair?) way to distribute wealth. All the while the free market, while crippled by liberal/socialist regulations and taxes, is working without the aid of the self-anointed "champions of compassion" moving the deserving from poverty to plenty.

HOW IS WEALTH CREATED?

Controlled or socialist societies operate on the principle of compulsion. The government takes your property and redistributes it according to a politically derived formula. A Liberty-Based Society operates on the principle of freedom. The government is limited to a very small role in society and the free citizen is

---

9. Thomas Sowell, "Hard Times for Envy" (www.jewishworldreview.com, Jan. 20, 2003).

allowed to dispose of, invest, transfer, or save his property as he freely chooses. In the free market, commercial transactions do not occur unless both parties freely consent. In addition, that consent is obtained only when both parties determine that they would be better off after the exchange than before it—both parties gain. In a socialist society, someone must give up something (usually in the form of taxes and/or liberty) in order for the government to give something (usually entitlements or special privileges) to someone else—the productive element suffers in order to reward those who are not productive. Socialism is great for distributing wealth already created, but it cannot, never has, and never will create wealth. The free market is the wealth-generating system that has given us virtually all the benefits that we enjoy in the modern world.

Let's look at the marvels that occurred as a result of the free market "doing its thing" in the past century. Financial and social improvement became such a standard part of our lives that we grew to expect it. Marvels of technology became commonplace, but they were the product of the free market. Government did not produce them. Free people working for their own betterment (Austrian economists sometimes refer to this as "enlightened self-interest") produced them and through the market process made them available to all of us. For example, the life expectancy in 1900 was forty-seven years, but today it is seventy-seven years. Infant mortality at the beginning of the twentieth century was 1 in 10, but by the end of the century it had dropped to 1 in 150. In the early part of the century, an average worker had to labor two hours to earn enough money to buy a chicken to feed his family, but by the end of the century he had to work about twenty minutes.[10] Did socialism produce this radical improvement? No. It was the free market at work. Yes, many men became very rich in the process. Henry Ford amassed a large fortune, but in the process he made the automobile a common item in families across America. The gains reaped by the common man as a result of Ford's labors and investments far outweigh his personal fortune. In America today even most of the "poor" have air conditioning. An immigrant who was asked why he wanted to come to America declared, "I wanted to come to a country where even the poor are fat." *The free market is the engine of wealth production because it allows*

10. Walter Williams, "The Politics of Envy" (www.jewishworldreview.com, Nov. 6, 2002).

individuals to harness their own creativity, energies, and dreams. It rewards people for taking risks, and it does so without regard to race, creed, color, sex, national origin, or any other element not directly related to the marketplace.

IF THE SOUTH WERE AS FREE AS HONG KONG

In the last few years of the twentieth century, Nobel Prize-winning economist Milton Friedman wrote an editorial in which he pointed out how much better off we would be if the United States were as free as Hong Kong.[11] The point he made was that even though Hong Kong had very little in the way of natural resources, its citizens were better off than we were because their government maintained a policy of limited taxation and little regulation of the business process. (Austrian economists would certainly agree with Friedman on this point, but they diverge when it comes to sound monetary policy because he believes in fiat money—inflationary paper money not backed by gold.)

Let us apply the Hong Kong principle to the South and see what could happen. First, look at Hong Kong. In 1950 the United States' per-capita GDP (gross domestic product) was almost six times Hong Kong's, but after years of liberal-inspired socialism, it was only 7 percent greater than Hong Kong's![12] Hong Kong's economic strength is further proof that liberals cannot tax a society rich, but they can impoverish the productive element of a society. According to Friedman, Hong Kong's direct government spending is less than 15 percent of its national income, whereas the United States' direct spending is 40 percent. Hong Kong's government's indirect spending—unfunded mandates, regulations, etc.—is virtually nonexistent, but in the United States it accounts for around 10 percent. Friedman's estimate for the latter does not account for the federalization of the money supply, with the resulting cost of unsupported paper currency and unsupported credit. His conservative estimate of the United States being 50 percent socialized actually understates the full effect. In reality we are closer to 70 percent, when the socializing impact of government's unsound monetary policies is factored into the equation. But even with Friedman's more conservative estimate, the impact is devastating.

As he wrote:

The marginal contribution in going from 15% of the national

---

11. Milton Friedman, "If Only the U.S. Were as Free as Hong Kong," *Wall Street Journal,* July 8, 1997, editorial page.
   12. Ibid.

income to 50% has been negative. I firmly believe that we would be better off if we were free to use that part of our production in accordance with our individual tastes and values rather than turning control of it over to the political authorities. The results would be a GDP per capita 70%, not 7%, higher than Hong Kong's.[13]

Hong Kong is not the only example of the free market's potential for producing wealth. India provides an example of how misguided, although perhaps well-intentioned, liberal/socialist laws can destroy even the hope for prosperity, while liberty, once unleashed, can turn poverty and despair into hope and progress. In 1947 India gained its independence from Great Britain. It was an era of anti-capitalism in the nations of the Third World. Socialism was seen as the wave of the future, and India bought in to the lie. After the nation accepted the political primacy of socialism, it became very hard for Indian entrepreneurs to compete in the marketplace. Before they could bring new products or services to the market, they had to work through endless government rules, regulations, and guidelines, and/or they had to pay large bribes to government agents. It was common knowledge that in order to do business, an Indian entrepreneur would be forced to bribe up to forty government bureaucrats. What most people do not realize is that the entire society bears the cost of lost opportunity when government places barriers in the path of entrepreneurs working to expand and grow the economy. Thomas Sowell wrote:

> The Birla family was likewise refused the government permissions needed to expand. The net result was that they bought pulp in Canada, had it converted to fiber in Thailand, had the fiber converted to yarn in Indonesia and then had the yarn made into carpets in Belgium. All the while, India remained a very poor country in need of economic growth and the jobs and incomes that these operations could have provided.[14]

All of that began to change after the reforms of 1991 were enacted. It was the first time that the government recognized the pernicious effect it was having on the Indian economy. The small change that took place was not a result of socialists or liberals learning their lesson from the sad experiences of the poor.

13. Ibid.
14. Thomas Sowell, "India Unbound" (www.jewishworldreview.com, July 12, 2001). Copyright 2001. Used by permission of Thomas Sowell and Creators Syndicate, Inc.

Change was forced on them because of the failure of their social-ist system. The reforms were a boost to the free market, and as new jobs began to open up, the poor found new opportunities to improve their standard of living. But one can be assured that there are socialists eagerly awaiting an opportunity to reinstate socialist dogma as soon as they can find a new way to harness envy and generate hatred for "greedy" businesspeople who "take advantage" of the poor. As we have seen, the free market helps the poor—it is the socialists and liberals who take advantage of the poor.

An important point to remember is that all of these laws and government regulations, regardless of what nation we are study-ing, were enacted at the insistence of liberals and socialists who thought (or claimed) they were doing the best thing for the poor. However, in reality they made life even more miserable than it otherwise would have been. For example, liberals want to pass laws to protect the environment because they assume they are the only people with pure motives. They claim that businesspeople are only motivated by greed (we would call it the profit motive). The Environmental Protection Agency (EPA) provides numerous examples. In Convent, Louisiana, the EPA held up the opening of a new plastics plant because of what it called "environmental racism." This $700 million plant would provide numerous jobs to the local community, a community composed of many low-income blacks. The local NAACP conducted a poll of Convent's black community and found that 73 percent favored the proposed plant. Yet, the will of *we the people* at the local level is of no concern to liberals. Even though the Louisiana Department of Environmental Quality certified that the proposed plant met its strict emissions standards, the EPA refused to permit the plant. Henry Payne wrote, "But Greenpeace and its allies, determined to stop the plant, invoked President Clinton's 1994 executive order on environmental injustice, which compels federal agencies to consider whether minorities bear an unfair burden in the loca-tion of industrial facilities."[15]

Liberals know that if they throw up enough barriers to entrepre-neurial activity, eventually they will be able to deter the efforts of businessmen. Sadly, this has happened more than once. In anoth-er Louisiana case, the Federal Atomic Energy Board held up the

15. Henry Payne, "'Environmental Justice' Kills Jobs for the Poor," *Wall Street Journal*, Sept. 16, 1997, editorial page.

permit for a proposed $850 million nuclear fuel enrichment facility, citing "environmental injustice" as the reason. After seven years of struggle, the out-of-state investors gave up and moved on to other opportunities.[16]

Government's massive intervention in day-to-day business decisions has reduced our enterprises to near copies of the sluggish federal bureaucratic behemoths that now sap so much of our entrepreneurial energy. In 1962, the Austrian economist Ludwig von Mises commented, "When a concern must pay heed to the political prejudices and sensibilities of all kinds in order to avoid being continually harassed by various organs of the state, it soon finds that it is no longer in a position to base its calculations on the solid ground of profit and loss."[17] Not being able to calculate and project profit and loss adds a new risk in any speculative adventure—so much so that it may discourage otherwise bold investors.

One can begin to consider the impact all the new federal regulations have on prospective investors when one realizes that since 1980 these regulations have more than tripled! American businesses face 10,000 more regulations today than they did in 1980.[18] Yet liberals/socialists continue to pass more regulations that do little to help our society but do much to make it difficult for us to compete with foreign companies that are not burdened with our legal system. As Mises stated, "The cost of diverting a corporation's managerial workforce from producing better-quality and less expensive products to catering to the whims of regulators is impossible to measure precisely, but it is bound to be huge."[19]

Yet the cost does not end there. Mises continued:

> With so much regulation, there is no free speech in the business world, either. Very few business people will speak out against government regulation for fear of retribution by regulators. In fact, they will often support harmful and counterproductive regulations for fear that they may get something worse if they don't.[20]

16. Ibid.

17. Ludwig von Mises, as cited in Thomas J. DiLorenzo, "Regulation and the Stock Market" (www.mises.org, Aug. 20, 2002).

18. Ibid.

19. Ibid.

20. Ibid.

As we have seen from the examples of Hong Kong and India, the free market is the only way to produce wealth. As India and the United States demonstrate, liberalism and socialism via tax policy and intrusive regulations hinder the free market's natural tendency to develop a wealthy and prosperous society. How can we put this knowledge to use in the South? What can we do from a political point of view that would encourage the development a vigorous economy? As we point out in chapter 10, in a Liberty-Based Society, the total government taxing authority must be kept to no more than 10 percent of the GDP. This would be well below the 15 percent that Hong Kong enjoys. In addition, in a Liberty-Based Society, government regulations would be kept to a bare minimum. With our sound money policy, we would completely wipe out inflation. From this you should begin to get an idea of what a free Southern economy would be like. We would be an international powerhouse fueled not only by abundant Southern natural resources but by the energy and intellectual capital of our people working in an unencumbered free market. The best thing government can do to increase personal wealth and remove poverty is to get out of the way and allow *we the people* to develop our economic potential.

THE FREE MARKET'S WEALTH GENERATOR

Every time Congress convenes, the debate over increasing taxes versus cutting taxes begins. Liberals/socialists frame the debate with the claim that "we" cannot afford to pay for tax cuts. They maintain that the only way to resolve society's perplexing problems, such as the high cost of health care or prescription drugs, is by increasing the amount of your income that government is allowed to seize. But liberals/socialists will never tell us how they plan to increase society's output of goods and services. In a Liberty-Based Society, the individual wealth of laborers, professionals, and entrepreneurs will be increased by an expanding and sustainable economy. The sidebar at the beginning of this chapter gives a simple outline of how the free market economy will respond when government gets off the backs and out of the pockets of its citizens.

The only way government can assure an unhampered free market is by lowering taxes to a minimal level (say around 10 percent of the GDP maximum), refraining from deficit spending, and avoiding intrusive governmental regulations. Decreasing interest rates on loans stimulates expansion of capital-goods industry.[21] Capital expansion in turn creates more jobs.

Increased savings and jobs are a direct result of decreased government interventions and tax levies. Robust savings are a sign that the economy is healthy and that consumers have sufficient money to pay for essentials (food, shelter, and clothing) with enough remaining to allow for discretionary spending/saving. This signals to entrepreneurs that there is a reservoir of discretionary funds available to purchase goods and services well into the future. This sustainable future purchasing power indicates to entrepreneurs that the economy will stay healthy long enough to consume the new goods created by the long-term capital expenditures—expenditures usually made to acquire new factories, expensive production equipment, and a skilled workforce to build and deliver future goods and services. As you can see, this system works only if government is not allowed to inject unsupported credit or inflated fiat currency into the economy. If government is allowed to distort the system, it will produce an initial economic boom, but it will be unsustainable and cause tremendous numbers of bad investments (caused by relying on government-corrupted savings/interest signals). Sooner or later these bad investments must be removed from the economy, producing a bust, and as we have seen, it is not those close to the government and their favored banking and business clientele who will pay the price. As with all things dealing with government, those who are close to government are protected, but the taxpayer is ultimately forced to pay the cost. And then the politicians signal their favored clients to start the Ponzi scheme all over again.

This is the reason why men such as Thomas Jefferson and Andrew Jackson were opposed to the concept of a national bank.

---

21. Capital goods are used by industry to turn out finished consumer goods. For example, the production of a machine press allows the wood industry to turn out particle board that the Home Depot will sell to consumers. Generally, investments in capital-goods industries require more time before the entrepreneur/investor/businessperson earns a profit. This is why the liberal/socialist boom/bust business cycle is so detrimental to our economy. During the boom, investors supply their capital for what appears to be a good business prospect, but the bust arrives before enough time has passed to allow for an adequate return on investment. Then management and investors are faced with the prospect of losing all of their investments. This is when industries "retrench" with layoffs and downsizing. At that point all they can do is wait for the Fed to initiate the next boom and start the cycle all over again. See Ludwig von Mises, *Human Action: A Treatise on Economics* (1949; reprint, Auburn, Ala.: Ludwig von Mises Institute, 1998), 490.

They knew that the bankers and commercial interests would always have political connections in "high" places to protect them and eventually shift their loss to *we the people*.

QUESTIONS AND ANSWERS

Q. You make the point that the South is the poorest section in the entire country, but if you improve its per-capita income, won't the South just be taking jobs away from non-Southern states?

A. One of the many fallacies promoted by liberals/socialists is that the only way one group can prosper is at the expense of another group. Wealth, in their world, is limited and therefore government must intervene to make sure the little wealth we have is "fairly" divided. A liberal/socialist system cannot create wealth—all it can do is seize what wealth is available and forcefully redistribute it. On the other hand, the free market will create more wealth and thereby enrich society as a whole. The free market is the wealth generator that has elevated modern civilization. As investors, businesspeople, and entrepreneurs develop new products, they create new jobs that allow workers to enjoy an ever-increasing standard of living. Liberals/socialists see the economy as a win/loss proposition, whereas those of us who advocate an unhampered free market see a society in which everyone wins.

Q. You mentioned in this chapter that if the South were as free as Hong Kong, it would become an economic powerhouse. Isn't this really an argument in favor of Southern independence?

A. Yes, but remember our goal is to offer to all Americans an opportunity to join the people of the South as we remove America's failed liberal/socialist political model and replace it with one based on liberty. The South has always been an advocate of limited federalism, states' rights, and constitutional government. *We the people* of the Sovereign States of the South are now in an enviable position. The fallacies of the past (slavery and Jim Crow segregation) that were used by our enemies to discredit our defense of states' rights and limited government no longer exist. We are now free to offer Americans the precious gift of a Liberty-Based Society. Will they accept it? Who knows? But one thing is for sure—the next generation of Southerners will grow up in a nation based upon the principles of liberty. Hopefully the vast majority of states will join us in this movement, but if not, we plan to be free nonetheless.

Q. Many years ago, I recall how an economics professor claimed that free market advocates argue against government taking action to allay the hardships created by market crashes, panics, recessions, and depressions. How can you expect people to support your position of doing nothing while working people are out of work and suffering through no fault of their own? Shouldn't government intervene to jumpstart the economy?

A. Those of us who follow Austrian economic teachings are opposed to government interventions completely, not just during the bust or economic slowdown. If government had refrained from injecting unsupported credit into the economy in the first place, then the unsupportable boom that leads to the bust would not have occurred. But as a result of our liberal/socialist government interventions, the unsupportable boom does occur and therefore sooner or later the bad investments made during the heady days of the boom must be liquidated. The longer this "market adjustment" is put off, the worse or more prolonged the recession/depression will be. The best way to prevent all of this is to establish a system of government (a Liberty-Based Society) that does not permit government interventions in the economy.

Q. You claim that with reduced taxes, workers will save more, interest rates will fall, and investors will read this as a signal for additional or new investments. Don't you think that instead of saving the increased dollars in their paychecks, workers will just go out and spend it?

A. With a tax decrease, workers will have more discretionary income. Some may elect to spend all of it at first, but others will elect to save a portion or invest it for future spending for such things as retirement or their children's college tuitions. Eventually the money will end up in the hands of businesspeople, who will use it to increase production or save it via investment instruments such as stocks and bonds. The primary point to remember is that working people's income does not belong to government—it belongs to the people who work hard to earn it! Any government that deprives its citizens of more than 10 percent of their income (regardless of what method we may yet elect to measure this by) is guilty of extortion. The bulk of monies currently collected by government are used to assure reelection of incumbents. Incumbents pass out other people's money to special interest groups and businesses, such as clients of the central bank (the Fed) and corporations with strong political connections with government power brokers in Washington, D.C. When all is said and done the ultimate question must be answered: Whose money is it? In a Liberty-Based Society the vast majority of our income stays with the individual who, by working or investing, earned it! The time has come to tell the fat-cat politicians, special interest groups, and politically well connected corporations to get off the dole and learn how the rest of us gain our living. We earn it—and by God, we intend to keep it!

Race Relations in a Community That Cares[1]

Back in the early 1960s everyone knew that Mississippi was populated by white people who hated blacks—or at least that was the general impression given to the world by the mainline media. No doubt there were some difficult social issues that needed to be resolved, but the following true story gives a different view of just how unimportant race really is to most Southerners.

During the civil rights era of the 1960s, most Southerners lived normal, peaceful lives, unaware of the national perception of an agitated South. A few years back two sisters in their fifties told me their "civil rights" story. Sometime during the early 1960s they decided to go to town to do a little shopping. They were surprised to find the town full of blacks—usually the population was about equally black and white. Little had they known that they had planned their shopping trip on the very day that one of the largest civil rights demonstrations in the county's history was to take place.

Both were concerned for their safety, but they were determined to complete their shopping. To avoid the large and boisterous crowd, they took the long way around to reach their shopping destination. As they began walking the final block to their favorite store, they felt confident that they had picked a safe route. But to their alarm, suddenly around the opposite corner at the end of the block emerged one of the largest black men they had ever seen. Fear and apprehension overtook them as they slowed their pace and wondered what they should do. Should they cross the street? Should they turn and go back? No, they reasoned. This is ridiculous. We will hold our heads high and walk right past him. But by then they noticed that he had fixed a wide-eyed stare on them! They clutched each other's hand and momentarily stood motionless in the middle of the sidewalk. The irrational fear was suddenly broken by shouts of surprise and joy. The three ran toward each other and embraced. It was Big Bob, who as an orphan had been taken in by the sisters' mother and father. As good Christians, they could not bear to see an innocent child suffer. They did their Christian duty despite the hardships and poverty that typified rural Mississippi in the early 1900s. When he was sufficiently grown, Big Bob set off on his own and eventually became a successful small-business owner. He would come by the old place each year at Christmastime to check on his "white parents" and to swap child-rearing stories with his white brothers and sisters.

"What are you two doing coming around by this route?" asked Big Bob.

With a note of embarrassment in their voices, they explained, "Well, actually, we were trying to avoid the mob of people over at the courthouse. What are *you* doing around here?"

"Well," he said, "I was trying to avoid getting mixed up in that big crowd at the courthouse. I need to get back to my store and don't have time to waste over there. Just listen to'em—all that shouting and demonstrating. They are trying to get what we've always had!"

---

1. This account of race relations in the state of Mississippi during the early 1960s was told to the author by the individuals involved.

CHAPTER 6

Making Race a Nonissue

Liberals have made race a major issue in America today. Before we can address how to make race a nonissue, we must first determine the veracity of liberalism's claims against the white middle class as they relate to the issue of race.

ARE WE A RACIST SOCIETY?

Allegations of racism had become the most contentious, emotional, and highly charged subject of American life by the end of the twentieth century. Liberal talking heads assured all that racism was endemic in America, with occasional outbreaks in epidemic portions. Self-appointed "experts" and spokesmen for the offended flooded nightly news programs and mainline print media with virulent accusations that evil is only slightly disguised in the attitudes of America's white middle class. Every social, civic, or political issue had to be dissected by liberal experts looking for evidence of institutionalized racism. Self-appointed black leaders thought of nothing but race and, by applying their personal logic to society at large, assumed that the middle class, especially the white middle class, was equally transfixed by the race issue. It was and still is an illogical assumption—but one that fitted nicely with their political agenda and one that had become very profitable for the self-appointed black leadership.

In the meantime, America was attempting to move beyond the subject, which of course would result in the loss of a major political weapon in liberalism's arsenal, not to mention the loss of substantial income for the self-appointed black leaders. By the end of the twentieth century, a black female entertainer, Oprah Winfrey, was the most popular daytime host on American television. Yet we were constantly reminded by liberals that we were a racist society or at least harbored unconscious racist attitudes. By the end of the twentieth century, the majority of viewers of professional sports were white but the vast majority of professional players were black (not to mention university sports). Yet the likes of Jesse Jackson and Al Sharpton continued to remind us that the lynch rope was only slightly hidden within closets all across white America. In the same year that an avowed racist made headlines in a highly visible election in Louisiana—an incident that was a godsend for the coffers of the professional "see I told you America is a racist nation" crowd—an opinion poll conducted in there demonstrated that the vast majority of the state's voters would vote for a black candidate, Colin Powell, if he ran for president! In 2003 voters in Louisiana selected Bobby Jindal, a young man of non-European ancestry, as one of its two candidates for governor. Jindal's parents are from India and his dark skin sets him apart (by color) from the vast majority of his supporters. Does racism permeate American society, or does the use of race permeate liberal/socialist political campaigns?

The unspoken truth is that by the end of the twentieth century racism had become big business and big politics in America. The propaganda ministry[1] of the liberal establishment, the mainline media, and the high priesthood of liberal theology, academia, were kept busy revving their powerful engines to perpetuate race as one of the key weapons in assuring liberal victories in the electoral process. Of course, conservative leaders were so intimidated by the subject that they dared not defend the integrity of America's white middle class. Thus, liberalism's accusations of white middle-class racism remained unchallenged—*conservative silence* validated or at least gave credence to these unfounded liberal accusations!

Liberals and self-appointed black leaders found it politically useful to allege that the social pathologies affecting blacks during the past century were a direct legacy of white-inspired discrimination and slavery. One black politician, while demanding greater tax funding for Aid to Dependent Children, told a Southern state legislature committee, "We owe these people." I witnessed this harangue and was struck by the sheer terror on the faces of the white committee members. You could almost see their thoughts—"How can we make him shut up before this threat becomes an embarrassing public discourse?" This one black liberal cowed five white officials, all of whom were elected from reasonably conservative

1. Kennedy and Kennedy, *Why Not Freedom!*, 42-43.

districts. Do you think these elected officials' first or even second thoughts were how to protect their middle-class constituents' income from yet another socialist raid? No way! Their only concern was how to avoid becoming involved in a race fight that would be fueled and waged upon them by the liberal propaganda ministry. The cowardly, timid, and unmanly (though who in our age still remembers what *unmanly* means?) failure of conservative leadership to constantly confront this issue has resulted in race becoming liberalism's talisman—*like a magic wand they can wave it and immediately conservative leaders and elected officials will scurry for cover!* By the end of the twentieth century, the race card had become liberalism's trump card. It was, in fact, an unintended gift to liberalism from the cowardly leadership of the conservative movement.

ARE WHITES TO BLAME FOR BLACK SOCIAL PROBLEMS?

Are social pathologies such as crime, drugs, illegitimacy, broken families, and unemployment a result of white-inspired discrimination and slavery? If so, do groups that have suffered civil wrongs in the past have a legitimate claim for restitution in the present? And is it fair to hold one generation accountable for the sins of prior generations? If not, then both white and black America has been defrauded by the socialists! Let's look at some data.

Currently, black illegitimacy hovers around 70 percent, but in the 1920s it was a fraction of that rate.[2] Today fewer than 40 percent of black children live in two-parent families; in the 1920s that rate was between 75 and 85 percent. In the 1920s, the crime rate for black Americans was a fraction of what it is today. Currently, 50 percent of homicides, around 50 percent of rapes, 59 percent of robberies, and 38 percent of assaults are committed by blacks— even though blacks make up less than 13 percent of our population! Making these statistics even more depressing for black Americans is that they are most often the victims of these crimes. Department of Justice data for 1976 to 1999 reveal that 46 percent of murder victims were black and 94 percent of black murder victims were murdered by blacks.[3]

During the 1940s, black students in a Harlem school had scores equal to and sometimes superior to those of white working-class students on New York's east side. Black scores from Harlem

2. Walter Williams, "Family Secrets" (www.jewishworldreview.com, Nov. 20, 2002).
3. Walter Williams, "An Evil Racist Plot" (www.jewishworldreview.com, Jan. 31, 2001).

schools are much lower today after years of civil-rights activism and political black power![4] If white-inspired discrimination and slavery are the causative factors in modern black social patholo- gies, then why is it that as you go back in time—that is, the closer you get to the era of slavery or the era in which the white political structure was ignoring black issues—the less social pathology you discover in the black community? Asking this question will not make you any friends in the liberal ministry of propaganda or among their high priests in academia, but it is germane to the question of race and American society.

Another point made by liberals is that minorities are less likely to benefit from help offered unless it comes as a result of minori- ty political power. In other words, the allegation is that blacks can- not improve their social and economic condition in our society without black political power. In this view the black politician is seen as a key element to black social progress. We need to test the this liberal assertion by asking, "If black political power helps decrease poverty, crime, and illegitimacy, then do parts of the country that enjoy black political dominance demonstrate lower rates of these social pathologies?" As the eminent black economist Prof. Walter Williams commented, "That's a nice theory, but the result is the exact opposite."[5] The harsh and thus-far unspoken reality is that blacks have been sold a bill of goods by the white lib- eral establishment and sold out by their own self-appointed lead- ers and politicos. Professor Williams notes, "For 50 years, the well meaning leftist agenda has been able to do to blacks what Jim Crow and harsh discrimination could never have done: family breakdown, illegitimacy and low academic achievement."[6] With "friends" like these who push the liberal agenda, do black Americans really need enemies?

The civil rights movement reached its zenith with the passage of the 1964 Civil Rights Act. One would think that this would elim- inate black mistrust, but only thirteen days later the Harlem race riots began. Black leaders from Stokely Carmichael to Rap Brown to Martin Luther King all blamed these types of riots on white society! During the Watts riots, "enlightened" liberal print media

4. Thomas Sowell, "'Friends' of Blacks" (www.jewishworldreview.com, Sept. 4, 2002).

5. Williams, "An Evil Racist Plot."

6. Walter Williams, "A New Racist Strategy" (www.jewishworldreview.com, Feb. 28, 2002).

such as *Newsweek* ran the results of an opinion poll asking white people to give the cause of the riots. The results were reported under headings of "intelligent" and "less perceptive" answers. Those who blamed white society were listed under the "intelligent" section and those who answered that the rioters were criminals who deserved to be punished for their actions were listed under the "less perceptive" section.[7] Charles Murray wrote in his book:

> The National Commission on Civil Disorders . . . conclud[ed] that . . . "white racism is essentially responsible for the explosive mixture which has been accumulating in our cities since the end of World War II." The report presented no proof for this statement, but few objected. Its truth was self-evident.[8]

EQUALITY OF RESULTS REPLACES EQUALITY OF OPPORTUNITY

This attitude of white guilt and responsibility advanced by the liberal propaganda ministry, its high priests in academia, and its political leadership changed the focus of civil rights from equality of opportunity—a pro-liberty approach—to one of equality of outcome—an anti-liberty approach. Henceforward in America, equality must be measured in results, or else racism is presumed to be at work! Search all you want, but you will not find a single case where conservative leaders set and followed through with a plan to correct the false assumption of equality of results. This is yet another example of conservative failure.

THE ROLE OF GOVERNMENT

Black Americans tend to vote in a bloc for Democratic candidates. Why? Why have black Americans been historically wedded to politicians promising liberal/socialist schemes? If we want to make race a nonissue in our society,[9] we must first understand this phenomenon and then find a way to gradually reverse the historical trend. White and black Southerners, who share many social

7. Murray, *Losing Ground,* 31.
8. Ibid., 32.
9. When I use the term *our society,* I refer specifically to the South—not the white South or black South but our common homeland, the South. I have little hope that any attempt to strengthen the bridges of friendship between the races would work outside of the South. Indeed, the human condition in big cities of the North, in my opinion, would work against any hope of establishing a nonracial society.

attributes, have almost exactly the opposite view of the benefit or danger offered by government. This dichotomy of political belief is generally overlooked by casual observers. In the South we have two peoples who share a common homeland and whose history, for good or ill, has been intertwined for centuries. And liberal propaganda to the contrary, we are two peoples who generally live and work together in a peaceful and respectful manner. Yet we have such a different attitude toward the role of government in our society. Why?

Well, it's not genetic! It is in fact a learned tradition that arises from the distinct history of each group. The white South was set- tled primarily by Scotch-Irish people who were fleeing the tyranny of England. These immigrants brought with them a healthy dis- trust (skepticism) of government. After all, it was big government in London that sent armies to rape, plunder, kill, and conquer the Celtic peoples of Wales, Ireland, and Scotland. In order to be free, these people had to flee big government. They settled in the back- country of the South and Pennsylvania and were enjoying a self- sufficient life until the English once again began to oppress these free-spirited Americans. The descendants of those Scotch-Irish immigrants who had fled big government in order to be free found themselves in a battle with big government (the Revolutionary War) in order to maintain their liberty. This whole sequence of events reoccurred in the 1860s; however, this time the big govern- ment was closer to home—Washington, D.C.

The white South has a long experience with government and its tendency to take away the civil liberties and property rights of a free people. Thus, we have tended to favor a limited government where most of the relatively few decisions required of government are made at the local level.[10] Our history has the beneficial effect of supporting liberty, but this is not true of every group's history!

For black Southerners, it was government that destroyed the insti- tution of slavery and government that organized the freed slaves and promised them a better life ("forty acres and a mule"). It was big government that eventually helped them to break down the Jim Crow barriers. During the war on poverty, it was big government that provided them with "free" entitlements. The perception of most black Southerners is that government is a useful tool that they can use to raise up their communities.

10. Kennedy and Kennedy, *The South Was Right!*, 21, 23.

However, as I have already noted, all of these recent "government" entitlements have had the very opposite effect they were supposed to have. Instead of raising the standard of living within the black community and making the members more self-sufficient, they have made them more dependent—dependent on the man in the "big house" but this time it's the White House. But what do conservatives have to offer? We must remember that liberty does not allow government to take the property from one person in order to benefit another. This is another area where conservative leaders have been remiss. Historically, conservative leaders have attempted to gain black support by "buying" it with more social entitlements. In other words, the conservative plan has been a weak "me too" of the liberal/socialist plan for black Americans. We can do better!

AN ECONOMY FULL OF OPPORTUNITY

It's strange, but even young liberals tend to become conservative as they age. This usually revolves around the fact that when you are young the tax collector is of little concern—you are living off your parents or you work at an entry-level job where the tax bite is too small to notice. But as you begin to work your way up the income ladder, you soon discover that more and more of your hard-earned income is being "stolen" from you by the tax collector. Thus, the cost of all of those socialist programs comes home, and suddenly it just does not seem fair.

How do we make pro-liberty conservatives out of black Southerners? It is really simple; we must provide a system that encourages economic activity. As more black Southerners enter the economic middle class, they will begin to realize the natural injustice of a government that appropriates more and more of their income. The fact is that liberals have an incentive to keep blacks dependent on government entitlements. As blacks become more self-sufficient, they would be far less likely to vote for liberal candidates. Without black support, liberals would not be able to maintain their political power. On the other hand, the best way for white society to protect their income from big government is to encourage an economy that will increase black economic achievement.

Why do many blacks think it is important to go out to the polls and vote in an organized bloc for liberal/socialist candidates? It is because they intuitively understand that the current American system of mass democracy has deteriorated into a one of political spoils. Because of their lower economic standing (as a group—many individuals within the black community are exceptions to this general observation), black Americans bear a disproportionately smaller part of the tax burden arising from government redistribution of income while they gain a disproportionately larger portion of the "redistributed" income. From this perspective, big government is a great deal! But someone must ask—is it really working? Is it benefiting black economic standing? The answer is a resounding no! LBJ's Great Society transferred nearly one trillion dollars of upper- and middle-class income in an effort to improve the economic status of the poor (a larger proportion being black Americans, especially in the South). If a trillion dollars worth of socialism won't do the trick, perhaps we need to look to a better model for economic improvement. But wait! You can rest assured that liberals/socialists will cry that one trillion dollars was not enough. But the truth is that under a socialist model (which is what our political system based on spoils is), no amount of money nor coercion would be enough. As was proven in the Eastern European experiment with socialism, no amount of centrally controlled resources is enough to make a failed socialist system successful. According to Murray Rothbard, the total amount of taxpayers' dollars spent by federal, state, and local governments since LBJ's Great Society is *seven trillion dollars,* and still liberalism/socialism is a *failure!*[11]

All the modern improvements that we have grown accustomed to today are a direct result of the workings of the free market. Centrally planned government did not invent the automobile, the radio, or microwave ovens, nor did it produce the marvels of modern medicine and technology we are accustomed to enjoying. The free market did it, in spite of the perverting influences of government. What would have happened to our economy if instead of spending between one and seven trillion dollars on socialist welfare programs, that money had stayed with the Americans who had earned it? Would they have taken their money and buried it in jars in the backyard? No, the money would have been saved and invested back into the economy. Jobs and opportunity would have flourished. Instead, the socialists spent between one and seven trillion dollars of other people's money teaching people to fill potholes, making others

---

11. Murray Rothbard, as cited in Adam Young, "A Retrospective on Johnson's Poverty War" (www.mises.org, Dec. 31, 2002).

more dependent on government, and generally destroying black families and communities.

But will black Southerners believe us? It's unlikely that they will, at least in the beginning. But we must argue for a new economy based on a free market, limited taxation, and very little government interference. I will demonstrate in chapter 10 that limited taxation means taxation no greater than 10 percent GDP. Under these conditions, the Southern economy could compete with any in the world.

During the debate over whether or not Mississippi should keep her state flag, which contains the Confederate Battle Flag, many blacks were interviewed and they expressed little concern about the flag but did express concern about their economic condition. We all have a vested interest in advancing our economic condition. Government programs have been shown to be the failure that all socialist programs eventually become. An unhampered free market where citizens enjoy limited taxation and limited governmental interventions can do what the free market does best—create economic miracles.

REMOVE THE SPOILS SYSTEM AND
RACE BECOMES A NONISSUE

Race is an issue in American politics because it benefits those who want to control big government (liberals/socialists) and because many blacks perceive that they benefit from government entitlements and special privileges that flow to them from big government. If we cut government down to size and prevent it from using its police power to extort income from citizens, if we constantly challenge the liberal/socialist claim that they are trying to help the disadvantaged "left behind" in our society and explain how liberal/socialist programs are destroying black families and communities, and if we offer a viable free market alternative to our current economic standing, then over time we will see more black Southerners move into the middle and upper economic classes. As this occurs, the possibility of "conservatives" winning black votes will dramatically increase and the likelihood of black Southerners marching lockstep to the polls and voting for liberal/socialist candidates will dramatically decrease. By removing the spoils system, we take race out of politics. But we must offer black Southerners something to replace their erstwhile misplaced faith in big government. The South is the poorest section of this country and black Southerners as a group have the lowest per-capita income in the South. A growing and expanding Southern economy will provide what trillions of dollars of socialism could not—unimagined economic opportunity for all Southerners but especially for the poorest segment of Southern society!

Race is an issue because conservative leaders in the twentieth century allowed it to become an issue. By refusing to courageously address it and find alternatives to socialist income-redistribution schemes, i.e., the political spoils system, they allowed black votes to become the "property" of the left. Over time we can make race a nonissue. We will do this by removing the political spoils system, instituting a true free-market economy where government tax collectors are allowed a maximum taxation of no more than 10 percent GDP. This new economy nurtured in a Liberty-Based Society will encourage and reward entrepreneurs for risk-taking, thereby expanding the economy. This in turn will improve the economic standing of Southerners in the lower economic class. As this happens, they will become less attached to the idea of big government and more concerned about keeping the government's tax collector away from their hard-earned income.

As a society, we must move away from race-centered politics. Under the socialist system of income redistribution, also known as entitlements, this will never happen. If it does, liberals/socialists will lose their grasp on political power. Their power depends on keeping as many Americans as possible dependent on big government—regardless of the social cost! Contrast this with my position. The surest way we have to protect our income from the government's tax collector is to convert as many tax consumers (the current recipients of government entitlements) as possible into taxpayers belonging to the middle and upper income group of our society.

Realistically, we all know, for good or ill, that throughout the world, some form of race consciousness will always be with us. Our goal should be to remove race from the political arena. No longer will one racial group attempt to capture control of government in order to repress the other, nor will one group be allowed to use the political process to steal the income of the other. A growing economy, with opportunity for all who wish to compete, will provide a much greater reward for the average Southerner than any entitlement program of the past. Seven trillion dollars of other people's money (OPM) and generations of failed liberal/socialist programs have not done the job. Their socialist model is a proven failure, while mine, a Liberty-Based model, is a logical and proven wealth producer that lifts the living standards of all society.

QUESTIONS AND ANSWERS

Q. How can we prevent the spread of racism without a strong federal government?

A. Your question implies that the federal government has been responsible for a dramatic decline in hostile racial attitudes. The facts are the exact opposite. By focusing on race as opposed to merit, the federal government has increased the level of racial hostility. Affirmative action plans, minority-preference contracting, busing, and hate-crime laws have divided America into two groups. One is given special treatment and privileges, while the other must sacrifice opportunities that merit would have conferred on individual members of the group, as well as income in order for the federal government to finance those special privileges. Racial hostility will never be removed by government interventions. All that government can do is provide one group with unearned benefits while forcing the other group to pay for those benefits. Regardless of which group is benefiting, these government actions are anti-liberty. In a Liberty-Based Society, people are free to choose, and because of a sustainable, expanding economy, they also have the income needed to finance their choice. The liberal/socialist political system may pass a law giving an oppressed minority the "right" to something, but it cannot give that group the resources necessary to finance their free choice. All that government can do is raise expectations that will ultimately be dashed by hard economic reality. Liberty principles such as noninterference and a sustainable, expanding economy will do more to remove discrimination based on race than generations of well-intentioned liberal/socialist laws.

Q. Aren't you really trying to undo the gains made during the civil rights struggle?

A. What gains? Yes, more blacks vote today than before 1965, and this has been a godsend for incumbent Democratic politicians. But has it helped the black community? The rise in crime, drug use, single-parent families, gangs, and sexually transmitted diseases does not support your claim of "gains" resulting from the much-vaunted civil rights movement. Who has benefited the most from the civil rights struggle? The answer is liberal/socialist politicians, but most of them are white! They do a great job feeding the black community empty words, but their politics and government programs cannot reward black entrepreneurs, businesspeople, and workers. After the

War for Southern Independence, they promised blacks "forty acres and a mule" if they would vote for Radical Republicans. During Reconstruction, black Southerners did just that, but the politicians never lived up to the promises they made to naïve, newly freed black voters. What was true yesterday is still true today. In a Liberty-Based Society, it will not matter what color our elected politicians are. In a Liberty-Based Society, government will not dispense other people's money. In a Liberty-Based Society, consumers are sovereign, and with ever-increasing wealth at their disposal, they will be able to freely choose from a vast marketplace with very little if any consideration of skin color. All of this will be accomplished without the use of government compulsion.

Q. You advocate equality of opportunity, but how can members of an oppressed minority have equal opportunity when they have been exploited and impoverished by this capitalist system?

A. You are making an argument against the current liberal/socialist system! Yes, all average people, i.e., those who do not have political connections with the central government, have suffered under the current system. Everyone suffers from the loss of income arising for unreasonable taxes; everyone suffers from the loss arising out of unsound monetary policy such as inflation; everyone suffers from the loss that occurs when an unsustainable boom turns into a bust and workers subsequently lose their jobs; everyone suffers from the opportunity cost of jobs that are not created due to indirect government taxes; and everyone suffers from government interventions that distort normal market tendencies to lower prices over time. All of these things and more are a result of anti-free market actions of the current liberal/socialist political system. A free market distorted by government interventions finds it difficult to expand opportunity. But you are wrong if you think that more government will resolve the problem that government interventions created in the first place. If you want more opportunity, then you need to join the struggle to overthrow the current liberal/socialist political system and replace it with a Liberty-Based Society.

Q. Do you really think that an unhampered free market where people are allowed to freely choose whom they want to deal with will result in less racial antagonism?

A. How could it do worse than the current liberal/socialist political system with its boom/bust economy? The current system has spent seven trillion dollars of our money in an attempt to socially engineer a better society. Since the 1950s, we have witnessed a steady increase in crime, drug abuse, and family breakdown and generally a loss of civility—not just in black communities but in communities all across America! Yes, I do believe that *we the people* of the Sovereign States working within our local communities, keeping more of our money, and enjoying a sustainable and expanding economy will be better equipped to perfect our communities than some self-appointed expert and bureaucrat in Washington, D.C. Our political masters seem to think that we are a timid, docile, and dependent people who are not fit for freedom. We are better than that! Americans have been known worldwide as self-reliant individualists who take care of their own. These are the types of people who will thrive in our Liberty-Based Society.

Q. But what about the poor? How will they survive if government is not there to provide food, shelter, and healthcare for those who cannot afford it?

A. As we have stated repeatedly—in a Liberty-Based Society, an expanding and sustainable economy will create more wealth for all of society. Jobs will be created where none can exist today in the liberal/socialist political system.

Q. But what about the truly disadvantaged, those who cannot work even if jobs are available? Who will care for them?

A. Americans have always been a charitable people. As personal wealth increases, there will be a commensurate increase in giving at the community level. In a recent survey of charitable giving, Southern people were shown to be the most generous people in the nation! Mississippi and Arkansas, the states with the lowest and second-lowest per-capita income respectively, were listed as the states where people gave the most. I am certain that as Southerners (and other Americans) gain more wealth in our Liberty-Based Society, they will continue their charitable giving. The truly disadvantaged will be able to find private groups, churches, and synagogues that will provide more than a handout—they will provide human compassion, encouragement, and connection to their community. This is something that the current liberal/socialist welfare worker cannot supply.

Q. But if the poor, disadvantaged, or sick must apply to a private charity for relief, then wouldn't they be subject to the rules of the private charity? In other words, relief may not be "freely" given to all who apply.

A. I would certainly hope so! Private charities could require those seeking relief to make a radical change in their life, and they may even offer the aid of religious faith to assist the individual in making that change. As William Booth, the founder of the Salvation Army, once said, "Before you can get the man out of the gutter you must first get the gutter out of the man."

Government is ill equipped to get the gutter out of the man. Indeed, government interventions often increase the probability of the man remaining in the gutter. Before the advent of government-sponsored welfare, private groups assumed the task of working within their communities to provide relief to those truly in need. The St. Louis Provident Association had the following rules for their volunteers, to assist them in preventing fraud on the part of applicants and to assure that the applicants were working hard to regain their independent status, i.e., to make sure those on relief would not remain on relief but only use the resources provided to help them back to a productive life.

- To give relief only after personal investigation of each case . . .
- To give necessary articles and only what is immediately necessary . . .
- To give only in small quantities in proportion to immediate need; and less than might be procured by labor, except in cases of sickness.
- To give assistance at the right moment; not to prolong it beyond duration of the necessity which calls for it . . .
- To require of each beneficiary abstinence from intoxicating liquors . . .
- To discontinue relieving all who manifest a purpose to depend on alms rather than their own exertions for support.[12]

Private charity given and administered by the people within the local community tends to strengthen bonds within the community. Government welfare administered by bureaucrats with a left-of-center political and social agenda tends to destroy not only the bonds of community but the very fabric of the family itself. This

12. Marvin Olasky, *The Tragedy of American Compassion* (Washington, D.C.: Regnery, 1992), 108.

alone is reason enough to overthrow the current liberal/socialist political system and replace it with a Liberty-Based Society!

Teddy Kennedy Defends Minimal Voting Qualifications

Archliberal Teddy Kennedy awakes to find himself standing before a court of inquiry. The panel of interrogators consists of English libertarian John Stuart Mill (1806-73), French political philosopher Frederic Bastiat (1801-50), and Sen. John C. Calhoun (1782-1850). The Senate Chambers look vaguely familiar but are filled with an eerie, almost ghostly presence.

"Senator Kennedy," a commanding voice begins, "I am Sen. John C. Calhoun, and my friends Mr. Mill and Mr. Bastiat have brought you before us to determine your reasoning for the imposition of minimal requirements for the franchise in the United States."

Teddy begins with a note of confidence in his voice. "It is very simple. In America we believe in one man, one vote—oh, I mean one person, one vote."

"Senator Kennedy," Mr. Bastiat says, "it is my opinion that the privilege of voting should be based upon the supposition of incapacity. If voting is a human right, then it would be wrong for you to prevent the youngest child from voting. But you will have to admit that even under your current system you recognize the principle of incapacity. After all, even you have not yet demanded that the privilege of the franchise be extended to young children. The privilege must be limited because the voter does not suffer alone if he makes a bad choice, but the entire society is forced to suffer."

"But," interrupts Senator Kennedy, "America is a democracy! Our system of government is based on everyone having the right to vote."

"A democracy, Senator Kennedy, or a mobocracy?" Senator Calhoun asks. "I am well aware of the nature of government to abuse its powers. Government is nothing more than the corporate will of the numerical majority, and if the numerical majority in a democracy votes to infringe on or encumber the rights of the numerical minority, then the rights of the numerical minority are as much at risk in your form of government as they would be in any other form of tyranny!"

"People need political power in order to gain economic power," protests Senator Kennedy.

"Citizens need the right to vote in order to make sure they are not misgoverned," declares Mr. Mill. "Your system puts as high a value on ignorance as it does knowledge. How can a citizen make an informed selection between issues and candidates if he cannot read or write or has no real knowledge of history, political theories, mathematical calculations, and international affairs? Your system is in fact a system of legal plunder where the numerical majority, by way of an unlimited franchise, is encouraged to use government's tax collectors to deprive the numerical minority of its property."

Senator Kennedy stands speechless before his judges. Never before has he met such conservatives. They were prepared with facts and logic, were not intimidated by the left-wing media, and spoke with an authority derived from intense study and a passion for their cause.

"When will this nightmare end?" he thinks.

CHAPTER 7

Voting: A Privilege to Be Earned

In modern America's mass democracy, it is heresy to even suggest that voting is anything less than a universal right. Under such a system, the "have nots" are encouraged to flock to the polls and vote for the candidates who will use government's police power to forcefully remove property from the "haves" and lavish OPM (other people's money) on them via government programs and entitlements."

As I noted in chapter 6, a system of political spoils is key to maintaining liberalism's hold on our society. As one nineteenth-century social commentator noted, "public welfare is the poor man's plunder." In America's mass democracy, this plunder is obtained by electing liberal/socialist politicians who will reward their constituents with generous government outlays of other people's money. But is this the proper role of the franchise in a society ordered on liberty?

VOTING FRAUD—OUR CURRENT STATUS

The 1993 motor voter law pushed through Congress by the Democratic party opened a whole new era of potential voting irregularities. Today you can register to vote when you get a driver's license or when you sign up for welfare. Liberals/socialists are determined to keep the requirement for voting as simple as possible. Their hope is to have more tax consumers voting than taxpayers. As demonstrated in the graph below, the top 50 percent of America's taxpayers pay a whopping 96 percent of the tax load! The bottom 50 percent pay only 4 percent of America's tax burden. But they vote— usually in blocs for the more liberal/socialist candidate—and their votes decide how much of your income they will help themselves to for the next four years! This will assure the election of candidates who favor liberal/socialist income redistribution schemes such as

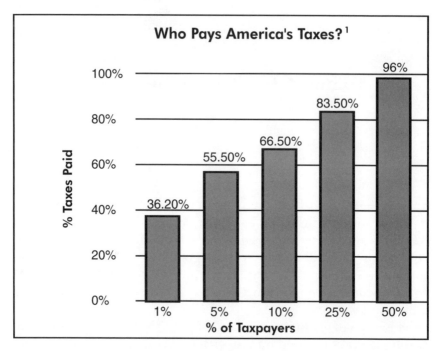

entitlements and unfunded federal mandates. Some liberals have suggested that we should not register people to vote but merely allow them to walk in on election day and cast their ballot! While the voter-registration system is difficult to police, even with good laws, our current liberal system provides major incentives for abuse by less than honest individuals.

The *Miami Herald* published a report on December 1, 2000, showing that at least 445 convicted felons in Florida voted illegally in the November 2000 general election. This occurred even after Florida had conducted a "multimillion-dollar effort to prevent election fraud by eliminating dead and illegal voters from the registration rolls."[2] Almost 75 percent of those fraudulent voters were registered as Democrats. The state of Alabama recently concluded a thirteen-year project to clean up its voter list. It resulted in the removal of 150,000 names of people who were dead and 50,000 who had moved away.[3]

1. "Share of Federal Individual Income Taxes Paid by Income Group, 1999" (www.cato.org/research/fiscal_policy/2002/indiv4.html, Dec. 2, 2002).

2. Kidwell, Long, and Dougherty, "Hundreds of Felons Cast Votes Illegally" (www.herald.com).

3. Phyllis Schlafly, "Foreign Language Ballots Are a Bad Idea" (www.eagleforum.org, Aug. 28, 2002).

This issue is important because the potential for misuse could threaten the veracity of the electoral process. As Phyllis Schlafly wrote, "Failure to purge ineligible persons from the voter lists is an open door to fraud. In the primary for Pennsylvania Governor on May 21, Philadelphia Democrats handed out a record $450,000 in election-day 'street money.'"[4]

Added to the potential for fraud is the new unfunded federal mandate requiring states to print ballots in foreign languages for those "Americans" who cannot read English! It is estimated that this will cost taxpayers at least $27 million.[5] Now let's stop and think about this. Only citizens are supposed to vote. Before immigrants can become citizens, they must demonstrate an understanding of English, including the ability to read, write, and speak simple phrases. Why then do we need foreign-language ballots?

Recently, members of Congress attempted to add a small amount of security to the voting process by requiring all "motor voter" registrants to present identification the *first* time they vote after registering. Approximately 95 percent of "motor voter" registrants *don't* vote. This large reservoir of registered voters could be used by unscrupulous political operatives to throw a close election. So it would seem reasonable to have some form of security in place. Not so fast! The NAACP and other "civil rights" groups set up a loud howl about the ID requirement. They claimed it would be an undue burden on the individual to bring some form of identification. Remember this is the same country where you have to show an ID to rent a movie or buy a pack of cigarettes. So into the battle came Senate Democrat Chuck Schumer, who opposed an ID requirement. The New York Democrat declared that there was no evidence of fraud in his fair state. Yet his own *New York Post* had reported that in New York City alone there were 11,642 people registered in two different voting districts simultaneously. Nevertheless, Senate Democrats won a vote to remove the ID requirement.[6]

VOTING—CIVILITY OR SPOILS?

What is the purpose of voting in a free society? In a socialist sys-

4. Ibid.
5. Ibid.
6. "Should Dogs Vote?" *Wall Street Journal*, March 1, 2002, sec. A, p. 14.

tem, such as we currently have in America, voting is a lottery used to determine which group gets benefits and which group pays for those benefits. Socialism is in fact a system of political spoils—to the victor go the spoils. But as I noted in chapter 3, the first requirement for a free society is civility—a sense of social responsibility. Voting is a civic duty in which the informed citizen attempts to direct the political course of his society. The result of setting low qualifications for voting is that the society's politics degenerate into a system of public plunder. The desire to gain at someone else's expense gives rise to a generation of pork-barrel politicians and fellow travelers whose sole purpose is to gain and retain political power and then use that power for personal aggrandizement. The primary argument in favor of low voting qualifications is that it is "democratic" and brings more people into the political process. But a lynch mob is in its own way also democratic—though majority rule will not be of much solace to the hanged victim. Society has the duty to set minimum qualifications for voting just as it sets them for driving an automobile. Liberty is in danger if voting qualifications are set too high or too low. Our task is to determine what they should be.

MINIMUM VOTING QUALIFICATIONS

Keep in mind that we are setting voting qualifications for a Liberty-Based Society. The current system of political spoils will be removed or at least limited by our low taxation policy (equal to or less than 10 percent GDP—as described in chapter 10), sound money that prevents politically inspired inflation (as described in chapter 8), and a free market economy where government regulations are kept to a minimum (as described in chapter 12). In our Liberty-Based Society, the motivation to vote will be based on civic duty, not a sense of greed. Civility will replace spoils as the reason to voting.

The Founding Fathers made a distinction between the American republic they created and the pernicious effect of "mobocracy," which sooner or later will develop in an unrestricted democracy. As James Madison, of Virginia, said, "A pure democracy . . . a common passion or interest will, in almost every case, be felt by a majority of the whole. . . . [Pure democracies or monocracies] have ever been found incompatible with personal security or the rights of *property* [emphasis mine]."[7] Benjamin

---

7. James Madison, as cited in Kennedy and Kennedy, *Why Not Freedom!*, 181.

Franklin shared this view but explained it with his typical flair: "Democracy is two wolves and a lamb voting on what to have for dinner. Liberty is a well armed lamb contesting the election."

This skepticism of mass democracy was not just an American concern. Nineteenth-century English civil libertarian John Stuart Mill had this to say about the potential dangers posed by what he called, most prophetically, "the Demos" in America: "The natural tendency of representative government, as of modern civilization, is towards collective mediocrity: and this tendency increased by all reductions and extensions of the franchise, their effect being to place the principal power in the hands of classes more and more below the highest level of instruction in the community."[8] Note that Mill sees the danger of the underclass using the vote to overrule the good judgment of the educated classes. Madison sees that the result of such a scheme is that eventually those who hold power will be motivated by jealousy and greed to use government police power to do what they could not—rob their neighbor of his property! What the law would not allow them to do with a gun, it facilitates via the ballot.

The concept that voting is an automatic right, instead of a privilege to be obtained after demonstrating certain, nonarbitrary qualifications, is the primary dividing line between a mobocracy and the democratic Republic of Republics as established by the Founding Fathers. The liberal/socialist establishment uses the "one man, one vote" universal franchise scheme to ensure the electoral victory of its favored candidates. Once a society starts down the road to an unlimited franchise, it opens itself up to massive election frauds. This is the result of a society that replaces civility at the voting booth with a system of political spoils. Frederic Bastiat, a nineteenth-century French civil libertarian, also noted the dangers:

> This controversy over universal suffrage . . . would lose nearly all of its importance if the law had always been what it ought to be. . . . In fact, if law were restricted to protecting all persons, all liberties, and all property; if law were nothing more than the organized combination of the individual's right to self defense; if law were the obstacle, the check, the punisher of all oppression and plunder—is it likely that we citizens would then argue much about the extent of the franchise?

8. John Stuart Mill, as cited in Kennedy and Kennedy, *Why Not Freedom!*, 181.

[Instead] the law takes property from one person and gives it to another. . . . Under these circumstances, then certainly every class will aspire to grasp the law, and logically so.[9]

There are three important points to remember when discussing (or debating) the proper role of voting qualifications in a free society.

1. There is always a danger that the control of even a good government can be obtained by a special interest group (liberals and socialists, for example) and used as a "legal" excuse to plunder the property of private citizens.
2. The right to vote is not a purely private right but is exercised by the individual as part of his duty to the community/society in which he resides and as such affects society at large.
3. Some individuals are incapable of exercising the right to vote in a manner that would maintain a free society, i.e., the principle of incapacity.

Many Americans find the principle of incapacity shocking. At first they draw back from it as if it were an unheard-of, alien idea. But the reality is that we already have the principle of incapacity built into the current "universal" franchise, "one man, one vote" mass democracy. Even most liberals and socialists will admit that infants, the criminally insane, or illegal aliens (though that might be stretching it too far) should not be allowed to vote. We currently have some form of qualifiers and disqualifiers. Our problem is that they do not address the major potential problem in a mass democracy—the desires of some to use the good name of the law as a vehicle for plunder.

FOUR ESSENTIAL QUALIFIERS FOR VOTING[10]
Please note that any of these qualifiers may be overcome if an individual so choose.

1. Anyone who desires to exercise the privilege of voting must be able to read and write as well as have acquired basic knowledge in

---

9. Frederic Bastiat, as cited in Kennedy and Kennedy, *Why Not Freedom!*, 184-85.
10. A complete chapter is dedicated to this subject in Kennedy and Kennedy, *Why Not Freedom!:* chapter 19, "Mob Rule at the Voting Booth," 181-93.

history, geography, and mathematics typical of that obtained by successful completion of a high-school education or equivalent.

2. No one may qualify to vote if he gains his existence via public relief, such as welfare, public housing, Aid to Dependent Children, entitlements, and so on. [Corporate welfare would also be a disqualifier for corporate officers, but in a Liberty-Based Society this type of welfare would be the first and easiest one to remove from our society.]

3. No one who has within the last five years made use of the bankruptcy act may exercise the privilege of voting. [The logic here is that the purpose of voting is to help manage government, and one who has demonstrated his inability to manage his personal business affairs and has shifted his individual obligations on to the public via bankruptcy has no current claim to the right to manage society's business.]

4. The privilege of voting will be suspended for those convicted on a felony charge until the completion of five years, with no additional convictions, after the running of their assigned sentence.

In a Liberty-Based Society, greed and jealousy will no longer be the primary motivating political factors. The need of one group to control the government in order to expand its own wealth at the expense of the out-of-power group will no longer exist. After a century of conservative failure and liberal/socialist triumph, the personal income of America's workers and entrepreneurs will at last be safe. Southerners such as John C. Calhoun had long ago forecast the dangers of mass democracy, even before the era of socialism:

> Nothing [is] more easy than to pervert its powers into instruments to aggrandize and enrich one or more interests by oppressing and impoverishing the others; and this too, under the operation of laws, couched in general terms; and which, on their face, appear fair and equal. Nor is this the case in some particular communities only. It is so in all.[11]

Let us not forget that the purpose of this book is to set the stage for political action necessary to install a Liberty-Based Society. No

11. Kennedy and Kennedy, *Why Not Freedom!*, 188.

matter how logical and historically well documented my facts may be, they are useless until I convince my fellow citizens of the necessity of overthrowing the current liberal/socialist political system and put these ideas into practice!

It is probably a good idea once again to explain the meaning of "overthrow" when discussing the removal of our current system. "Overthrow" is used in a social and political—not violent—context. Dedication to civility precludes the use of violence, except in self-defense in response to an obvious threat. In order for "civil and political" disobedience to be legitimate, it must be nonviolent.[12] This movement has much more in common with Gandhi than it does with the Unabomber or Lenin.

QUESTIONS AND ANSWERS

Q. America is a democracy; shouldn't everyone be allowed to vote?

A. No! Even under the current liberal/socialist system, many people are denied the right to vote. For example, many seventeen-year-olds are intellectually better equipped to vote than many registered voters, yet we do not allow them to vote. People who are mentally ill and confined to mental institutions are not allowed to vote. Illegal aliens are not allowed to vote. People who would otherwise be qualified to vote but have not taken the time to register are not allowed to vote on election day. So as we can see, even in a mass democracy such as we now have in the United States there are restrictions placed on who is allowed to vote.

Refusal of the privilege of voting should be based upon the principle of incapacity. Some people are not capable of casting a learned, knowledgeable, and socially rational ballot. For example, a young child is incapable of discerning which candidate would be the best for society. Therefore, the child's incapacity precludes her from voting. This incapacity is not permanent. With the passage of time (maturity) and the gaining of knowledge (education), the child becomes an adult and is able to rationally influence the governance of society by voting.

As demonstrated in this chapter, other things could cause an incapacity that would temporarily preclude a citizen from voting. Lack of formal education at a minimum level—say, completion of

---

12. For a discussion of the use of political civil disobedience, see Kennedy and Kennedy, *Why Not Freedom!*, 262-66.

high school—would be an example, but this could be removed by the individual. It is not a permanent incapacity. Acquiring one's sustenance from public or private welfare or charity would also be an example of incapacity that would preclude one from voting. But this too would be within the power of the individual to correct.

Remember the privilege of voting is granted to all who qualify, using nonarbitrary qualifications that apply to all citizens. The privilege is granted to help us ensure we are not misgoverned—not to assure that we elect the politician who will bring the most pork-barrel government projects back to our district. When we cast our ballot, we have an effect upon all of society. Therefore, society has a duty to ensure that those who vote are the best qualified and least likely to try to use the ballot box as a means to loot their fellow citizens via pork-barrel government handouts.

Q. Aren't you really trying to undo the gains we have made as a result of the passage of the Voting Rights Act of 1965?

A. Once again we come back to the issue of "laws" pushed through to remedy "problems" that arose from the intentional distortion of America's political system by liberals/socialists and their eighteenth- and nineteenth-century antecedents. No one can say how the United States would have resolved its pressing social issues of the past three centuries had the constitutionally limited Republic of Republics been allowed to survive. But the original Republic of Republics composed of a constitutionally limited federal government and Sovereign States was destroyed by advocates of an "energetic" federal government, such as Alexander Hamilton; by advocates of centralized federal supremacy, such as Daniel Webster and Joseph Story; by advocates of an American empire that crushes free men and women who refuse to obey its orders, such as Abraham Lincoln; and advocates of federalized socialism, such as FDR and LBJ! Advocates of liberty are not interested in debating the utility of laws passed by this liberal/socialist regime. Every law passed has been an attempt to shore up a debased, immoral, and failing political system. The alternative is to establish a Liberty-Based Society in which energetic individuals can increase their personal wealth by exercising their God-given rights and liberties. We will not need a Voting Rights Act, because in our new society, voting will not be a means to loot your neighbor—it will be a means to assure that we are not misgoverned! The incentive to use the voting booth as a "legal" means to seize other people's money and redistribute to those who just happen to vote for the right "incumbent" will no longer exist.

Q. Don't you think that you put too much faith in humans? After all, if there is no strong central government around, would not people of the states be tempted to oppress minorities within their states?

A. I have no faith in the theory of man's inherent goodness. I believe that the history of the last century, with its rivers of blood, death, and destruction—man against man—is vivid evidence of man's fallen nature. Left to his own devices, man tends to do evil and eschew good. John C. Calhoun, in the mid-1800s, noted that there is a tendency in man to sacrifice the public good in order to advance his own personal gain.

Many seem to think that if a man is sanctified by a plurality of the vote in a democratic election, his nature will magically change and he becomes an angel (figuratively speaking). After gaining office, according to liberal/socialist reasoning, men and women will do no harm, put aside divisive thinking and personal prejudices, and work honestly to solve society's problems without regard to their own betterment. People who believe that must also still believe in the Tooth Fairy! It does not happen. What happens is that people get into public office, find it much more lucrative than working productively in the free market, and begin to use their office to assure their incumbency. In other words, they become political prostitutes—they sell their souls to whoever will guarantee them the most votes in the upcoming election.

You seem to think that society needs a strong federal government to prevent people at the local level from doing evil. Your assumption is that the federal government is controlled by angelic beings who will never do evil like those fallen men and women down at the local and state level. Yes, people at the local and state level at one time passed anti-liberty Jim Crow laws. But what about anti-liberty federal affirmative action laws, court-ordered busing, or seizure of private property in the name of wetland protection? What is the difference? These are all anti-liberty acts of government. If anything, the anti-liberty acts of one or more states are less evil, in that *we the people* could still vote with our feet by leaving that state. But how do we leave the entire country when the federal government enacts anti-liberty laws? No, we do not need more government, state or federal. We need more liberty!

Good as Gold?

Suppose you were a citizen of an ancient kingdom. Your day-to-day life as a trader at the local harbor is profitable and peaceful. You trade goods produced or grown by local craftsmen or farmers for goods from beyond your quiet kingdom. Gold coins minted by local and foreign craftsmen serve as your medium of exchange—i.e., money. It does not matter who produced the coin because gold is interchangeable. The only consideration is its weight. Local gold warehouses make profits by providing a secure place for merchants to deposit their gold, giving the depositor a paper receipt for the exact amount, and returning the deposited gold to the bearer of the receipt on demand.

Your king requires a specific amount of gold every month as taxes due the kingdom. Although the taxes are onerous, everyone pays them on time because after all, the king has troops stationed at the tax collector's office that will punish severely anyone who attempts to avoid paying the king's taxes.

The king is ambitious and wants to finance an invasion of a neighboring country, but his advisors tell him that it would be dangerous to increase taxes. He gives his advisors an ultimatum—"Find me a way to gain more money or else!" None of the king's advisors wants to find out what is meant by "or else."

One very devious advisor comes up with a foolproof plan to get as much money as the king needs without raising taxes. "All you have to do," explains the advisor, "is require that every coin used to pay the king's taxes or used as 'legal tender' in this kingdom bear the king's mark. So every coin must be delivered to the king's mint, melted down, and recast with the king's image on it. But 10 percent of the coin's pure gold will be replaced with a base metal when it is recast. The king will be making a 10 percent profit on every gold coin brought into the kingdom!"

The king has now succeeded in monopolizing the kingdom's money. No longer is the marketplace allowed to select its medium of exchange—government is in control. But as a merchant, you now begin to notice that what once took an ounce of gold to purchase now takes 1.10 ounces of gold. You are paying a tax, despite the fact that the king never raised taxes! As years go by you notice that your grandchildren are paying three or four gold coins for articles that once only cost you a single gold coin. Meanwhile, the king's palaces have grown in size and luxury, numerous wars have been waged, and tax collectors and other government bureaucrats have multiplied.

Question: Is the debasement of the kingdom's free market gold coins different from the gradual devaluation of the U.S. dollar via government-sponsored inflation?

Question: Is debasement of privately owned gold coins any less of a crime because it is done by the king's agents?

Question: Is government-sponsored inflation the same as taxation without consent?

CHAPTER 8

Sound Money

In human society, there is an irreconcilable conflict between the concept of financial wellbeing of the individual and the pernicious desire for increased wealth of the politically well connected. Like fire and ice, the two are set at odds by nature itself. They cannot be reconciled. One shall dominate the other.

Note I am not equating the profit motive of businesspeople and entrepreneurs in a free market with the greed of the politically well connected. The politically connected may be referred to as "special interest groups." In a free market, the consumer is sovereign. But the politically connected use their influence and the exchanging of favors to gain an unfair advantage over the individual citizen. In other words, the private property of the citizen/consumer is at risk anytime government and the politically connected conspire. For example, lobbyists exchange favors with their friends in Congress to gain special favors for their clients. Their clients may be large military-industrial corporations seeking lucrative contracts with the government or large voting blocs seeking an even larger distribution of OPM (other people's money) in exchange for their votes in upcoming elections. In both cases, the individual citizen is not represented. The organized special interest has something the politician desires (usually money or votes), but to "help" the special interest, the politician must obtain the personal property of the individual citizen and transfer it to the politically well connected.

Taxes are the primary way that modern politicians confiscate private property. But raising more taxes becomes difficult even for socialists when a nation, such as the United States, gets to the point that over 50 percent of our income must be used to satisfy government. That is why socialist politicians favor—no, demand—the abandonment of sound-money policies in favor of fiat money[1] and central banking. This allows them to provide huge profits to their favored banking clients, and via inflation they can provide entitlements to large blocs of voters without the messy necessity of raising taxes. But in the final analysis, we know who pays the bill. It is the individual citizen—the one person who did not have a seat at the table where politicians and their special-interest clients devised the plans to divide the personal property of the unrepresented citizen.

This is not something new in America. As I pointed out in chapter 1, it was Alexander Hamilton who first used the concept of "loose construction" to read into the Constitution authority for the federal government to establish a central bank. Thomas Jefferson resisted Hamilton's proposal because he knew bankers with government connections would use this new power to defraud private citizens who had no close working relationship with the central government. The pattern continues even to this day. As George Reisman wrote:

> A vast array of pressure groups want money from the government, and [government] can obtain their support by giving [money] to them. In other words, the government inflates the money supply in order to buy votes. This inflation of the money supply makes the value of the monetary unit decline. Prices rise despite the great success of businessmen in making goods ever more abundant and less expensive in real terms, because paper money becomes more abundant and cheaper at an even faster rate.[2]

A Liberty-Based Society with a sound monetary policy based on gold would prevent this "legalized" looting. Unfortunately today very few people have ever heard about sound money and cannot conceive of a society where inflation not only did not occur but where falling prices was the norm.

WHAT IS SOUND MONEY?

Ask the average American, "What is money?" and he will most likely repeat the line taken in the early 1950s by the U.S. Chamber

---

1. Fiat money is money that has no real value. For example, a gold coin or paper certificate that is redeemable by the holder in gold has direct value (as in the gold coin) or indirect value (as in the paper certificate). Printing-press money that is not redeemable by the holder in gold, silver, or some other commodity has no actual value.

2. George Reisman, "The Stock Market, Profits, and Credit Expansion" (www.mises.org, Aug. 2, 2002).

of Commerce: "Money is what the government says it is."[3] Money—a medium of exchange—is vital to our economic prosperity, yet we understand so little about it. Our governmental masters would prefer that we leave such an important issue alone and let them take care of it—so they can manipulate money to deprive us of our hard-earned income. That way they can enrich themselves and buy more elections or, more properly, reelections.

Money was not established by government. It was not mandated into being by a king, caesar, or democratically elected head of state. Money resulted from the need for some medium of exchange to replace or supplement the primitive barter system. For thousands of years, merchants used various commodities to facilitate exchange. In colonial America, tobacco and cotton were used. Tobacco and cotton warehouses would issue receipts, which were exchanged in lieu of actual tobacco or cotton. But every warehouse that issued a paper receipt was required to have the stated amount of the commodity on hand and to deliver it upon demand. The important point is that whatever the medium of exchange might be, it always began as a commodity that had a commercial purpose other than to serve as a medium of exchange. For centuries the market generally settled on gold as the best commodity to use as a medium of exchange, i.e., money. Gold had the basic requirements for a good medium of exchange: (1) it is fungible (interchangeable); (2) it is relatively light in weight, making it portable; (3) it is durable; and (4) it has a high ratio of value to unit of weight. By the beginning of the industrial revolution, gold had become the guarantor of sound money.

While government did not create money, government has always sought to control society's money. Coin clipping and debasement of gold with another metal are examples of early inflation. Political leaders who controlled government used its police power to take over creating money, thereby establishing government's monopoly over our money. The results has been a move away from gold as freely circulating money and eventually the abandonment of the gold standard, forced reliance upon fiat money (unsupported paper "money"), loss of purchasing power for the money held by average citizens, unsupported credit, and eventually inflation as an indirect tax on the income of citizens.

3. Murray N. Rothbard, *The Case for a 100 Percent Gold Dollar* (1962; reprint, Auburn, Ala.: Ludwig von Mises Institute, 2001), 20.

WHY IS SOUND MONEY IMPORTANT?

In a Liberty-Based Society, citizens would be free from government-sanctioned force, including monetary fraud. That is why I say that in a free market or Liberty-Based Society, the consumer is sovereign. But when government injects inflation into the economic system, it illegally taxes the earnings of citizens and perpetrates fraud upon society. This was understood early in our history. During the early part of the nineteenth century, voters understood the issue of sound money and the arguments in favor of and against easy credit via central banking and fractional reserve banking. But sadly today the topic is all but unheard of in conservative discourse.

Imagine what would happen if someone gave a family the right to print all the dollars they wanted. How long would it be before that family would begin to abuse its new power? While no one would tolerate even one family's manufacture of money, we have nevertheless quietly acquiesced to the granting of this right to politicians! Because of the loss of sound monetary policy, citizens have become accustomed to ever-increasing prices while struggling to find ways to maintain the purchasing power of their take-home pay. Even though this is a common condition today, *it is not the norm for the free market,* nor was it the norm prior to the establishment of central banking (the Fed) in America.

Falling prices are the normal byproduct of voluntary commercial transactions in the free market. Prices continued to fall during the nineteenth century as industry became more efficient. Even if wages remained constant,[4] workers' purchasing power would increase due to the gradual but steady decline in prices.[5] Even today in our highly regulated and taxed economy, we can still see the remnants of this market phenomenon. Look at the cost of a pocket or handheld calculator now as opposed to one in the mid-1970s. Today the consumer commands a higher-quality product at a much lower price. This is what economists call "growth deflation." As Christopher Mayer wrote:

> Growth deflation should be the prevailing trend in a healthy progressing economy. It is only because of years of rampant money supply growth, endemic under a fiat currency system, that inflation has become the accepted norm. As Salerno notes, "throughout the nineteenth century and up until the First World War, a mild deflationary trend prevailed in the industrialized nations as

---

4. A stable wage would be more likely in older jobs, while newer jobs requiring new skills would command higher pay rates.

5. Rothbard, *The Case Against the Fed*, 21.

rapid growth in the supplies of goods outpaced the gradual growth in money supply that occurred under the classical gold standard."[6]

This trend lasted roughly until the establishment of the Federal Reserve Bank in 1913, which restored the Second Bank of the United States that Andrew Jackson was successful in closing in the 1830s. Remember the reason for falling prices is that businesspeople/entrepreneurs work to satisfy the consumer's demand for quality at the lowest price. In a free market the consumer is sovereign—this is an example of how the free market working through a voluntary system encourages the development of better and less expensive goods and services. But taxes, regulations, and monetary fraud corrupt this process. There is a cost attached to governmental distortion, and that cost will eventually be paid by the consumer.

The liberal/socialist establishment has reduced the word "profit" or "profits" to something akin to evil. Ironically, any amount of profanity is acceptable in the media, but who would dare go on national television and defend the free market concept of the profit motive? The truth is that human progress is tied to profit. The major advancements of the nineteenth and twentieth centuries came as a result of the profit motive at work. It was not government that invented electric lights, the automobile, or the airplane or made one astounding scientific discovery after another—it was the free market at work!

In a free market economy, most profits are saved or reinvested in the commercial enterprise to acquire newer, higher, or more efficient production. In either case the money flows back into the economy to produce more jobs and eventually more wealth for society at large. Liberals/socialists look upon profits as excess money that "rich and greedy capitalists" hoard (bury in fruit jars in their backyards?), thus preventing it from flowing back to the "impoverished masses."

In a free market, a successful commercial enterprise provides benefits in three primary ways: (1) the businessperson is rewarded for taking the initial risk, (2) the workers are rewarded with better wages and new and improving work opportunities, and (3) society at large benefits from the added wealth, lowered prices, and increased quality. All of these are natural byproducts of the free market in action. This complicated free-market exchange, this allocation of scarce resources in order to produce more personal wealth, is

6. Christopher Mayer, "The Imaginary Evils of Deflation" (www.mises.org, Sept. 11, 2002).

accomplished by diverse individuals acting voluntarily on their own behalf to satisfy their own self-interest. Reisman noted:

> In a free market, the way one obtains money from others is by offering them something they judge to be valuable and desire to have. These are the kinds of things one seeks to produce and sell. In this way, the profit motive is the foundation of the continuous introduction of new and improved products and methods of production. The development of new and improved products that people will want to buy, and the more efficient, lower-cost production of what they already want to buy, are the leading ways in which businessmen make profits in a free market.[7]

In 1903, Henry Ford began with an investment of $25,000, and by 1946 he had turned it into over $1 billion. Profits made him rich, but what about the American worker? New job opportunities that were unimaginable in 1903 became commonplace by 1946. What did his investment do for society at large? It democratized the automobile, freed Americans from the chains of place, and gave the term "freedom of movement" a whole new meaning. Profits are not evil but are in fact the very source of our modern technological advancement. They are responsible for our current civilization. When government injects unsound monetary policies into society's economic system, then government becomes the enemy of profits, of the workers who obtain their families' sustenance from income, and of society at large. Government does all this in order to favor special interests that support the political establishment. Who pays? You pay!

Why is sound money important to the private citizen? It facilitates commercial activity necessary to advance civilization. That is, it encourages and assists free market activity that results in a continuingly improving standard of living. It makes it possible for businesspeople and workers to calculate with relative confidence the cost/benefit of doing business and estimate the potential future reward for current investments or savings. Historically, the greatest enemy of sound money has been government. Historically, those classes, groups, or individuals with close connections to government benefit when sound monetary policies are replaced with inflationary ones. Historically, the cost of unsound monetary policies has been paid by the average citizen, who has no close connections with the power brokers in government.

7. Reisman, "The Stock Market."

LIBERALS AND SOCIALISTS HATE SOUND MONEY

Once we gain even the most rudimentary knowledge of the role that sound money plays in preserving liberty, it becomes obvious why liberals/socialists hate sound monetary policies. If we had a sound monetary policy in the United States today, who would be the first to feel the effect? Liberals and socialists! Even before the economy could become healthy and expand, liberals/socialists would experience the withdrawal pains of suddenly having to give up their favorite pastime—spending your money. Overnight they would be denied a huge source of OPM (other people's money). Government would be forced to pay its bills by taxing the population. Liberals hate to deal with taxes because taxes tend to arouse the indignation of the taxpaying citizens. Liberals/socialists find it much easier to pay for government entitlements via inflation, which does not have to pass the constitutional muster of being introduced in the House of Representatives, approved in the Senate, and then signed into law by the president. Liberals/socialists find such democratic procedures to be very cumbersome—much better simply to turn on the printing press, run off a couple of billion dollars in counterfeit money, and go forward with their scheme to redistribute your wealth to their favored clients. Sound money limits their legalized looting of your private property. They can redistribute OPM only to the extent that *we the people* are willing to accept the direct tax burden imposed by government. Even under liberal leadership in Congress, they would run out of tax revenues before they were able to redistribute your income, and they would be forced to either give up or risk enraging the taxpayers by proposing higher taxes to pay for their schemes.

Many of us recall our mothers' warning that "the road to hell is paved with good intentions." The same is true about the road to serfdom—it too is paved with good intentions. Ideologically, true liberals/socialists really do have good intentions when they advocate the expenditure of more OPM via government entitlements to, for example, correct the sad condition of inner-city youths. How can anyone deny that these young people living in an area of crime, disease, broken homes, and general poverty would be better off if these social pathologies were corrected?

Advocates of a Liberty-Based Society do not argue or disagree with that point. What we do disagree with is the liberal/socialist contention that the way to accomplish the goal is via government. Indeed, we argue that using government to force private citizens to work without pay to "improve" someone else is nothing less than slavery! Our disagreement is based on the principle of *liberty*, not *utility.* Even if the free market would not provide a better solution than government, government still would not have the moral authority to force one citizen to labor for another's benefit! Too many Americans have been swept up in the emotional appeals of the liberal/socialist camp. These appeals are heavy on good intentions but are virtually absent any logical connections with moral authority or effective results! According to some estimates, you and I were robbed of over $600 billion[8] in order to fund liberal/socialist "war on poverty" programs. Yet even after the forceful confiscation of our money and years of government regulations, guidelines, and job training programs, we have the same poverty level as when this boondoggle began! Good intentions, bad results, less income for you and me, an enormous opportunity cost borne by society—and the headlong rush down the road to serfdom continues.

Even though it is apparent that war on poverty programs have not been successful, these programs and the high tax rate needed to pay for them continue. And the government uses its ability to create money out of thin air (fiat currency and unsupported credit) to pay for these programs, even though you and I also end up paying via income tax creep and higher prices due to government-sponsored inflation. The same holds true for all liberal/socialist programs. Busing has been an enormous failure. It has been a key ingredient in the destruction of educational excellence—all done to accomplish the "right" mix of white to black students without a thought or care as to how the loss of local neighborhood schools would affect educational quality. But even when you use the percentage of racially integrated classrooms as the measure, you will see that instead of producing integrated education,[9] busing has virtually resegregated many public schools. But failure is of no concern to the liberal/socialist political masters, and the buses continue to roll. After all, liberals "mean well" and their intentions are "good." They are the self-anointed, the experts. They care more than the mere average citizen and therefore they have seized the government to use its police power to compel our compliance.

The truth is that they do not trust us. They view us as uneducated,

8. Murray, *Losing Ground,* xviii.

9. I will not go into the discussion of how to determine if a classroom is integrated. A lunch counter is integrated when anyone can come in and make a purchase with no distinction based on race. But if that definition is applied to public schools, liberals/socialists declare it to be insufficient and mandate forced busing. An absence of logic continues to be a hallmark of liberal/socialist thinking.

uncultured, and unable to properly select the best course of social action for ourselves, our families, and our society. Therefore, they will make us do what they think is best for us, even if we do not agree with their choice. That is why they used the force of government to compel everyone to participate in the socialist "old-age security" pension plan (known as Social Security). Indeed it was a group of liberal/socialist "experts" who devised FDR's Social Security plan. Members of Congress did not even understand the plan when they voted on it![10] Would the average American invest the major part of his retirement funds into a system that teeters on the edge of insolvency (some would argue that it actually is insolvent) and only pays 1.5 percent return on the investment? No, of course not! But liberals/socialists who mean well and do not trust common citizens to make the right decisions regarding their retirement continue to force us into a Social Security scheme that has been demonstrated to be a failure.

Liberals/socialists not only distrust us but they also distrust the free market and the capitalist system. They equate profits with greed. As I have previously stated, in a true, unhampered, free market the consumer is sovereign. That means that if a businessperson does not offer consumers products or services they want, and at the lowest price and highest quality, that businessperson will be severely punished by the consumer—the consumer will not purchase from that businessperson. In short order even large corporations will face bankruptcy if they do not satisfy the consumer. The Kmarts of the world may want to do business their way, but if the Wal-Marts of the world find a way that consumers prefer and offer it, then the demise of the Kmarts of the world is assured. In a free market the consumer is sovereign. "Greedy" businesspeople do not last long in a free-market world where the consumer is sovereign. But liberals/socialists do not believe this and demand some type of central planning, governmental control, or redistribution of the wealth of the "rich capitalist." They redistribute your private property and at the same time eviscerate the ability of the capitalist system to continue to produce wealth and a higher standard of living for society.

Liberals/socialists hate sound money because it limits their ability to force us to pay for their income redistribution schemes. They hate sound money because it prevents them from counterfeiting money (fiat money) to pay for entitlements for their favored clients. Understanding this, we should ask ourselves, "Why aren't we doing something to return sound monetary principles to America?"

10. Bresiger, *The Revolution of 1935,* 61, 73, 78-79, 90, 93.

BOOM/BUST—HOW GOVERNMENT
TURNS YOUR 401KS INTO 201KS

During the 1990s we all experienced what economists refer to as an economic boom. It was a time of rapid increase in stock prices. Many people saw their economic worth greatly increase as market prices hit new heights. Austrian economists warned that sooner or later the boom would turn into a bust, because the boom was fueled not by real and sustainable economic growth but by the Fed's injection of false credit, i.e., credit not supported by savings. Anyone who followed the rise and then decline of his 401K or other stocks understands the reality of the boom/bust economic cycle. It has been reported that the equity market has declined over $8 trillion since 2000.[11] Who pays when government tinkers with our money? You pay!

The disastrous results of unsound monetary policy are not well understood in modern America. But if we do not understand this policy's ill effects, *we the people* will be condemned to continue paying the bill that is run up by the political elites during the boom phase. The key to real economic expansion is savings, because it represents excess capacity. When consumers and businesses begin to save[12] it sends a signal that there is additional capacity for consumption. Businesspeople understand this and they gear up to provide new and/or different goods and services. At the same time, the increased savings mean there is additional money (capital) available to lend to businesspeople to expand their capacity. The additional money in savings drives down the cost of borrowing (interest), which is the primary signal to businesspeople/entrepreneurs that there is potential for additional consumption in the economy. This works until government, by creating money and credit out of thin air, injects distorting signals into the economy.

As one writer said:

> In a free, unhampered market economy, there will be a harmonious and sustained change in the pattern of consumption with a rise in consumers' real wealth. This harmony, however, gets disrupted when the central bank pumps money via an artificial

11. Hans F. Sennholz, "The Fed Is Culpable" (www.mises.org, Nov. 12, 2002).

12. Savings in businesses are created by profits that are either reinvested in the business, invested in other businesses or savings instruments such as stocks and bonds, or paid out to stockholders who then save or reinvest it. Remember, even if the stock profits are spent by the recipients, they eventually flow through to a businessperson who will save or reinvest them.

lowering of interest rates. The monetary pumping disrupts the production of consumer goods because when money is injected, not everybody gets it first.

The injection of new money into the economy benefits individuals who receive the newly created money first, at the expense of those individuals who don't receive the new money at all, or who receive it late. . . . According to Rothbard, "The individuals who receive the new money first are the greatest gainers from the increased money; those who receive it last are the greatest losers."[13]

Those with close connections to the federal government are the first receivers of the newly created money, while those of us who merely pay the bill via taxes and inflation are the losers! This is why Thomas Jefferson and Andrew Jackson resisted federalized central banking. They knew that those close to government, the large bankers in the Northeast, would gain while the average citizen working away at his farm or in a factory would eventually be left with the bill to pay. They knew and indeed most farmers and small business-people in the nineteenth century understood the dangers of unsound monetary policy.

Inflation is a major cost of unsound monetary policy that is paid for by *we the people*. Because it is so insidious (it produces its deadly effects slowly, almost unnoticed over time) most people never stop to think about their loss. Most never realize that the federal government's unsound monetary policy has robbed them of a large portion of their pay. Let us consider an example of a registered nurse who earned $17,398 in 1980 and $46,782 in 2000.[14] At first glance it seems that the nurse did quite well. Over two decades this nurse added nearly $30,000 to *before taxes* pay! But wait—the federal government got to this wage earner's money, by way of inflation, even before deducting taxes. Now see what happens when this seemingly large increase is corrected for the effects of government-imposed inflation. The nurse's actual purchasing power increased over twenty years by slightly less than $6,000. On average this amounted to a raise of around $300 per year or around $25 per month—before taxes! Of course, the effect of government-imposed inflation is felt not just by nurses but by all Americans. Perhaps this is the reason that personal bankruptcy filings rose from 287,570 in 1980 to an alarming 1.5 million in 2002![15] Who pays? You pay!

13. "Why the Fed Should Not Lower Rates" (www.mises.org, Aug. 21, 2002).

14. www.nurseweek.com, May 28, 2001, 16.

15. "Non-business Bankruptcies Soar," *USA TODAY Snapshots*, March 13, 2003, sec. 1A.

THE PROBLEM WITH EASY CREDIT

Rich bankers knew that their money would influence government to guarantee their banks and insure them against bank runs. Bank runs occurred when bankers lent money while holding too little in reserve to pay depositors on demand. In other words, the bank would be insolvent—unable to meet the demands of its creditors. In general we would call this bad business. But if a banker could get the government to pay its creditors if necessary, then it turns out to be a very lucrative business—for the banker, that is! If a citizen deposited a bushel of wheat in a grain warehouse, and the warehouse then sold it and could not provide a bushel of wheat upon demand by the original depositor, we would label this fraud. Indeed, the owner of the warehouse would be seized by the local sheriff and held for trial. But this rule does not apply to banks that practice fractional reserve banking[16] via the Federal Reserve. Under a national banking system, America's taxpayers foot the bill for banks' failed business ventures.

In addition to footing the bill for failed banks (don't forget the S&L bailouts paid for by *we the people*), we also suffer the effects of the boom/bust economy as a result of the federal government injecting money and credit created out of thin air. Frank Shostak wrote:

> A major factor that distorts producers' judgments regarding the true conditions of the market is the central bank's's easy monetary policy. This policy leads to an artificial lowering of interest rates and thereby falsifies an important market signpost that producers pay attention to. Consequently, this triggers activities that are out of touch with reality; an economic "boom" is set in motion.
>
> Once the central bank tightens its monetary stance, however, the facts of reality are revealed, various activities that sprang up on the back of previous loose monetary policies are abandoned, and an economic bust emerges. From this we can infer that a recession is: *a process whereby business errors brought about by past easy monetary policies are revealed and liquidated once the central bank tightens its monetary stance.*[17]

There are real economic and social problems with easy credit,

16. Rothbard, *The Case Against the Fed*, 48-49.
17. Frank Shostak, "The Supply-Side Gold Standard: A Critique" (www.mises.org, June 27, 2002).

credit that is not backed up by real savings, and as we have seen, these problems are eventually paid for by the average taxpaying citizen via inflation and/or higher taxes. Large bankers who have a close working and business relationship with government use the scheme of "credit out of thin air" to enrich themselves. The average citizen on the other hand must rely upon a sustainable and growing economy to improve his economic wealth. *We the people,* the average taxpayers, are not part of government's special interest groups. Under the current political system, average taxpayers have no way to protect their income and therefore pay the bill for big government's unsound monetary policy.

Easy credit distorts economic signals and sets the stage for severe and nationwide boom/bust cycles. A free market economy can produce great wealth for society if government does not distort economic signals by injecting unsupported credit into the economy. Such distortion makes it impossible for businesspeople to calculate or project business ventures. Sean Corrigan wrote:

> As an aside, to know how much time one has to complete a process, one must know what savings are available for the sustenance of its factors. The means by which both are signaled is the natural rate of interest. That is why any interference with this regulatory influence by action of the central bank is so prejudicial to prosperity.[18]

The ill effect of government-created "money out of thin air" is eventually felt by workers who enter the market as consumers and attempt to make purchases with their hard-earned income. Liberals/socialists attempt to use the negative emotion of envy to divide the "working class" from businesspeople by claiming that advocates of a Liberty-Based Society are only concerned about the profits of rich and greedy businesspeople. This fits well into their basically Marxist class-warfare view of society. We must reject such outmoded and historically defunct ideologies. In a Liberty-Based Society, we do not divide people according to the manner in which they freely choose to earn their living. We view all members of our society ultimately as consumers, and as I have repetitively noted, in a true free market the consumer is sovereign.

That is why it is so important for society to insist on sound monetary policy. Ultimately all of us—hourly workers, businesspeople, or retirees—will bear the cost of unsound money as consumers.

18. Sean Corrigan, "Say's Law for Our Time" (www.mises.org, Sept. 5, 2002).

Professor Shostak notes:

> Problems emerge, however, whenever the central bank embarks
> on loose monetary policy and creates money out of "thin air."
> Since this type of money was never earned, it is therefore not
> "backed up," so to speak, by goods and services. When such
> money is exchanged for goods and services, it in fact results in
> consumption that is not supported by production. Consequently,
> a holder of "honest" money that wants to exercise his claim over
> goods discovers that he cannot get back all the goods he previ-
> ously produced and exchanged for money. In short, he discovers
> that the purchasing power of his money has fallen.[19]

Workers who earn "honest" money the old-fashioned way—they
work for it—are put at a disadvantage by central bank policy of easy
credit or "money out of thin air." Those of us who advocate a
Liberty-Based Society recognize this and want to do something to
protect all consumers. Liberals/socialists deny it and contemporary
conservative "leaders" ignore it.

SAVINGS—THE SOURCE OF SUSTAINABLE CREDIT

How is wealth produced in a free market economy? Savings are
the source of wealth. Let us review a simple example of how this
occurs.

Assume we are in a simple barter economy. A baker produces
four loaves of bread, two of which he consumes. And since he has
satisfied his hunger, he now has two excess loaves, which he saves.
The baker's feet are cold and he decides that he needs a pair of
wool socks to keep them warm. He takes his two saved (excess)
loaves over to his neighbor, who happens to be very good at knitting and who also happens to have a pair of socks in excess of her
needs—i.e., she saved them. She dislikes baking and would rather
spend her productive time knitting. So they barter and exchange—
two loaves of bread for a pair of socks. Note that both exchanged
an excess that they really did not need to get items they both
desired. The exchanges increased the wealth of both parties. Note
also that these exchanges were completely voluntary and could not
have occurred had it not been for the saving of excess capacity. The
government was not needed to accomplish the transaction, but it
would have created a loss to both parties had it inserted itself into
this free exchange. (For example, think of the distortion caused in

19. Frank Shostak, "Can More Yen Save Japan?" (www.mises.org, Sept. 25, 2002).

any business transaction when government interposes itself by using its police power to assess and collect a sales tax.)

Take the same scenario, but this time replace barter with an economy using money as a medium of exchange. The baker exchanges his excess loaves for money, saves the money until he finds someone who has excess socks, and makes his purchase with the money he has saved. Professor Shostak states, "All that money does through its role as the medium of exchange is to facilitate the flow of real wealth among various wealth producers. . . . The key to the expansion in real wealth is saving—which is an unconsumed production of goods."[20]

Savings and accumulated savings are also the source of capital that businesses need for start-ups or growth. Accumulated savings allow for the development of credit based upon prior production. This signals businesspeople that the economy is currently strong and will remain so long enough for them to get a good return on their investment. This encourages the development of new and expanded businesses, which means more and better jobs for those who gain their living from wage earnings. This normal market situation is distorted when government creates money or credit out of thin air and injects it into the economy. With credit developed from production and savings, society gains a sustainable economic expansion. With credit out of thin air (credit unsupported by savings and not linked to actual production), society experiences an initial boom, but the boom is unsustainable, causing bad investments that will not repay principle, much less interest. And these investments must eventually be cleared or corrected. These corrections (sometimes referred to as "market adjustments"), caused by the distorted signals sent by the injection of money out of thin air, are called the bust. It is important to remember that the first to receive this new money (money out of thin air) profit. But by the time the late receivers (average taxpayers) get the money, it has become apparent that the economy is in trouble, and they pay the price via inflation, devaluations of stocks and equities, and, for workers, layoffs and work slowdowns.

As I noted in chapter 1, the only economists who have successfully explained the origins of, and therefore how to avoid, the boom/bust cycle are the Austrians. Steve H. Hanke wrote:

> For the Austrians, things go wrong when a central bank sets short-term interest rates too low and allows credit to artificially expand.

---

20. Frank Shostak, "Why the Fed Should Not Lower Rates" (www.mises.org, Aug. 21, 2002).

Interest rates that are too low—lower than those that would be set in a free market—induce businesses to discount the future at artificially low rates. This pumps up the value of long-lived investments and generates an investment-led boom, one that is characterized by too much investment and investment that is biased towards projects that are too long-lived and too capital intensive.

An investment-led boom sows the seeds of its own destruction and is unsustainable, however. Indeed, on the eve of the downturn investors find that the loanable funds for investments are too expensive to justify commitments they made during the preceding monetary expansion. Some businesses engage in distress borrowing, profit margins collapse under the weight of too much costly debt, and—if that is not bad enough—many businesses are saddled with excess capacity, resulting from what turned out to be wrong-headed investment decisions. With that, the investment-driven boom turns into a bust. In short, artificially-created investment booms always end badly.[21]

Unsound monetary policy benefits liberals/socialists, special interest groups who have close working relations with the power elite in Washington, and hacks of both political parties. Who pays for the economic distress created by unsound money? You know who benefits, but just in case you have forgotten, who pays? You pay.

GOLD—ESSENTIAL FOR SOUND MONEY

Fiat currency and unsupported credit (unsound monetary policy or easy money—money that was not acquired through productive activity such as the production of goods or services) have much in common with socialism. Neither has lived up to its promises. To maintain either requires the adherent to continually ignore the facts of current history. Socialism and unsound monetary policy have both outlived their failures. Both remain because, as Rockwell said, "political elites had too much invested in them to change the system and the intellectual class worked overtime to shore up support for the failed system." A return to the gold standard is necessary, he continues, because:

> The monetary benefits of a gold standard are clear enough, and they include life without inflation, an end to the business cycle, rational economic calculation in accounting and international trade, an encouragement to savings, and a dethroning of the government-connected financial elite.

21. Steve H. Hanke, "A Hayekian Hangover" (www.cato.org, June 26, 2002).

> But it is also political considerations that draw people to support the gold standard. Gold limits the power of the state and puts power back in the hands of the people.[22]

Sound monetary policy based upon the gold standard is an essential element in a Liberty-Based Society. With it we can limit government control of our personal income and regain a healthy, sustainable, and expanding economy that creates wealth. This wealth creation benefits all of society. Without sound monetary policy, *we the people* pay, without ever giving our consent! Recall the words of the Declaration of Independence that declare a free government to be based upon the unfettered consent of the governed. It's time to return such government to *we the people*.

QUESTIONS AND ANSWERS

Q. I can remember when gasoline was twenty-seven cents per gallon. Today it's over two dollars a gallon, but I make more money now—more than at any time in my life. Why should I be worried about inflation?

A. Yes, you most likely do make more today than you did back in the late 1950s when gasoline cost around twenty-seven cents per gallon. But you are older now. My point is that as we mature we should be making more money than when we first began working. The question is how much of your increased income is real and how much is artificial, i.e., a result of inflation. Your real income is represented by your purchasing power. Every day that the government injects inflation into the economy is a day that the government devalues the money in your pocket, bank account, or retirement account and thereby decreases your purchasing power. What right does government have to devalue *your* savings? Where in the Constitution is the federal government granted the right to delegate the authority to regulate our money to a quasi government agency— the Federal Reserve? Your hard-earned money does not belong to you. The government has assumed the right to inflate the money supply at will, even though such action eventually devalues the money you earned and saved. In chapter 10 you will see an actual example of a professional's yearly salary that looks great, but when it is adjusted for inflation you see the startling results—almost no increase in purchasing power over twenty years of hard work.

---

22. Llewellyn H. Rockwell, Jr., "Is the Gold Standard History?" (www.mises.org, Sept. 27, 2003).

Working men and women must be given the means to prevent the federal government from devaluating their income via inflation. The only way to do this is to establish a society that demands that its government follow sound monetary principles. Neither the Republican nor the Democratic party will give this to us. It is up to *we the people* of the Sovereign States to establish a Liberty-Based Society.

Q. Are you advocating that we go back to using gold coins instead of paper money?

A. I am advocating that we return to gold-backed currency. For thousands of years gold has been used as a medium of exchange. Trial and error have proven that it is the best choice because it encourages voluntary trade. I would hope to see money in our Liberty-Based Society backed by gold. "Backed by gold" to me means fully redeemable in gold by the individual bearer on demand. When the United States was last on the gold standard, gold was not redeemable by individuals but only by governments. The question of just how to move from fiat currency to gold-backed currency will require the intellectual labor of Austrian economists. Such a discussion is well beyond the scope of this book, but it is well within the ability of *we the people* of the Sovereign States to oversee it to its successful completion.

Q. I'm confused—why is it that you think sound monetary policy is so important to liberty?

A. Governments since the dawn of time have always desired to control society's money. Remember that money was not instituted by government but by the marketplace. Men working for their enlightened self-interest needed some way other than barter to facilitate voluntary exchange. Different commodities began to be used as a medium of exchange, but eventually, as already explained in this chapter, gold was chosen as the best one. Governments have always wanted to control money because the king or other ruling elites could debase the coinage by "watering" down the kingdom's gold coin with base metals. This was the beginning of inflationary monetary policy. When paper money came into use, it was much simpler for government to merely turn on its printing presses and print up more money for its use. Gold coinage makes it harder for government to debase coins, and gold-backed paper makes it harder for government to inflate our money. When government is prevented from gaining its revenue by inflation (indirect taxation), then it must resort to the more difficult task of raising taxes (direct taxation), which will eventually cause the "serfs" to rally around the castle, pitchforks and torches in hand, demanding relief from oppressive taxation or else! Politicians don't like the term "or else!" Sound money is as important for limiting government as is states' rights coupled with the acknowledged right of the Sovereign State to nullify unconstitutional federal acts or secede if necessary. Remember, all governments are or would be inflationary if *we the people* allow them to control our money.

Q. What role, if any, would gold play in preventing the boom/bust business cycle?

A. As already noted, gold-backed currency would limit the central bank's ability to inject unsupported credit into the economy. It would prevent the government from printing unsupported fiat money. This would prevent the heady boom from ever occurring and therefore there would not be nationwide bad investment. Without that, there would be no need for a "market adjustment."

Gold will not prevent bad business investments. Even with daily, voluntary exchange in the marketplace, those who invested poorly will lose some if not all of their investments. Those who invest wisely will reap the reward determined by the market. Sound money prevents government from distorting normal market signals and clouding the vision of investors. Nationwide booms and busts will not occur, but the normal risk of investing will not be eliminated. Businesspeople, entrepreneurs, and average people who invest in stocks and bonds will be rewarded by the market for voluntarily assuming this normal risk of investing.

Free Public Newspaper and Free Public Education

Civic and progressive social leaders in the state of Oklarado decided that it would be socially beneficial for all citizens to have access to political, social, and cultural news. But not everyone could afford to pay for a subscription to a daily newspaper. To remedy this grievous social injustice, the state passed a law establishing a "free" state newspaper. With great fanfare the political leaders declared that now all citizens would have access to "free" news and social commentary.

As time passed, it became obvious that the "free" newspaper system had some major flaws. One problem was that it took increasingly more tax revenues to keep the paper operating. In addition, most people thought the quality and quantity of newsprint was decreasing, even though more and more tax money was poured into the paper. Small private papers were enjoying some success but were at a distinct price disadvantage. Many citizens who would have purchased a subscription to a private paper could not, due to the large tax burden they were bearing to support the "free" paper.

It also became apparent that whoever controlled the editorial policy of the "free" paper would have enormous power over the political climate in the state. The "free" paper's managers organized themselves into an effective political group and traded their support to those politicians who would support their quasi monopoly. Citizens slowly became aware that even though there were many good local reporters, the "free" paper's management was more concerned about political power than producing an efficient newspaper.

While such a state of affairs would be unthinkable for a newspaper, Americans have accepted it for public education. Competition in the free market produces new, better, and less expensive goods and services for consumers. Yet, administrators of quasi monopolistic public education insist that parents operating within the free market are not competent to provide for the education of their children. Is politics afoot?

CHAPTER 9

Education in a Liberty-Based Society

For over a century, public education has been considered a political "sacred cow" that few would dare to question. But the decline in test scores and increase in functional illiteracy in the latter half of the twentieth century have caused many parents and other taxpayers to question the efficiency of our system of "free" mass education. The question we are concerned with is: "In a Liberty-Based Society, what is the proper role for government in education?"

WHO IS RESPONSIBLE FOR THE CHILDREN— GOVERNMENT OR PARENTS?

Noninterference is a key ingredient for a Liberty-Based Society. When dealing with minors (children under the age of eighteen years), we must first establish who is responsible for the quality and quantity of their education. Who is responsible for making this decision? Who is best suited to assure that this quality and quantity is adequate? One would think that it must be either their parents or government.

In ancient Rome, the plebeians were considered so poor that they could own no property; in fact, they were so poor that they did not even "own" their children. In that society, government owned the children of the poor. The liberal/socialist view is similar to the ancient Roman view. Liberals/socialists think modern parents are so dumb that if they are empowered with the freedom to make choices regarding their children's education, they will make the wrong decisions. Therefore, liberals have appointed themselves as "experts" who will use government's police power to force parents to give their children the "right" (i.e., politically correct) education. In contrast, the classical Christian view is that children are a gift from God to parents. Parents are responsible to God for guiding children in the ways of righteousness. Parents who fail this duty are accountable to God and will be judged by God accordingly. The obvious distinction between the Roman and liberal/socialist views and the Christian view is that the latter does not recognize any role for government in how children are raised.

A Liberty-Based Society would have more in common with the Christian view[1] in that it would not recognize government as having a role in raising children—except in that rare case where a child is criminally abused by a parent. In a Liberty-Based Society, parents make all crucial decisions for their minor children. Other than the rare exception as noted above, any interference by government is a violation of the parents' right to freely choose on behalf of their children. A minor child's rights are exercised on his behalf by his parents. Any interference by government, even in the name of good, will ultimately result in the reduction and eventual destruction of liberty.

This being said, it still must be acknowledged that a proper education is a major prerequisite for success in a modern technological society. For this reason alone it is important that citizens in our society have access to educational opportunities. Yet, is the use of governmental force necessary for the provision of such opportunities? A Liberty-Based Society would look upon the so-called "free" public education system as a violation of liberty as well as an inefficient process for the provision of educational opportunities.

PUBLIC EDUCATION VIOLATES
THE PRINCIPLE OF LIBERTY

When viewed from the vantage point of liberty, it is evident that the contemporary system of "free" public education violates the principle of liberty on at least four points. First, government forces all citizens to pay for services that benefit a relatively small number of citizens. For example, a retired couple living on a fixed income pay taxes to support government and that government uses part of its tax base to provide "free" education; a married couple who do not have children will pay taxes their entire lives and part of their tax payments will go to pay for "free" education; or a single individual who may never have children is taxed to pay for this "free"

---

1. What is meant by *Christian view* is that traditional view as contained in both the Old and New Testaments of the Bible. Most Christian views about "family" derives from the Old Testament and would therefore be in agreement with other religions based upon the writings of the Old Testament. Therefore, *Christian view* should not be considered an exclusive term but only an explanatory statement. A Liberty-Based Society is inclusive of all people who accept the basic principles of liberty, i.e., civility, noninterference, skepticism of governmental power, and recognition of the immoral nature of socialism in any of its diverse forms.

education. In all cases it is obvious that some people are forcefully deprived of their income in order to subsidize the education of other people's children.

A second point is that government forces the relatively few who do benefit from "free" public education to surrender a substantial portion of their freedom to choose. The loss of freedom of choice is accomplished by government requirements that children attend schools within their district, federal busing court orders, or an oppressive tax structure that removes so much of average citizens' income that they cannot afford to send their child to a private school.

Thirdly, government forces some taxpayers to pay twice for the education of their children. Those who decide to send their children to a private school still must pay the tax burden assessed against them even though their children do not attend tax-supported government schools.

Fourthly, government forces all taxpayers to subsidize leftist propaganda used in "free" public schools by liberal teachers. For example, Southern schoolchildren are routinely instructed using textbooks that slander as racist their ancestors who wore the gray in the War for Southern Independence.[2]

The virulent attack by the politically correct education establishment is not confined only to the South. The University of Colorado provides an example of what is going on in public colleges and universities all across America. Colorado is a state where registered Republicans outnumber Democrats by more than one hundred thousand. The GOP has controlled both houses of the state's legislature for more than two decades and a majority of its congressional delegation are Republicans. Yet a recent study found that Democrats outnumbered Republicans in this tax-supported university's social sciences and humanities departments by a ratio of thirty-one to one![3] A *Wall Street Journal* columnist noted, "Students who study social sciences or the humanities at the University of Colorado, or who wish to become teachers or journalists, evidently find themselves in an environment in which liberal professors don't merely dominate the faculty, they essentially are the faculty."[4] With education's continuing fixation on "diversity," it is assured that new professors will be hired who have the correct "diversity" and thereby

2. Kennedy and Kennedy, *The South Was Right!*, 289-99.

3. Vincent Carroll, "Republican Professors? Sure, There's One," *Wall Street Journal,* May 11, 1998, sec. A, p. 22.

4. Ibid.

assure fewer conservative professors in the tax-supported centers of higher learning—the very centers that train our children's future teachers.

The liberal/socialist push for politically correct diversity and a reliance on irrational "junk science" has met with some resistance in the halls learning. Another *Wall Street Journal* columnist noted, "Last month, under the auspices of the New York Academy of Sciences, University of Virginia biologist Paul Gross and Rutgers mathematician Norman Levitt helped organize 'The Flight from Science and Reason,' a high-level conference of more than 200 scientists, physicians, and humanists who met 'to consider the contemporary flight from reason and its associated anti-science.'"[5] The fact is that liberals/socialists are not above sacrificing truth and scientific inquiry if it helps them promote their pet social schemes. Junk science and revisionist history are nothing more than socialist propaganda weapons used to destroy American liberty.

The public education establishment is now a part of the liberal/ socialist establishment. Liberals/socialists are now empowered by government to use taxpayer-financed schools to brainwash successive generations of American children, while conservative taxpayers are forced by the police power of government to fund the entire process. How did the liberal education establishment become so powerful?

GOVERNMENT'S QUASI MONOPOLY IN EDUCATION

"Free" public education is relatively new in the South. Prior to the War for Southern Independence, there were almost no "free" public schools. Many people think that this resulted in a high illiteracy rate in the South prior to the war. But in fact, at that time the South's literacy rate (and educational level) was almost as high as that of the North and major European nations. Noted Southern historian Frank L. Owsley reported that "if college attendance is any test of an educated people, the South had more educated men and women in proportion to population than the North or any other part of the world."[6]

The campaign to replace private schools with "free" public schools was begun in America during the mid-1800s in Massachusetts. The movement was led by Horace Mann, who was

5. Christina Hoff Sommers, "The Flight from Science and Reason," *Wall Street Journal,* July 10, 1995, sec. A, p. 12.
6. Frank L. Owsley, as cited in Grady McWhiney, *Cracker Culture: Celtic Ways in the Old South* (Tuscaloosa: The University of Alabama Press, 1988), 198.

known as the father of American public education. He wanted an educational system paid for and controlled by the state. Even in this early period, the special interest group of teachers and school administrators was the primary driving force behind this movement. It was an open secret that the movement's most appealing aspect for this special interest group was that they would have greater control of the educational system if government replaced parents as their paymaster.[7] Indeed the primary goal seems to have been to remove parental authority over their children. Rothbard wrote, "As early as 1785, the Rev. Jeremy Belknap, preaching before the New Hampshire General Court, advocated equal and compulsory education for all, emphasizing that the children belong to the State and not to their parents."[8] As a result of this movement, it gradually became an accepted "fact" in America that government, not parents, is responsible for the education of children. This attitude has its precursors in the nineteenth-century authoritarian European states of France and Prussia. The authoritarian European nation-state represents quite an ideological difference from the political traditions of liberty held by nineteenth-century Americans, yet the education establishment led us away from our American roots toward the compulsory power as exercised by the nation-states of Europe.

Public education in America has its origin in special interest politics. It should be of little surprise that the political nature of the public education system has increased with time. Practical educational results have taken a backseat to special interest politics. This is not a criticism of classroom teachers but an acknowledgment of the current priorities of public education administrators. The city of Philadelphia provides us with an example of how educational "leaders" use politics to protect their interest even when said interest works against the education of children. In 2001 the city's public schools were failing, as evidenced by a 50 percent dropout rate. The Republican governor of the state decided to step in, take over the city's schools, and turn them over to a private group to manage. The Democratic mayor and organized teachers made plans to sabotage the private management's efforts to turn the schools around.

The mayor prepared a memo outlining their plans: "Thus, under headings such as 'Making the Takeover Difficult,' the memo

---

7. Milton Friedman, *Free to Choose* (New York: Harcourt Brace Jovanovich, 1979), 153.

8. Murray N. Rothbard, *Education Free and Compulsory* (Auburn, Ala: Ludwig von Mises Institute, 1999), 44.

outlines a host of possible disruptions such as having the city refuse to collect taxes or stripping the school system of key personnel."[9] Special interest educational groups use their close connections with liberal political powerbrokers to maintain and enforce government's quasi monopoly in the field of education. But has this system of "free" public education delivered what it promised?

PUBLIC EDUCATION—A FAILED SYSTEM

Public educators in the 1940s were asked to list the major problems facing teachers in America's schools. At the top of this list were such issues as students running in the halls, chewing gum in class, and speaking out of turn! By contrast, today's list would include such items as students bringing guns and bombs to school with the intent of murdering their schoolmates and teachers, riots, teenage pregnancy, drug use, gang activity, and a general decline in academic achievement. The *Wall Street Journal* reported a survey conducted by a group called Public Agenda in which 43 percent of teachers noted that they spend more time keeping order than teaching.[10]

This failure is not an indictment of the classroom teacher but of the system of mass education and the socialist social setting in which government schools must function. Therefore, any attempt to "reform" public education will face ultimate failure until we reform our society—until *we the people* reclaim our natural right to control our local communities and bring about a revival of limited government and individual responsibility. In essence, we must restore a Liberty-Based Society in America, before the enormous problems facing education (as well as Social Security, healthcare, and so on) can be resolved. Schools, both public and private, have many dedicated educators who truly desire to impart a quality education to their students, but they do not work in a vacuum. Their efforts are influenced by the greater society. Gangs roaming the neighborhoods will have a negative effect on teachers' ability to educate their students. A prevailing attitude among adults that the world "owes me a living" coupled with liberal/socialist programs to provide "free" food, healthcare, and housing will convey a far stronger and in many cases more appealing "educational" message to students. This being said, it is still important to look at the failures of

9. "Street Justice," *Wall Street Journal,* Dec. 18, 2001, sec. A, p. 16.
10. Daniel Henninger, "Doing the Numbers on Public Schools Adds Up to Zero," *Wall Street Journal,* May 2, 2003, editorial page.

America's "free" public education system in order to determine the best method to provide education in a Liberty-Based Society.

Our current system of mass public education is partially responsible for the uniquely twentieth-century phenomenon of youth social disassociation. An example of this phenomenon is the lack of respect young people today have for adults *and* each other. When asked if students in public schools treat each other with respect, only 18 percent of teachers and 19 percent of students answered yes. As for respect for adults, only 9 percent of Americans surveyed say that young people today are respectful of adults.[11] This disastrous disassociation of children from the family that produced them and the community that nurtures them is chronicled daily in headlines across America. The genesis of this disassociation includes such social issues as

• an economy that is so overburdened with taxes and inflationary monetary policies that it now requires both parents to work outside of the home in order to "make ends meet,"

• a federal government that has supported an increasingly virulent politically correct attack against traditional family values,[12]

• a politically correct attack against the role of religion in the establishment of community standards of morality and social values, and

• a mass educational bureaucracy that supports the politically correct attack against traditional American values and that has attempted to usurp the parents' role in determining and defining what constitutes a proper education for children.

As I noted earlier in this chapter, public schools began as a movement to control the "education" of children and to use the power of the state to mold the minds of children. As long as there was no disagreement between education bureaucrats and parents regarding what was being taught, the system of mass public education seemed to work effectively. Unfortunately, the educational bureaucracy evolved into a particularly strong special interest group able to sway political debate relative to education and tax policy needed to support a ballooning eduation bureaucracy. Tax funds have been used to finance "experts" and liberal/socialist educational professionals who eagerly proclaim the new politically correct gospel that education is the responsibility of the state and its education "experts." In this new system, parents are responsible for paying the increasing tax burden needed to

11. Ibid.
12. Kennedy and Kennedy, *Why Not Freedom!*, 169-79.

finance "free" public education, while the experts hired by the state administer the mass education bureaucracy.

In this system there is a major disconnect between the people who pay for "free" public education and those who administer and provide the service. Anytime government comes between the consumer and the producer, it distorts the efficiency of the free market, and education is no exception. In America's mass public education system, parents no longer participate as consumers. The state is the consumer because it is the paymaster. The educational bureaucracy, which has a far more powerful voice in the halls of government than the average taxpayer, not only caters to the will of government but is instrumental in determining governmental policy. *We the people* pay the bill while our children are "molded" in a most politically correct manner. In a Liberty-Based Society, the educational system will be responsive to the consumer while supporting and enhancing the role of the family and community, thereby inculcating an attitude that lends to the development of citizens who understand and accept the importance of civility in society.

ACADEMIC RESULTS—A LEGACY OF SOCIALIST FAILURE

It bears repeating that by pointing out the failure of the current mass education establishment, the emphasis is on the failure of the system and the liberal/socialist political schemes that produced it. It is not an indictment of the numerous dedicated and talented teachers who are doing the best they can within a failed system. A Liberty-Based Society would dethrone the educational and liberal/socialist political bureaucracy, free talented teachers to fulfill their role, and allow talented teachers to be paid according to their true market value.

The slow demise of academic achievement in public schools is typical of the results one would expect from any socialist system. In the Public Agenda survey of the public's opinion of public education, 71 percent of the respondents believed that public school students performed at the bare minimal level necessary to "get by."[13] Even more telling are the reported views of potential employers and college professors. Only 42 percent of employers rated public education graduates as good or excellent, while 59 percent of college professors rated them as fair to poor. The results were even worse when employers and college professors were asked specific questions such as their rating of public education graduates' writing skills—74 percent fair to poor; math

13. Henninger, "Doing the Numbers."

skills—64 percent fair to poor; and personal organizational skills—69 percent fair to poor.

The inflation of grades given to students in contemporary centers of higher learning is another example of socialism at work. Again, remember liberals and socialists do not care about results; they only care about promoting their socialist schemes. Recently the Academy of Arts and Sciences noted that Harvard awarded As in 1996 to 46 percent of its students, as compared to only 22 percent in 1966.[14] How is it that we see students across the nation reporting increases in their grade point averages (GPA) and at the same time academic achievement scores keep falling? A January 30, 1997, article announced that a "bachelor of arts degree in 1997 may not be the equal of a graduation certificate from an academic high school in 1947." One can only wonder if the liberal/socialist establishment is operating on the theory that a dumbed-down citizenry would be more docile and easier to control.

MORE MONEY—DOES IT WORK?

Liberal social schemes are never evaluated on common-sense standards of efficiency or effectiveness. It does not matter to a liberal whether or not one of his pet social programs is working (i.e., if it resolved the perceived social pathology that gave rise to their demands for government intervention and the massive expenditure of private income confiscated by government as taxes). All that matters to him is that he is using the police power of government to do something about a perceived social problem. This is the standard mode of operation for liberals in all social experiments they foist upon society. For example, in the late 1990s and early 2000s, liberals anticipated the possibility that some healthcare institutions or workers would fail in their common law duty to protect the privacy of their patients' medical records. Never mind that every state in the union had long before enacted statutory laws to address this privacy. Liberals raised a cry and demanded that the federal government in effect "federalize" the private medical records of every citizen in the United States. The enforcement of these new (and basically useless) federal rules is costing untold millions of dollars each year. Is it making a significant improvement in the privacy of our medical records? No! But to liberals that is not important! What is important is that they feel better because they were able to use government's police power to force Americans to pay for added security

14. Walter Williams, "The Cost of Academic Integrity" (www.jewishworldreview.com, Feb. 20, 2002).

that the marketplace did not want nor need. We see this same illogic at work in environmental issues, education, social welfare, and every other area of liberal social intervention.

Liberals/socialists insist that more money spent on public education will result in improved educational opportunity for children. But what does the record show? Washington, D.C. spent more money per student in public schools than any state in the union, but what was the result? The academic achievement of its students ranked lower than any state![15] The state of Utah spent the smallest amount per student, but they ranked the highest in academic achievement. The graph below dramatically demonstrates the fall of SAT scores over a period when inflation-adjusted dollars (constant dollars) were actually increasing.[16] SAT scores are not the only measurements that show the "dumbing-down" phenomenon created by modern liberal/socialist public education establishment.

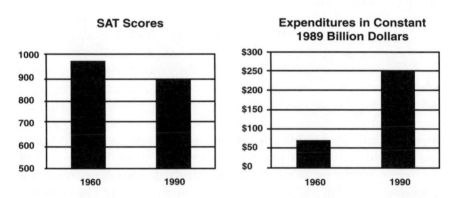

The National Assessment of Education Progress, an organization that measures educational "quality," announced in 2000 that 60 percent of poor children in the fourth grade could barely read. For black fourth graders, a full 63 percent scored below "basic."[17] Secretary of Education Roderick Paige summed it up: "After spending $125 billion of Title I money over 25 years, we have virtually nothing to show for it."[18] Obviously, money and socialism are not the solutions. The free market in a Liberty-Based Society

15. "Learning and Spending," *Wall Street Journal*, Dec. 15, 2003, sec. A, p. 14.

16. William J. Bennett, *The Index of Leading Cultural Indicators* (New York: Touchstone, 1994), 82.

17. Bill O'Reilly, "Racism in Public Education" (www.worldnetdaily.com, May 30, 2001).

18. Ibid.

would effectively and efficiently resolve problems created by the failed system of mass "free" public education.

WHERE THERE IS NO CHOICE, THERE IS NO FREEDOM

I noted at the beginning of this chapter that public education by its very nature—the use of government's police power to force people to hand over their income for some social purpose that they may have no interest in—decreases "free" people's ability to choose the proper course of education for their children. The very essence of freedom is the right and power to freely choose between various alternatives available in the marketplace. For example, if the government decides to help Kmart by imposing a "level-playing-field" tax on items purchased at Wal-Mart, then my freedom to freely choose is limited by this government-imposed tax. Items purchased at Wal-Mart will cost more, and therefore I am forced to either punish my family by spending our money foolishly at Wal-Mart or purchase the same items at an artificially lower price at Kmart. Liberals/socialists might argue that it is socially beneficial to keep Kmart open so that Wal-Mart will not become a monopoly. However, though liberals may say they want to prevent monopolies, monopolies cannot occur without the support of government! But who really suffers? Individuals have lost a small portion of their right to freely choose, and Kmart now knows that it does not have to try harder to please its customers. So society has lost not only in price but in choice of goods as well. The quality of service is reduced, and society also suffers due to the reduced potential for employment at Wal-Mart. Liberals/socialists are happy, but as always happens, *we the people* pay the price for their utopian schemes.

The same is true for public education. The tax burden paid by the average citizen is one of the many reasons that most parents cannot afford to seek other options, even when they know that their child would do better at a local private school. *We the people* are not free if government uses its police power to limit our freedom to make choices regarding our children's education. The power of government's tax collector is nil absent government's police force to compel us to "stand and deliver." As taxes increase, our residual income is reduced. Therefore we are less free, because government has limited our financial ability to choose.

VOUCHERS AS A USEFUL FIRST STEP

By the beginning of 2000, the decades-old debate over the utility of vouchers seemed to be turning in favor of the proponents. The argument has not changed much over the decades,[19] but what has changed is the public's realization that at least *some* of our public schools are a failure. Usually these failures are located in inner-city areas with predominately black populations. Numerous surveys have demonstrated that black citizens in these areas supported vouchers as a means to give them a choice over their children's education. Unfortunately for these citizens, the self-appointed black leadership is more concerned with the political alliances it has made with organizations such as the National Education Association (NEA) and Democratic party operatives than it is with the education of inner-city young people. Therefore, vouchers have received little support from these self-appointed black leaders.

Regardless of skin color, parents in America want to improve their ability to freely choose with regards to the education of their children. Philip Vassallo wrote, "A recent survey by Portrait of America found that 52 percent of adults believed that introducing competition by allowing parents to select schools would do more to improve education in America than spending money. Similarly, 54 percent favor school vouchers, and 59 percent say that allowing parents a choice in school selection is more likely to produce accountability than oversight by a school board."[20] The *Wall Street Journal* reported a poll of 1,000 black Milwaukee residents that demonstrated that 70 percent "believe that private and parochial schools provide a better education than public schools."[21] There is little doubt that people are beginning to realize that our mass public educational establishment is a failure and they are beginning to look around for solutions. The question remains: "Are vouchers the answer to the educational dilemma?"

From the vantage point of a Liberty-Based Society, it is easy to answer this question. Vouchers may be a good way to transition from public to private funding of education. They may be a means for providing citizens who are facing extreme problems in the inner cities with immediate but temporary relief. But vouchers are not the ultimate answer because they represent the political distribution of other people's income. The answer to education is to allow citizens to reap the benefits of a free market economy. This will provide economic opportunity that will allow free people to choose the best educational options for their children. It will also encourage the development of numerous educational choices that do not currently exist, while paying teachers

19. Friedman, *Free to Choose*, 158-75.

20. Philip Vassallo, "Empowering Parents Through School Choice" (www.cato.org/dailys/10/20/00).

21. "Saving City Schools," *Wall Street Journal*, May 12, 1995, sec. A, p. 12.

top dollar for their talents. As I will discuss in the next chapter, no government should be allowed to tax its citizens above 10 percent of GDP. The extra money (which rightfully belongs to the workers and investors who earned it) left in the pockets of our citizens will free them from the shackles of "free" public education.

QUESTIONS AND ANSWERS

Q. You are condemning all public schools just because of the failure of a few. Don't you think society would be better off if we simply fix the part of public education that is broken?

A. You are correct that there are many "blue ribbon" public schools that are relatively excellent. But the point I stress is that the principle of publicly financed education is flawed vis-à-vis the principle of liberty. If you force individuals to pay for something, you deprive them of (1) the freedom to choose whether or not to provide their financial support to "your" cause—and it may well be a laudable cause—and (2) their income that they could have used to finance other choices. Free men and women use their income to finance their personal choice(s), but serfs and slaves are told by their master what choice(s) to make.

Public schools are based upon the socialist theory of force. Individuals are not free to make their choice but government forces them to do what some "expert" or bureaucrat tells them to do. Even if by some stroke of magic every public school in America became a "blue ribbon" school, this still would not remove the anti-liberty stigma from public education. Putting this observation aside for the moment, how could we "fix" the broken part of public education? If money were the solution, we would have already solved the problems. If more administrative personnel were the answer, we would have already solved the problems. If stricter truancy laws or more police presence in schools were the solution, we would have already solved the problems. The point is that without competition, where parents are empowered via liberty to freely choose the best school for their children, education will never rise to the level that our well-trained and motivated classroom teachers could achieve.

Q. We've tried charter schools and they have been only mildly successful. Yet the vast majority of public-school students still remain in the educational trap that modern education has become. Vouchers are a political impossibility. What else can we try?

A. Charter schools and vouchers are examples of "Band-Aid" political efforts meant to ease the pain created by the liberal/socialist system.

Actually these efforts are not so much intended to "ease the pain" as to pacify the populace. These types of efforts are all that current conservative "leaders" can come up with because they are trapped in the liberal/socialist political system. They most likely are doing the best they can within the system. Our aim should be to get out of the system! In a Liberty-Based Society, individual wealth will greatly increase first as a result of a radically reduced tax burden and secondly as a result of sustainable economic growth. As a result, parents will have the financial resources necessary to purchase educational services that they feel will be most beneficial for their children. Charter schools and vouchers should be viewed as an initial step in the right direction, but eventually—and this will occur only after we have overthrown the current liberal/socialist political system—education must be subjected to the rigors of market competition.

Q. What will happen to all of our teachers who are now employed in public education?

A. The demand for educational services is a function of the number of children and young people demanding (though usually via their parents) an education. If overnight all public schools were turned into private schools, the number of students demanding an education would remain relatively the same. The type of education demanded may change—parents may decide to demand one that puts more stress on arts, athletics, or some special craft or profession. But the demand for well-trained and motivated teachers would actually increase. For the first time in modern history, the better teachers would be in higher demand and therefore would command higher wages. The free market would reward merit and quality in education just as it does in technology fields. Good teachers would have more choice as to where to teach and they would receive compensation established by the forces of supply and demand—just like everyone else in the private sector. Educators in a Liberty-Based Society will receive better pay; they will perform their professional duties in an atmosphere where students want to learn and where parents are spending their money and are therefore interested in the value they are purchasing; and they will have more employment choices in their local communities.

Because living Americans have never seen an educational system that is not based on the socialist system, it is hard for some of us even to comprehend an educational system based on individual choice, where parents use their income to purchase educational services. In many respects we are like the citizens of the former Soviet Union and its Eastern European bloc nations, who grew up under socialism and then one day their system was suddenly gone! They had no idea how to order their society—they had never been free. Freedom is wonderful, it is challenging, and it demands that individuals be willing to take personal responsibility for their choices. Americans have a proud history of individualism and self-reliance. I am confident that *we the people* of the Sovereign States will rise to the demands of building a Liberty-Based Society. Our well-trained and highly motivated educators will be a key part of this new society—and society will reward them accordingly.

Theft Made Legal—A Story of Lords and Vassals

In ancient Europe, during a time long since forgotten, there existed a small village in the fiefdom of Vassalland. The vassals were a contented people happily living out their commoner existence. Food and shelter were barely sufficient, and survival depended on every man working his small crops during the growing season and saving his excess production to see himself and his family through the cold winter.

One day a belligerent band of men claiming to be the agents of the fiefdom's lord entered the village. These men carried cruel weapons and made it clear that they would use them on anyone who refused to comply with the lord's new decree. And what was that decree? At the end of each growing season, all vassals would turn over one-third of their produce to the agents. The lord would use it to finance new castles, crusading in the Holy Land, and a larger army.

"But how can we survive the cold winters? How will we be able to trade for shoes for our children? How will we maintain our meager homes?" the poor vassals cried.

Their pleas were to no avail. The agents were armed and determined to get what they considered belonged to the lord. The vassals' pitiful supplications were met with the cruel reply that if the vassals worked harder and put their wives in the fields with them, they would be able to survive.

Enraged, the vassals accused the agents of being thieves and robbers bent on pillaging their village. The agents placed their hands firmly upon their cruel weapons and arrogantly assured the vassals that they were actually doing the vassals a favor! "Just think about all the new projects the lord will be able to do with your contributions," they said.

The vassals murmured among themselves, wondering what good new castles would bring them. They could not see any advantage that large forts in faraway places would bring their village. And as much as they would like to see the Holy Land in Christian hands, they did not think it was expected of them to starve their children in order to bring this about. And as for a larger army—well, they suspected that the lord intended to use it to extort more of the vassals' private property.

It was all to no avail. The agents collected the vassals' private property and left them to manage as best they could. They also warned them to be ready—for next year they would return and most likely demand an even larger share.

Question: As far as the vassals were concerned, was there any difference between the lord's agents and robbers?

Question: If someone compels you to surrender a portion of your private property for a "good cause," does this change that person's status from a thief to a moral person bent on doing good?

Question: If it is wrong for an individual to force another person to surrender his private property, would it be right for a majority of individuals to force the minority to surrender their private property?

Question: Are you a vassal?

CHAPTER 10

Taxes and Other Ways to Steal Other People's Money

Money is the mother's milk of American politics. Politicians need money to enter or maintain themselves in office, to grant favors to the special interest groups that provide votes in elections, to support business ventures of the politically connected, and to support the ever enlarging bureaucracy required to maintain their political empire. Most contemporary politicians are rich compared to the average taxpayer, but this should not lead one to believe that they will use their personal fortunes to support the liberal/socialist goals they vote for every day. No, their fortunes are safe; it's your income they desire. This basic fact of American politics will remain as long as we maintain the current liberal/socialist scheme of government. As I pointed out in chapter 1, the election of a "conservative" president or majority in Congress has done nothing to roll back liberal/socialist gains previously won. Indeed, conservatives' main role in American government is to serve as the preservers of past liberal/socialist gains. So regardless of who is in power—conservative, liberal, Republican, or Democrat—under the current liberal/socialist political system, your income is always at risk!

THE INHERENT EVIL NATURE OF TAXES

As was demonstrated in the sidebar at the beginning of this chapter, the taking of private goods for the use of government is based upon a system of force. When you pay your taxes, you cannot direct how your money will be spent. The government may intend to transfer your property to the Sexual Minority Youth Assistance League even though you may be opposed to many of the goals of that organization. If you had the freedom to do with your hard-earned property as you saw fit, you might never give it to such an organization. Yet government intervenes, and with the backing of its police powers it forces you to support ideas and organizations that you might never freely choose to support. Coercion, intimidation, threats, and brutal force are the common denominators of tax collectors in all governments. Frederic Bastiat (1801-50), a French political philosopher, noted:

> We must remember that law is force, and that, consequently, the proper functions of the law cannot lawfully extend beyond the proper functions of force.
> When law and force keep a person within the bounds of justice, they impose nothing but a mere negation. They oblige him only to abstain from harming others. They violate neither his personality, his liberty, nor his property. They are *defensive;* they defend equally the rights of all. . . .[1]
> Sometimes the law defends plunder and participates in it. Thus the beneficiaries are spared the shame, danger, and scruple which their acts would otherwise involve. Sometimes the law places the whole apparatus of judges, police, prisons, and gendarmes at the service of the plunderers, and treats the victim—when he defends himself—as a criminal. In short, there is a *legal plunder.*[2]

In a Liberty-Based Society, total taxation (national, state, and local) above 10 percent of GDP will be considered as illegal plundering of the population by the political classes. As I noted in chapter 5, the free market will work economic miracles only if the productive elements of the population are allowed to invest their property as they see fit. Reducing the current tax burden imposed upon Americans will eliminate the tremendous opportunity cost that is currently imposed by government on the economy. It will also remove the insidious and oppressive nature of taxes from society. Refer to the table below for a partial listing of taxes that individuals are currently forced to pay.

A Partial Listing of Taxes Working Americans Pay

Accounts Receivable Tax	Corporate Income Tax (cost of doing business passed on to consumer via higher prices)	Federal Unemployment Tax
Building Permit Tax	Court Fees	Fishing License Tax
Capital Gains Tax	Dog License Tax	Fuel Permit Tax
Cigarette Tax	Drivers License Tax	Gasoline Tax
Commercial Drivers License Tax	Federal Income Tax	Hunting License Tax—Federal

1. Frederic Bastiat, *The Law* (1850; reprint, New York: The Foundation for Economic Education, 1979), 28.
2. Ibid., 20.

Hunting License Tax—State	Real Estate Tax	Telephone Recurring and Nonrecurring Charges Tax
Inheritance Tax Interest Expense	Recreational Vehicle Tax	Toll Bridge Tax
Inventory Tax	Road Toll Booth Tax	Toll Tunnel Tax
IRS Interest Charges	Sales Tax	Traffic Fines
IRS Penalties	Septic Permit Tax	Trailer Registration Tax
Judicial Fines	Service Charge Tax	Utility Tax
Judicial Interest	School Tax	Vehicle Registration Tax
Liquor Tax	Social Security Tax	Water Craft Registration Tax
Luxury Tax	State Income Tax	Well Permit Tax
Marriage Tax	State Unemployment Tax	Workers Compensation Tax
Medicare Tax	Telephone Federal Excise Tax	
Municipal Income Tax	Telephone Federal Universal Service Fee Tax	
Property Tax	Telephone Minimum Usage Surcharge Tax	

ARE AMERICANS TAX SLAVES OR ONLY TAX SERFS?

Slaves, such as those currently in bondage in the African nation of Sudan, have no right to the product of their labor. They work for their master. Their master has first claim to the slaves' productive output or income. A serf is only a little better off in that he owes a large percentage of his productive output to the lord of the manor—typically between 30 to 60 percent. Substitute "taxpayer" for "serf" and "federal government" for "lord of the manor" in the prior sentence and you will begin to get an idea of the logic in calling contemporary Americans "Uncle Sam's tax serfs."

St. George Tucker from Virginia was an early-nineteenth-century expert on the United States Constitution. He was against slavery and sought to find a peaceful solution to the issue. In his treatise on slavery, he described three forms: (1) domestic slavery—the ownership of one person by another; (2) civil slavery—the reduction of an individual's liberty by an abusive government; and (3) political slavery—the denial by one nation of another nation's right of self-government.[3] Note that even in the early 1800s, an American writer had

3. Kennedy, *Myths of American Slavery*, 178.

demonstrated that a free people would become civil slaves if government encroached on the rights of the people. Thus the term "tax slaves" as applied to modern American taxpayers is not an abuse of the term, if government confiscates privately earned income and property above a certain amount. In a Liberty-Based Society *we the people* will establish that limit at no more than 10 percent of GDP. But how does that future condition, under a Liberty-Based Society, compare to the burden that an average American taxpayer currently endures?

Assume you are an average industrial worker who receives a payroll check twice a month. Your gross earnings each payday in 1998 would be somewhere around $1,290. After the federal government takes its portion via income and Social Security taxes and other payroll taxes that your employer must pay on your behalf (a cost of labor that in an unhampered free market would have gone to the worker via higher wages or the consumer as lower prices), you have only $935 to take home! Remember that Master, i.e., the federal government, gets his first. In other words, government has staked a claim to the first 38 percent of your income! And remember that you still are required to pay real-estate taxes, gasoline taxes, sales taxes, and other taxes out of your remaining income. To make matters even worse, remember that you must use your $935 to pay for government-imposed inflation and the cost of government regulations and save enough to ride out government-imposed recession and unemployment.[4]

A study published by the Cato Institute demonstrated that government-mandated employer costs reduce the average industrial worker's salary by almost 30 percent! And that is without taking into account the cost of regulatory compliance.[5] What does that mean for the average worker? It means that if we were to reduce the size and scope of government to one costing no more than 10 percent of GDP, then workers could expect a wage increase (or purchasing-power increase) of between 20 to 30 percent. The question is—"Is it really a more important, patriotic, or wiser investment to allow government to extort your income, or would you and your family be better off if you kept your property and used it as you see fit?" If you think it would be better for you to keep your income, then the only way it will ever happen is to establish a Liberty-Based Society.

TAXPAYERS' BURDEN

Most workers do not understand just how much they are paying for

4. Dean Stansel, "The Hidden Burden of Taxation: How the Government Reduces Take-Home Pay" (www.cato.org), Cato Institute Policy Analysis No. 302, 4.
5. Ibid., 8.

government. Most workers pay more for government than they do for food, shelter, and clothing combined![6] A simple look at the difference between what shows on your "gross" versus your "net" pay on your payroll check will demonstrate this in part. I say *in part* because your check does not include the 7.65 percent matching taxes your employer must pay on your behalf. The total cost the employer must pay is the employer's cost for your labor. This is money that in a free market would have gone to the worker as (1) higher wages or (2) higher purchasing power arising from lower prices caused by lower production costs. In either case, assuming sound monetary policy, which would result in zero inflation, the worker wins. Gary Galles wrote, "Benefits which the government mandates employers to provide their workers also really come out of workers' pockets, because that cost is part of their total compensation package, which must be covered by the value of worker output to their employer. Similarly, the productivity-reducing costs of complying with regulatory burdens (a 'tax' of hundreds of billions dollars a year) reduce take home pay."[7] Another "invisible" cost (tax) paid by American workers without their consent is the opportunity cost that occurs when private savings dry up and the economy's ability to sustain long-term capital growth is destroyed. The table below shows the stunning growth during the last century of the government's interference in the economy.

Total Federal Revenue
Percent of Gross Domestic Product
1900-2000[8]

Year	1900	1925	1950	1975	2000
Percent of GDP	3.0%	9.4%	14.4%	19%	20.8%

With this kind of governmental interference, American industry becomes old and uncompetitive, and eventually jobs are lost or are never created. And a heavy tax burden that reduces saving and

6. Gary Galles, "'Less for Our Labor' Day?" (www.mises.org, Sept. 2, 2002).

7. Ibid.

8. Data from "Fiscal Facts & Figures" (www.cato.org/research/fiscal_policy/2002/factsfigs.html). Data for years 1925 and 1975 extrapolated from cited data. Note that this represents only direct federal revenues. It does not include the cost of indirect federal taxation via inflation, the cost of unfunded federal mandates, the cost associated with complying with intrusive federal regulations, or the opportunity cost our economy pays when private funds are confiscated and used by government instead of being invested in productive enterprises that will result in creating real jobs and driving down prices.

investment also holds back the accumulation of capital over time. Fewer tools mean less production, and therefore less income for workers.[9]

Note that it is not the workers' fault that they become less productive and their products become less competitive, and it is not the business owners' or investors' fault either. Who then is to blame? The blame lies squarely at the feet of greedy, self-absorbed politicians! How do we solve the problem? It is impossible to solve it under the current business-as-usual, patronage political system that has controlled the United States for over a hundred years! What is needed is a revival of the original constitutional Republic of Republics, which I have described as a Liberty-Based Society. Conservatives are wasting their time and limited resources when they engage in political activities that are not specifically aimed at the radical restoration of the original constitutional Republic of Republics. If we continue to do what we have been doing for the past century, it should be of no surprise that we end up with the same mess that we have suffered under since the days of Lincoln.

Some "conservatives" (and at this point we should begin to question what they are trying to "conserve"—other than past liberal/socialist victories) may think the prior comment is too critical of the many hard-working conservative Republicans serving in the federal government. They may ask, "What about the famous Newt Gingrich Republican 'revolution' of 1994?" The problem was that the newly elected conservative Republicans came with the intent to reduce government but stayed to oversee what was to become the largest growth in federal spending since LBJ's Great Society! What went wrong? Jeffrey Tucker wrote:

> First, there was Haley Barbour, chairman of the Republican Party, who was concerned that if the GOP cuts taxes, Clinton would . . . benefit politically. Barbour promised that the GOP could "outmaneuver" Clinton by calling off all discussion of tax cuts. Now there's an idea: outmaneuver Clinton by doing what he would otherwise want you to do!
>
> Second, there was William Kristol, then running a D.C. policy boutique, who advised the GOP not to do anything "reckless" like actually cut the government. Why? Because the most important priority of the Republicans ought not to be cutting government but rather preparing itself for taking back the presidency in 1996, after which, he implied, government can finally be cut.[10]

After reading this far, you should know that the above reasoning

9. www.cato.org/research/fiscal_policy/2002/factsfigs.html.
10. Jeffrey Tucker, "The Spoils of Victory" (www.mises.org, Nov. 18, 2002).

by "conservative" leadership is not new. It did not start in the 1990s but has been a hallmark of conservative thinking (if you can call it thinking) since the turn of the twentieth century. Sad is the fate of a people whose leaders have sacrificed principle at the altar of pragmatism and political expediency. And what difference does it make for the average citizen if our "conservative" politicians become more concerned about winning their next election than about working to control the growth of government? It makes no difference at all—unless you happen to be someone who objects to the steady evolution from being a freeman to a tax serf and ultimately to Uncle Sam's tax slave! (See the table below.)

Total Federal Revenue
Per Capita—1900-2000[11]

Year	1900	1925	1950	1975	2000
Per Capita Taxes	$151	$401	$2,139	$4,430	$7,668

Tucker points out, "The [GOP] has been running on a platform of cutting government in every election since World War II. During that time, the overall tax burden on the American family has risen from 17 percent to 40 percent."[12] Colonial Americans revolted against King George because they considered his taxes to be a badge of slavery. Today we endure a tax load that is so large it makes us look like slaves in the antebellum South, working on the task system, in which the master allowed the slave to keep half of everything he produced—provided of course that the slave surrendered his first earnings to his master. Then the slave was allowed to take what was left (similar to payroll deductions).

TAX FREEDOM DAY

Tax freedom day—the day average Americans stop working to pay taxes for the year and begin working for themselves—in 1902 was January 31. By 1998 tax freedom day had moved toward the middle of the calendar to May 10! In other words, under the watchful eyes

11. Data from "Fiscal Facts & Figures" (www.cato.org/research/fiscal_policy/2002/factsfigs.html). Data for years 1925 and 1975 extrapolated from cited data. Note that at the beginning of the twentieth century, an average American family of four would pay $604 each year to the federal government. By the end of the century, a similar family would pay $30,672! Note also that this table represents federal taxes only, not our total tax burden.

12. Tucker, "The Spoils of Victory."

of "conservative" leaders, liberals/socialists have forced Americans to go from working one-twelfth of their lives for government to five-twelfths.[13] And this does not take into account the indirect taxes imposed upon us, such as inflation, the cost of complying with unfunded mandates, and the enormous opportunity cost of direct and indirect taxation. For twenty-first-century Americans, the glory of being a freeman is all but gone. The only question is whether we are tax serfs or tax slaves. For this new American, it is no longer a question of tax freedom day but of tax serf-obligation completion day, with the fear that tax slavery day is just over the horizon.

> There is an old saying that describes the feelings of workers in difficult economic times: my take-home pay won't take me home. One reason for the squeeze on workers is the rising tax burden at all levels of government. Since 1990 the federal government has enacted a five-year $200 billion tax increase and the states have added $40 billion in taxes to the total.[14]

The above quote was written in 1992. The authors, George Nastas and Stephen Moore, were lamenting the fact that the percentage of income paid by the average American family to the government in taxes had grown from less than 30 percent in 1960 to 40 percent in 1992. This trend has not reversed itself since; if anything, it has gotten even worse.

Nor should we think that it is all the fault of liberals/socialists. We can't even blame it on the neoconservatives! The Republican party is as responsible as the liberal/socialist party (a.k.a. the Democratic party). For example, in New Jersey, the Republican governor and legislature increased that state's budget by over 50 percent in eight years. For the same period, inflation increased 20 percent.[15] The rise in state and local taxes from 1960 to 2001 resulted in the average family paying twice as much of their income to state and local tax collectors than they had in 1960. Overall, state and local governments have bought into the tax-and-spend doctrine that now emanates from our masters in Washington, D.C. The federal tax-and-spend mentality has infected politicians across the spectrum of American politics. The idea has taken root throughout the political system that *we the people* owe our taxes to the political class, who will be responsible for deciding who should benefit from our income. Talk of tax cuts brings hoots of derision from the liberal/socialist

13. Charles Adams, "Taxes in America," *The Free Market* 18, no. 4 (April 2000).

14. George Nastas and Stephen Moore, "A Consumer's Guide to Taxes: How Much Do You Really Pay in Taxes?" Cato Institute Briefing Paper No. 15,April 15, 1992.

15. "The Fifty State Hangover," *Wall Street Journal,* Dec. 18, 2001, sec. A, p. 16.

propaganda ministry (a.k.a. the mainline media) demanding to know how we plan to pay for these tax cuts! *We the people* pay for our income with our labor and investments. It's our money in the first place. Anyone who has it without our unfettered consent is a thief! In an editorial, the *Wall Street Journal* warned:

> There are some useful lessons to be learned from all of this. One is that if surpluses aren't returned in tax cuts, the politicians will spend them and then during hard economic times they will claim the only solution is to raise taxes again. Another is that rainy-day funds turn out to be leaky budget vessels; tax cuts are a better way to restrain spending. The best way to avoid a hangover is not get drunk in the first place.[16]

Big government requires big taxes. Professional politicians require huge amounts of OPM in order to grease the skids of reelection. How else do you think they can maintain an almost 95 percent incumbent reelection record in Congress? The question is, do you need big government and its big taxes?

HIDDEN TAXES—CALMING THE SHEEP BEFORE YOU FLEECE THEM

In a Liberty-Based Society, taxation above 10 percent of GDP is the moral equivalent of theft! In the liberal/socialist society there are no moral barriers against onerous taxation. Despite this, our modern-day politicians make every effort to hide their private income-confiscation schemes. Crafty politicians realize that during the past century American tax serfs began to rebel when the visible tax burden approached 50 percent of their income. Somewhere in the dark, cold recesses of society's political leaders' subconscious stirs the dread that perhaps this will be the night when their Washington, D.C. castle will be surrounded by enraged tax serfs with pitchforks and torches in hand demanding a final settlement with their political persecutors. To prevent a tax-serf rebellion, our political leaders have devised measures to hide their onerous tax burden from America's working men and women.

The twentieth century, with its mass industrialization and concentration of America's workforce, provided politicians with their first real opportunity to hide taxation from average workers. Take for example average manufacturing workers toward the end of the century.[17] Their employers' yearly cost averaged $30,971 per employee.[18]

16. Ibid.
17. Stansel, "The Hidden Burden of Taxation," 8.
18. I used 2,080 hours per work year in this calculation.

This represented the value of the worker's labor to the employer—what the employer was willing to pay in order to obtain the productive results of the worker's labor for one year. But of this $30,971, the worker only saw $27,206 in his gross pay. The difference between what the employer was willing to pay for the worker's productive output and what the worker saw in his gross pay represents government-imposed costs that the employer was forced to pay. This government-imposed tax is hidden from the vast majority of Americans. America's political leaders know that if taxpayers don't see the tax, they won't protest the tax!

After allowing for the government-imposed cost that average American manufacturing workers never see, these workers then receive payroll checks that list their gross (yearly) pay as $27,206. But these workers know that they will not be able to take this amount home. No, the government has devised another way to keep its tax serfs ignorant and pacified—it's called payroll deductions. It's the tax collectors' easy-payment plan. Recall the tax collector's logic—if the tax serf never holds the money in his hand, he will never protest the loss of something he never really ever had! The average manufacturing worker's net pay, his take-home pay, has been reduced to $22,443 per year. This means that the government has reduced the worker's pay from $13.08 per hour down to $10.79 per hour. The difference of $2.29 per hour represents the serf's obligation to the lord of the manor. Every day each worker labors eight hours at $2.29 per hour for the government. That means that each day the first $18.32 earned by the average manufacturing worker goes directly to the government! The tax collector quietly removes the worker's income without even so much as a sigh of despair coming from the tax serf. No doubt government agents view this as quite an efficient system. What would happen if the system was changed, and each day as workers filed out a government agent stood at the gate and forced them to pay $18.32 before they could go home? We all know what would happen. It would not be long before government castles in Washington, D.C. were surrounded by angry serfs with pitchforks and torches in hand!

The result of over a half-century of government-imposed taxes and employer-mandated benefits, rules, and regulations is that America's working men and women end up with less real take-home pay even though total employee compensation has increased. These additional employment costs and employee taxes were established either as hidden taxes or quietly removed from our take-home pay in a manner that would most likely preclude protest from the workers. For example, during the 1943 debate regarding the passing of the

Current Tax Payment Act, the politicians' main goal clearly was to create a taxing mechanism that would cause the least amount of tax-payer resentment. Look at the record and see how Senator Clark and a representative of the Federal Treasury Department, Mr. Paul, described the tax act:

> *Senator Clark:* Psychology almost certainly ought to be considered in the tax year. Some British Chancellor of the Exchequer once said: "Taxation consists of getting the greatest amount of money with the least amount of squawks."
> *Mr. Paul:* Do you think if we cut down the squawking under this method we could raise the individual tax rates?
> *Senator Clark:* That's what I am trying to find out.[19]

The combination of hidden taxes and "easy pay" taxes does more than just deprive working people of their hard-earned income. It also masks the real cost of government. This allows unscrupulous politicians to expand the size of government without "unduly" alarming the serfs.

Inflation is another hidden tax. It hampers the ability of the economy to sustain growth, decreases long-term investments that bring about more jobs, and robs workers of any salary increase they may earn. (Recall the description in chapter 5 of how the free market creates wealth that benefits our society at large. Inflation reduces or hinders the ability of the free market to increase wealth in our society.) It also gives the population the impression of economic growth when growth really does not exist. Just because we take home more money does not mean that our real wages (our purchasing power) have increased. Inflation allows politicians to tax without passing legislation. And it has the salutatory effect (from the politician's point of view) of keeping the serfs quiet because they have more money in their pay-checks—even though their purchasing power is the same or reduced!

In chapter 8 we looked at the average salary of a registered nurse from 1980 to 2000.[20] During that time the average nurse's salary "jumped" from $17,398 to $46,782 annually. Of course, as the nurse made more money she moved into a higher income tax bracket. But look at what inflation did to the nurse's real salary, i.e., her purchasing power. Inflation causes all goods and services to become more costly to purchase. Even though the nurse brings

19. Stansel, "The Hidden Burden of Taxation," 17.
20. Heather Stringer, "Frozen Assets: For Nurses, a Solid Financial Future Remains Elusive as Salaries Fail to Keep Up with Inflation" (www.nurseweek.com, May 28, 2001), 16. Copyright 2001. Nurseweek. All rights reserved. Used with permission.

home more dollars, each individual dollar has less purchasing power! When we adjust the nurse's 2000 salary for inflation—constant 1980 dollars—we see that her real salary went from $17,398 in 1980 to only $23,369 in 2000 (see the table below). In other words, the nurse received an increase of 3.4 percent over twenty years of work! No wonder so many Americans complain that it seems that our take-home pay won't take us home.

Inflation-Adjusted Take-Home Pay (1980-2000)[21]

Year	Average Nursing Salary	Real Salary—Purchasing Power in 1980 Constant Dollars
1980	$17,398	$17,398*
1984	23,505	19,079
1988	28,383	20,839
1992	37,738	23,166
1996	42,071	23,103
2000	46,782	23,369

Note: This representation assumes the purchasing power of 1980 dollars to be equal to 1980 salary. In reality this is not the case. The purchasing power of the 1980 salary would have been reduced by the effects for prior inflation. But for simplicity's sake I assume that inflation began subsequent to 1980. In actuality the results for American workers are worse than the table indicates.

Inflation has been a boon to big-government politicians of both parties. Gene Callahan wrote:

> If the government is in charge of creating money, its interest generally will run toward inflating the money supply. It can use the new money for increased spending, without having to go through the unpopular measure of raising taxes. That helps explain why prices have been more volatile since governments have replaced the gold standard with fiat [unsupported paper] money.[22]

Austrian economists have warned us that one of the primary dangers of inflation is that when government creates new money, it alters the economic system. Those who get the new money first—government and those special interests close to government—benefit from it,

21. Ibid.

22. Gene Callahan, *Economics for Real People: An Introduction to the Austrian School* (Auburn, Ala.: Ludwig von Mises Institute, 2002), 146.

but those of us who are not close to government are hurt by government-sponsored inflation. Special-interest groups get the benefit, politicians use it as a vote buying scheme, and the serfs who don't know any better eventually pay the bill!

The following table gives you an idea of just how much of your hard-earned income is used by politicians to curry favor, i.e., votes and financial contributions, from special interest groups. Modern politicians call these donations "public subsidies." The question for you is, do you want your income spent on such left-of-center causes?[23] If not, then what can taxpayers do about it? Write their congressman! Liberal or conservative, all politicians have bought into the "tax and spend, curry favors, and get reelected" theme of the contemporary American liberal/socialist democracy. Asking contemporary politicians to stop using taxpayers' income for their political advantage is like asking the proverbial fox to stop raiding the henhouse. If we are to change our current circumstances, we need to change the system in which our elected leaders operate. Merely tinkering with symptoms will not cure the problem. The only solution is to change the current liberal/socialist-based political system back to one based on liberty, individual responsibility, sound monetary principles, and a free market economy—in other words, a Liberty-Based Society.

How Politicians Spend Your Income (1996-2000)[24]

Gay Men's Health Crisis	$428,835
Sexual Minority Youth Assistance League	154,470
Center for Women's Policy Studies	813,881
NOW Legal Defense and Education Fund	1,168,252
NAACP	1,280,751
National Council of Churches	18,423,588
National Association of People with AIDS	1,862,670
League of Women Voters	2,329,328
National Education Association	3,655,052
National Urban League	123,855,505
National Council of Senior Citizens	333,482,287

It should be of no surprise that the one thing all of these organizations

23. Left of center or right of center—neither has a legitimate claim upon private citizens' income.

24. John Samples, Christopher Yablonski, and Ivan G. Osorio, "More Government for All: How Taxpayers Subsidize Anti-Tax Advocacy," Cato Institute Policy Analysis No. 407, July 10, 2001, 5. Keep in mind that this is not an exhaustive list. There are many more, but you can get a general idea of what's going on by reviewing this list.

have in common is their ability to turn out voters who will support the liberal/socialist agenda. Just remember that those votes were bought with income extorted from you and your family.

THE IRS—AMERICA'S "TAX GESTAPO"

One can only wonder if the federal government had been as intent on preventing terrorists and other illegal aliens from entering the country as it is on making sure that we all pay our taxes, would 9/11 have ever happened? The loss of civil liberties as a result of an intrusive and arrogant IRS is something most Americans never think about until the notice of an IRS audit appears. In its usual quiet and insidious way, the federal bureaucracy has slowly expanded its "right" to keep a watchful eye on America's tax serfs. Charles Adams wrote:

> Each fact that follows is pervasive in today's economic life but was non-existent in 1970. All banking records are photographed for Big Brother to see. All stock and securities transactions, real estate transactions, and interest and dividends are reported to the tax man. All part-time, even babysitters and teenage garden helpers, are reported. All barter transactions and gambling winnings of significance are reported. All foreign accounts, holdings, and trusts are reported.
>
> The above list of enslaving intrusions and punishments is by no means exhaustive. There are a myriad of other spying devices and punitive measures for tax enforcement. Special units prey on lawyers to keep them off-balance. A small town lawyer in California was sent to jail when he sent in a proper tax return without a check. Rather than send the matter to the powerful collection division, the IRS simply threw him in jail under a rare, almost unknown provision of the tax code.[25]

Big government requires big taxes. Big taxes lead to tax serfdom and eventually tax slavery. When taxes are low, there will be little need or effort to avoid paying them and therefore little need for an intrusive and oppressive agency to collect them. But when taxes become oppressive, people will begin to rebel by seeking mostly legal ways (loopholes) to avoid paying so much of their income to the government. As this happens, the government is forced to (1) reduce the size, role, and scope of government—something career politicians are loath to do—or (2) organize a special security force to compel citizens to "stand and deliver!" The federal government has elected to carry out the second option.

25. Adams, "Taxes in America."

Southerners should seize every opportunity to stress the fact that the income tax was first introduced in America by the federal president Abraham Lincoln in order to finance his invasion and conquest of the South. Even the Northern-dominated federal Supreme Court found the income tax hard to accept and in 1895 declared it unconstitutional. Politicians overcame this in 1913 by passing the Sixteenth Amendment, all the while assuring Americans that it was safe to support this new tax because it would be limited to only 1 percent of income and only the rich would have to pay. From such a humble beginning, it has grown into a monster with vast powers of intimidation. Today the income tax and its necessary enforcement agencies violate numerous principles of civil liberty. See the table below.

The IRS: Six Violations of Liberty[26]

Civil Liberty Principle Violated	Violation Explained
Equal protection under the law per Fourteenth Amendment of U.S. Constitution	The income tax subjects financially successful and economically productive people to a higher tax rate than less successful people. This unequal treatment also masks the real cost of government. This causes the less successful to view government services as "free" and they tend to demand more "free" services paid for by the successful elements of society.
Right to be secure in our papers and effects per Fifth Amendment of U.S. Constitution	Federal courts have sanctioned the IRS's "powers of inquisition" as claimed by the agency in its tax code section 7602, which states the IRS has the right to obtain any and all records it needs to carry out its function as the government's tax collector.
Right to be secure from coerced self-incrimination per Fifth Amendment of U.S. Constitution	Every taxpaying citizen must sign a document under threat of perjury completely describing any and all facts that might be needed for tax collecting or

26. Data from Chris Edwards, "Top Ten Civil Liberties Abuses of the Income Tax" (www.cato.org, Apr. 11, 2002).

	prosecuting purposes. Failure to submit such document is actionable—therefore the citizen must self-incriminate or else.
U.S. Declaration of Independence indictment #10 regarding confusing rules that are difficult if not impossible for the average citizen to understand or follow. "He has erected a multitude of new officers, and sent hither swarms of officers to harass our people, and eat out their substance" (Declaration of Independence).	Current IRS rules are complex and confusing, over 45,000 pages, designed for social engineering purposes—income redistribution—as opposed to revenue gathering, its own error rates run as high as 60 percent on audits. Tax code is enormous and constantly changing yet average citizen is required to abide by it. There were 441 changes in 2001 alone, and rules for pension have changed almost every year since 1980.
Presumption of innocence and due process of the law per common law tradition and Fifth Amendment of U.S. Constitution	A citizen is required to prove to the IRS that he is not guilty of the violation that the IRS is charging him with. The citizen enters the IRS's administrative courts with the burden of proving his innocence. The IRS engages in many summary actions, and the very nature of the administrative tax courts violates due process principles by placing the citizen at the mercy of a court that is controlled by the accusing agency.
Common law tradition of trial by jury	There is no trial by jury in Federal Tax Court. Before a citizen can fight the government, he must first pay disputed taxes, penalties, and interest in full. The citizen can then take whatever resources he has left and file a claim in the Federal District Court— good luck!

Direct taxes in 1999 consumed nearly 38 percent of the average dual-income family's income.[27] The tax code is now composed of more than 45,000 pages of incomprehensible bureaucratic verbiage that contains more than 703 different forms that taxpayers must choose from. File the wrong form and who knows what might happen to you! The tax history of the twentieth century (see the graph below) is one in which freemen devolved from freedom to serfdom, and who knows when our chains of tax slavery—already forged—will be fastened securely upon us.

From Liberty to Tax Slavery[28]

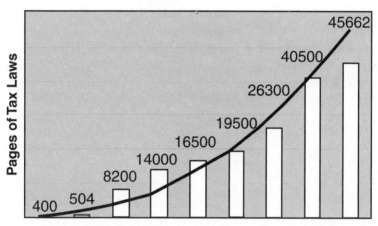

The distance from the trend line to the top of the graph can be thought of as your area of personal liberty. As the federal government enacts more tax "laws" that taxpayers must comply with, the area in which citizens exercise personal liberty is diminished. Because this occurs over time, it is very difficult for the average person to realize just how much personal liberty he has lost. If the twentieth-century trend continues, by the end of the twenty-first century there will be over 6 million pages of federal tax "laws" that *we the people* must obey! Liberalism/socialism is anti-liberty. If we are to regain lost liberty, *we the people* must take bold action!

27. Veronique de Rugy, "The Latest IRS Scare Campaign" (www.cato.org, Apr. 12, 2002).

28. "Total Number of Pages of Federal Tax Rules, 1913-2001" (www.cato.org/research/fiscal_policy?2001/code1.html, Dec. 2, 2002).

A LIBERTY-BASED SOCIETY IS THE ONLY SOLUTION

This chapter demonstrates the dangers to liberty inherent in all governments, even governments that are ruled in the most democratic fashion. It is the nature of men to attempt to expand their power, prestige, and financial status. In the free market we deal with people only if they have a good or service that we want and we have something that they want. But government injects "legalized" force into the human community. Government allows politicians to "justify" their extortion of private income by claiming that your money will be used to fight poverty, supply healthcare, or protect the nation from terrorists. Yet these same leaders always end up with more power and prestige and an improved financial status—not to mention an almost iron guarantee of reelection! And the serfs never think to ask if poverty has been eliminated, or if healthcare has been made more affordable, or if we have won the war on terrorism. It's time we began to ask pointed question and demand honest answers.

America's current political system is designed to maintain the status quo. Attempting to reform it will be no more successful than Mikhail Gorbachev's effort to reform the socialist system of the former U.S.S.R. The only solution is to change from a liberal/socialist-based system to one based on the concepts of liberty. A Liberty-Based Society would give us a political establishment that seldom intrudes into our lives, with a tax burden no greater than 10 percent of GDP and a society based on civility and merit.

The choice is ours to make—pay our taxes, both direct and indirect, in ever-increasing portions and continue to be pacified tax serfs or recast the entire political process by demanding a Liberty-Based Society. In the first scenario, we continue to play by their rules. With the second choice, we change the entire game, write our own rules, and become the masters of our own destiny!

QUESTIONS AND ANSWERS

Q. How dare you call Americans serfs! Who do you think you are?

A. What I said was that over the past century Americans have moved from being free people to becoming *tax* serfs and if the liberal/socialist trend continues, we will soon become Uncle Sam's *tax* slaves! Occasionally the truth hurts, but to ignore the facts will result in more than a perceived insult. As I noted in this chapter, since World War II the tax burden of an average American family has increased from 17 percent to 40 percent. Some of the slaves in the prewar South who worked under the task system were allowed to keep a higher percentage of the income they produced for their master. You tell me—are we really free?

Q. What about all of the tax cuts that have been pushed through by the Republicans?

A. Yes, we have benefited from these small tax cuts, but one point that conservatives conveniently ignore is that the Republicans have not decreased federal spending. They did the politically popular thing by cutting taxes but have been too cowardly to take the next necessary step of cutting back federal spending. Eventually the illogical disconnect between reduced federal revenuess and increased federal spending will have to be addressed. The political temptation will be to address it not through direct taxation—thereby incurring the wrath of taxpayers—but through indirect taxation. The resulting inflation will reduce our personal wealth by lowering the purchasing power of the dollars we have saved or invested, or lowering the purchasing power of the dollars in our paychecks. Our mothers told us when we were children that we can't have our cake and eat it too. Unfortunately for working men and women of America, contemporary politicians have devised a way to make taxpayers think they can have tax cuts without lowering federal spending. Although *we the people* are forced to pay the price, our political leaders have devised a way that they can have their cake and eat it too. I think it is time that we put an end to their party!

Q. What plans do you have for the IRS in a Liberty-Based Society?

A. The IRS has become one of America's most hated federal institutions. Historically, tax collectors have been looked upon at best as a necessary evil and at worst as evil and cruel people. In our Liberty-Based Society, we will not allow any payroll taxes. Taxes on income will not occur at the federal level, while *we the people* of the Sovereign States will make our own decision regarding state payroll taxes. Personally I favor a prohibition on all payroll taxes, but the people of each state will have to make their own decision on this. Because we will not allow federal income tax and other federal payroll taxes, the role of the IRS in a Liberty-Based Society will become moot. Their services will no longer be needed or allowed!

There is also good news for those who currently work for the IRS. In a Liberty-Based Society, with its sustainable and expanding economy, there will be a greater demand for the services of those with financial and accounting backgrounds. They will be able to use their talents for productive services in our society.

Q. How do you propose to collect the revenues required for necessary government services?

A. Taxes are a necessary evil of any society. The aim of a Liberty-Based Society is to limit the "necessary" to as small as possible. Any taxation that deprives citizens of more than 10 percent of their wealth will be considered illegal—with the exception of national emergency such as imminent threat of invasion. The technique used to measure this "10 percent" has yet to be firmly established. I have suggested measuring total annual tax burden against annual GDP. Others have suggested different methods. But the point is that we must not allow government to exceed our 10 percent barrier, and if our economy grows as expected, 10 percent may be too high! Remember 10 percent is the maximum tax level; the actual tax level should be gradually reduced as the economy grows.

One method would be to rely on revenue-producing tariffs, not to be confused with trade-protecting tariffs. Another way would be to tax consumption—as opposed to savings and investments—via a percentage increase in the state sales tax that would be remitted to the federal government. Oh my! Just think of it, our agent the federal government having to rely upon its creator, the Sovereign States, for its operating revenues.

Q. What about the national debt? How will we be able to pay off this huge amount on such a low tax base?

A. Good point, but under the current liberal/socialist system, are there any plans to pay off this huge debt? As I will discuss in chapter 13, we will fulfill our obligations to people currently or soon-to-become eligible for Social Security benefits. We, unlike our liberal/socialist opponents, will not cheat people who had no choice but to pay into the federal government's Old Age Pension Plan. The same will be true for those individuals who hold government bonds and other federal securities. The federal debt will be retired over time due to the government's increasing tax receipts from a growing and expanding economy. Once the debt is retired, taxes can be lowered from the 10 percent maximum level, which will generate even more economic growth and personal wealth.

The Death of a Good Business Contract

Thirteen men who had similar businesses decided that they could make a better living if they combined their diverse talents into a single business. They each brought into the business different assets, but they knew that together they would make more money than if they continued to operate separately. So, like good businessmen, they sat down as equals and negotiated a contract to create their new business. These thirteen men had some concern that this new business could be used by the most influential of the thirteen to enrich the majority by taking profits away from the less influential. Therefore, the contract was carefully designed to prevent this from happening. The contract outlined the general duties and limitations of the new business and also created a three-man management structure to run the business. One manager would be responsible for making any new rules or procedures required to operate the business, another would be responsible for the general operations of the business and for making sure the rules and procedures were followed, while the third would be responsible for clarifying any confusion in business rules and to assure that the business performed according to the limitations specified in the contract.

From the very beginning it was evident that the more influential partners were trying to capture control of the business to promote their own interests. But the less influential were confident that they had negotiated a sound contract. Unfortunately, the three men who made up the management structure were all too human. It became apparent to them that their worth to the organization, and therefore their personal power, would be increased if the strength and authority of the organization could be increased. The less influential members refused to alter the contract and so it appeared to them that their interests would be safe. But as questions of authority came up, the partners, who had no common judge to interpret the contract, would submit the question to the one manager who was responsible for interpreting and clarifying questions under the original contract. It was not long before the contract was being read in a manner that would increase the authority of the business—a business that just happened to enrich the more influential partners at the expense of the less influential partners while bestowing more personal power and influence on the three-man management structure. Soon the business was controlled by the three agents, whose positions had been created by the contract among the original thirteen independent businessmen! How could otherwise knowledgeable businessmen put themselves in a position where their agents would interpret the contract that outlined the agents' authority?

Substitute thirteen independent and Sovereign States for the thirteen businessmen, and in place of the three-man management team substitute the federal executive, Congress, and Supreme Court, and you find yourself asking the same question. How did *we the people* of the Sovereign States put ourselves in the position of having the agent of the states, the federal government, become the sole judge for the extent of the agent's power?

What has this new federal supremacy done to our liberties? Are we more free today than Americans were prior to 1861? Do we have command of our income to the same degree our grandfathers did at the beginning of the twentieth century? In contemporary liberal/socialist America, who has greater authority—*we the people* of the once Sovereign States or special interest groups with paid lobbyists in Washington, the unelected Federal Reserve and their banking associates, and career politicians?

CHAPTER 11

Federal Supreme Court vs.
Middle-Class Values

Since the mid-1950s, the United States Supreme Court has established itself as the ultimate enemy of American middle-class values. Operating under robes of judicial "activism," federal courts have demonstrated their unchallengeable authority to socially engineered American society. During the 1950s and 1960s, conservatives would excuse such federal activities as the result of liberal judges appointed by evil Democrats. "Just wait until we [conservatives] have a chance to appoint our judges; then we will correct the evil done to our society," conservative leaders promised America. Political campaign after political campaign was wasted with conservative busywork as we worked to elect conservatives to governors' offices, Congress, and the presidency. The net effect was that we elected numerous "conservatives" while our efforts amounted to no more than busywork calculated by modern political "leaders" to keep the middle class pacified as the majority toed the party line, refusing to jump ship from the GOP.[1] But when measured against the standard of successfully protecting middle-class social values, did these efforts accomplish anything? No doubt GOP politicians won numerous elections, special interests in finance houses that depend on new money from the Fed certainly prospered, and all manner of special interest groups were rewarded with more OPM and new federal regulations. But did average people gain by these efforts?

The undeniable answer from the United States Supreme Court came in 2002 in a decision that all but shouted, "No! You have gained nothing and in fact have been fools to place your dreams and hopes on a court appointed by conservatives." In this decision, the court once again instructed us that *we the people* no longer have the right to legislate in our states on matters regarding social accountability. The court declared that child pornography was protected by

1. The Wallace presidential campaign in the late 1960s and the Perot campaign in the 1980s are rare exceptions to conservative loyalty to the GOP.

the United States Constitution if it involved "virtual" child pornography—computer-generated graphic displays that are virtually indistinguishable from the real filth.[2] The court that handed down this disgusting ruling was not a liberal court appointed by Bill Clinton or Jimmy Carter or LBJ. No, it was a court created by Mr. Conservative Ronald Reagan and his sidekick George Bush I! It was our dreamed-of, hoped-for, and prayed-for conservative court. And just in case the serfs did not get the message, this same court subsequently added a benediction to American social values with its decision to open the door to federalizing the issue of same-sex marriages. Even the most ardent conservative Republican partisan should be getting the picture by now. Even the most vigorous flag-waving conservative should be able to read the handwriting on the wall. We don't need a Daniel to interpret the message—contemporary conservative leaders have failed the majority of America's conservatives!

The United States Supreme Court has conducted a virtual campaign against middle-class values since the 1960s. All the while conservative leaders seemed more concerned about issues relating to reelection and budgetary outlays than middle-class social issues. In the absence of staunch resistance from conservative elected leaders, the federal Supreme Court has marched virtually unopposed over the right of *we the people* to govern ourselves.

BUSING—IGNORE IT AND THE MIDDLE CLASS
WILL FORGET ABOUT IT

In the 1968 presidential election, the conservative standard bearer Richard Nixon assured middle-class voters across America that he was opposed to federal-court-ordered forced busing—at that time busing was a major social issue for most Americans. Nixon tapped into the anxiety expressed by the middle class over this issue and garnered our support. What most Americans have forgotten is that as far as busing is concerned, under Nixon nothing changed—lied to again! In 1969 one of Nixon's lieutenants met with a group of civil-rights leaders who were concerned that Nixon would undo some of their liberal/socialist gains. This lieutenant told the group, "Watch what we do, not what we say." Shortly later, Nixon's secretary of labor issued an order mandating (for the first time in American history) quotas in federal contracts.[3] Thus began the quota/affirmative action era—initiated not by a liberal but by a conservative leader whom we all had worked so hard

---

2. National Review Editors, "Virtual Porn, Real Corruption—The Court's Reasoning" (www.nationalreview.com/20may02/editorial052002b.asp, May 20, 2002)

3. Kennedy and Kennedy, *Why Not Freedom!*, 51.

to elect! While a conservative president was advancing the cause of anti-middle-class reverse discrimination, other elected conservative leaders were meekly silent—lied to again! With the passage of time, the buses continued to roll and cowardly conservative leaders were able to quietly move away from the discussion of this sticky subject. (Federal-court-ordered forced busing is still an issue, but no elected conservative leader is willing to recognize it and therefore it does not exist! For those who desire more information, I have a complete discussion of busing in chapter 8 of *Why Not Freedom!*)

CRIME—LAW AND ORDER

The United States Supreme Court's *Miranda*[4] decision dealt another blow to the right of *we the people* of the (once) Sovereign States to police local communities. Again the court successfully asserted the federal government's right to dictate to local authorities and state legislatures on matters that are vital to the health and well-being of society. And of course, the dictates from the federal Supreme Court are always couched in rulings that tend to promote anti-middle-class class values. Despite the harm inflicted by this federal court ruling, no conservative leader has challenged this socialist victory with a plan to roll it back— lied to again. Very few, if any, have even called upon the federal court to give an account of the evil that has resulted within local communities from the court's decision. The *Wall Street Journal* noted, "Each year *Miranda* results in lost cases against approximately 30,000 violent criminals and 90,000 property offenders for FBI-indexed crimess. In addition, prosecutors lose cases against 62,000 drunk drivers, 46,000 drug dealers and users, and several hundred thousand lesser criminals."[5]

Yes, there have been incidents of police abuse in questioning suspects. Our modern technological society provides new and more efficient ways to prevent this from happening. For instance, a state could pass a law requiring all interrogations of suspects to be conducted under the watchful and permanent eye of a video camera and requiring audio recordings of all confessions and discussions leading up to the confession. The duly elected representatives of *we the people* are more than capable of protecting our civil liberties if the federal courts would only allow this natural process to operate.

Crime in America has become so commonplace that, just like busing, we no longer demand that our elected leaders address the issue.

4. *Miranda* v. *Arizona*, 384 U.S. 436 (1966).
5. Paul G. Cassell, "How Many Criminals Has *Miranda* Set Free?" *Wall Street Journal*, March 1, 1995, sec. A, p. 17.

But it remains an important issue, one that has caused a dramatic degeneration in the quality of our social life. In many parts of the United States, people live in fear. Too many Americans live behind iron bars and double-locked doors, guarded by electronic security systems—an additional cost we pay because the federal courts have shown more concern about the "rights" of criminals than about middle-class values. How bad is crime in America today? Every minute of every hour of every day in the United States of America three people die due to violent crime, two people are robbed, twelve homes are burglarized, and twelve women are raped![6] Remember this is happening every minute in America. The United States federal courts have abandoned the middle class to the mercies of criminal elements that now dominate much of society.

FEDERAL COURTS SEIZE CONTROL OF STATE PRISONS

As of 1998, federal courts had seized control of prisons in some thirty states.[7] Federal judges have extended themselves far beyond their mere constitutionally mandated role of interpreting the Constitution into the role of social activists and legislators. They now impose their opinions as to what constitutes a socially acceptable prison in place of the opinions of duly elected representatives of *we the people* of the (once) Sovereign States. A *Wall Street Journal* column noted:

> The case before the Second Circuit is a perfect example. It contains the consent decree governing virtually every aspect of New York City's jails since the 1970s. The court-ordered regulations, now thicker than two Manhattan phone books, extend to amenities unknown to constitutional scholarship, such as sports television and the regular washing of prison windows. New York isn't an anomaly. Federal courts control state and local prisons in more than 30 states.[8]

But the sad story of unconstitutional federal judicial activism does not end there. When a federal judge orders the local community to provide prisoners with sports television or other amenities, who has to pay for these amenities? *We the people,* who no longer have a voice in the decision, must of course pay the bill. Wasn't taxation without representation a complaint Americans leveled against tyrants of old?

6. Kennedy and Kennedy, *Why Not Freedom!*, 95.
7. David Schoenbrod and Ross Sandler, "By What Right Do Judges Run Prisons?" *Wall Street Journal,* Aug. 31, 1998, sec. A, p. 19.
8. Ibid.

The column continues, "But if federal judges can order increases in state spending just because they think it's a good idea, government can grow without check. Judges who go beyond remedying violations of rights and become policy makers violate the most fundamental of constitutional rights—the right of voters to hold elected officials accountable for government policy."[9] The ability of federal court judges to compel the local population to increase local taxes to pay for federal court orders has already been demonstrated in a Missouri busing case.[10] An arrogance of power now surrounds federal courts. Under the present political system, they are not answerable to *we the people* of the (once) Sovereign States. The hard question must be asked—and I am going to ask it: "Do you really want to keep this current liberal/socialist political system?"

FEDERAL COURTS TO MIDDLE CLASS: "JUST SAY NO TO GOD"

The recent (2003) controversy over whether or not the Alabama state supreme court had a constitutional right to place a copy of the Ten Commands in the state's Supreme Court Building ended as we all should have expected. Read the Constitution as closely as you might, but you will never find the authority explicitly granted to the federal government to countermand the decorating decisions of a branch of government in a Sovereign State. Power-hungry and ideologically driven judges can read into a document any power they truly desire—and so it is with our federal masters.

The federal courts' attack against middle-class religious values did not begin in 2003. It began in earnest under the Warren court (Chief Justice Earl Warren was appointed by Republican president Eisenhower), but it has not been relinquished, much less reversed, under conservative-appointed federal judges. Indeed, the federal courts have become an extension of liberal/socialist legislative efforts. The following is a sample of some of the more noteworthy anti-God federal court decisions.

Case	Vote	Description
Engel v. *Vitale* 370 US 421 (1962)	6:1	Outlawed prayer in public schools (the prayer in question was a twenty-one-word nondenominational prayer)

9. Ibid.
10. Kennedy and Kennedy, *Why Not Freedom!*, 212.

Abington School *District* v. *Schempp* 374 US 203 (1963)	8:1	Outlawed reading Lord's Prayer and Bible in public schools
Stone v. *Graham* 449 US 39 (1980)	5:4	Forbid the posting of the Ten Commandments in public schools
Wallace v. *Jaffree* 472 US 38 (1985)	6:3	Outlawed one minute of voluntary silence for private prayer or meditation in public schools
Lee v. *Weisman* 112 S. Ct. 2649 (1992)	5:4	Outlawed invocations and benedictions at public-school graduation ceremonies

U.S. SUPREME COURT VOIDS RIGHT OF STATES TO DETERMINE WHEN LIFE BEGINS

In *Roe* v. *Wade,* the United States Supreme Court nullified the right of (once) Sovereign States to determine when life begins. If you accept the contention that federal courts are the ultimate arbiters of the Constitution, then you are left with a political system in which the agent created by the Sovereign States via the Constitution becomes the one that decides if the agent has the authority for its actions. Today we have a situation in which the federal government decided that it wanted to nullify a long-existing states' right and then read into the Constitution a new right that the federal government would then force each state to honor.

The constitutional crisis created by *Roe* v. *Wade* is not new! It arises from the destruction of states' rights that for the first seventy years of our national history served as a check on federal excesses.[11] But today that check no longer exists. The result is that the federal Supreme Court can in effect legislate on any social matter it desires. It only needs to dream up a new constitutional test or bizarre constitutional theory, and presto—the nine judges in black can reshape our society according to the latest social fad. It is all neatly done, without the messy necessity of answering to the voting public, who must endure the leftist court's social engineering!

We the people of the Sovereign States, via the original Constitution, reserved unto ourselves the right to determine when life begins.

11. See discussion of Virginia and Kentucky Resolutions of 1798 in Kennedy and Kennedy, *Was Jefferson Davis Right?*, 281-85.

"Really?" one may ask. "Where in the Constitution is such a right declared?" It is not in the Constitution as such, and to modern eyes this apparent absence is why so many have failed to recognize it. Under the Tenth Amendment, *we the people* of the Sovereign States expressly reserved unto ourselves *all* "powers not delegated to the United States by the Constitution, nor prohibited by it to the States." A question we must first answer is whether the right to determine the moment when life begins is "prohibited" to the states by the Constitution. The clear answer is no. Then the logical conclusion is that the right to determine when life begins remains with *we the people* of the Sovereign States. Just to make sure that the federal government properly understood its role with regards to enumerated and nonenumerated rights reserved to *we the people* of the Sovereign States, the Founding Fathers enacted the Ninth Amendment, which declared, "The enumeration in the Constitution, of certain rights, shall not be construed to deny or disparage others retained by the people." *Roe* v. *Wade* is a clear example of why the constitutional doctrine of states' rights is a critical element in maintaining a free Republic of Republics—the United States of America as handed to us from the Founding Fathers.

Some may contend that this constitutional argument ignores the moral issue involved with *Roe* v. *Wade.* They would argue that without a national standard enforced by the federal government that protects life, some states may choose to terminate life at will. Yes, in a Liberty-Based Society the people of each state could pass laws governing their society that they deemed necessary. However, it is not true that if a state passed a law that people of other states found morally reprehensible, those people would be powerless to influence a change in a reprehensible law. Take for example a law passed by the citizens of our fictitious state of Oklarado.

The citizens of Oklarado decided that their state was becoming too crowded due to an exceptionally high birth rate. To prevent the consumption and spoliation of their environment, they decided to pass a law to reduce their population. Each day, 10 percent of all children born would have their lives terminated. The people in the rest of the country were horrified. What could they do? They could:

1. Express in various legal ways their moral indignation.

2. Organize a boycott of commercial transactions with Oklarado.

3. Assist those in Oklarado who opposed the law in peaceful non-cooperation.

4. Assist citizens of Oklarado in conducting campaigns of nonviolent civil disobedience.

5. Assist citizens of Oklarado who wanted to "vote with their feet"—that is, help people leave the state.

Note that all of these efforts to revoke a reprehensible law in a neighboring state are peaceful actions of private individuals, not the action of government. If the people of Oklarado persist in maintaining their immoral environmental protection law, then eventually the question will arise of whether or not the people of the other states want to remain in union with such a people. In a Liberty-Based Society as I describe in this book, we have a procedure by which we could pass a constitutional amendment forbidding a law such as the one enacted in Oklarado. Oklarado could choose to nullify the amendment. If three-fourths of the states do not vote to override Oklarado's nullification, then the law remains valid in Oklarado. If three-fourths of the states vote to override Oklarodo's nullification, then Oklarado must remove its law or remove itself from the union. But it does not end there. Suppose only a small minority of states voted to override Oklarado's nullification (hard to imagine because three-fourths of the states had previously voted to pass the amendment). Now this small minority must decide if they want to remain "unequally yoked together with unbelievers."[12] In a Liberty-Based Society *we the people* of the Sovereign States *always* have at our disposal a means of escape (nullification or secession) if we feel our rights, liberty, or moral beliefs are endangered by the larger society. Quirk and Bridwell wrote:

> The American Revolution is not finished yet. Near the heart of America is the unresolved conflict between our two most basic principles: one, that all power derives from the people, and two, that certain inalienable rights are immune from government power. This conflict, in some way, has to be resolved and the critical issue is *who will decide* if government has gone beyond its proper powers and is disturbing inalienable rights.[13]

THE FEDERAL SUPREME COURT'S ROLE IN A LIBERTY-BASED SOCIETY

What would be the role of the federal courts in a Liberty-Based Society? Interestingly enough, their role would not be too different from the one they now serve, but with two major exceptions. In a Liberty-Based Society *we the people* of the Sovereign States are the

12. 2 Cor. 6:14 King James Version.
13. William J. Quirk and R. Randall Bridwell, *Judicial Dictatorship* (New Brunswick, N.J.: Transaction, 1995), 129.

ultimate decider of questions of constitutional rights. The federal courts would serve as the primary vehicle by which such questions are adjudicated. In the vast majority of such cases their decision would be mandatory. But because *we the people* of the Sovereign States are the originators of sovereign authority—not the United States government—*we the people* must be the final arbitrator of social questions bearing on our reserved rights. In other words, a decision rendered by the United States Supreme Court would be conditionally mandatory. Its authority would be contingent upon the acceptance of *we the people* of the Sovereign States. The process by which *we the people* could reject a court's decision is outlined in the constitutional amendment I described in chapter 4.[14] The second exception is that under a Liberty-Based Society, the role of all government, including the federal government, will be greatly reduced. With a limited federal government, we will have fewer issues requiring a hearing before federal tribunals.

Nothing strikes terror in the heart of liberals/socialists more than the thought that they might no longer be able to use their control of the federal courts as an instrument to force liberal/socialist social engineering schemes upon America's citizens. Nothing should encourage us more than the dream of the day when *we the people* of the Sovereign States will be able to exercise authority over the unelected judiciary of the federal courts. This dream will not happen, though—unless you help to make it happen!

QUESTIONS AND ANSWERS

Q. You spend a great deal of time talking about busing, crime, and other old issues. Why are you trying to resurrect forgotten political issues?

A. These and numerous other issues were ones that the middle class wanted their political leaders to resolve. The sad truth is that these leaders have never successfully done so. When it was politically expedient, they did give lip service to resolving them—all in an attempt to pacify middle-class rage. With the passage of time, conservative leaders could move on to other issues that were less controversial and therefore less likely to endanger their reelection. Each of these issues represents an intrusion of the federal government into the reserved rights of *we the people* of the Sovereign States. Just because the leadership of the current liberal/socialist political system

14. For a complete discussion of the reasoning and historical justification for such an amendment, see Kennedy and Kennedy, *Why Not Freedom!*, 19-55.

decided to ignore the demands of the people is no reason to assume that these issues have been successfully resolved. The issues remain; ineffective conservative leaders remain; and the liberal/socialist political system that foisted these burdens upon us remain. Once *we the people* overthrow the liberal/socialist system and dethrone ineffective incumbents, then *we the people* will elect representatives who will successfully resolve all of these issues.

Q. The federal Supreme Court is responsible for removing the mere mention of God and the Holy Bible from our public schools, forbidding the mention of God in all public meetings, and most lately the removal of the Ten Commandments from a State Supreme Court building. It seems that the entire federal bureaucracy is aligned against traditional American religious faith. What can we do?

A. First remember that in chapter 9 I noted that one of the reasons that liberal/socialist educators and politicians wanted to establish a system of "public" education was so that they, not parents, could control the education (indoctrination) of America's children. Complaints against federal court orders banning religion in schools will be impossible in a Liberty-Based Society because education will not be "public" but will be purchased in the free market by parents. The current issues of public prayer and Bible reading in schools will be resolved in a Liberty-Based Society by removing "public" monies from education. (But note that if the demand is sufficient, atheists and agnostics may develop their own schools, where their children will be protected from the moral influence of religion. In our society, everyone has the freedom to choose—even if it is by your personal standards a stupid choice.)

Second, remember that in a Liberty-Based Society, *we the people* of the Sovereign States are the ultimate arbiter of the constitutional limits of the federal government. If Judge Roy Moore (the Alabama Supreme Court justice who placed the Ten Commandments in the state's Supreme Court Building) had been practicing in a Liberty-Based Society, the Sovereign State of Alabama could have nullified the federal Supreme Court decision.

Currently, the federal government answers to no one. It is the supreme and ultimate judge of the limits of its powers. The federal government is the protector not of reserved rights under the Ninth and Tenth Amendments but of the current liberal/socialist political system. It will allow no one to challenge its authority. As long as we continue to play by the rules established by the liberal/socialist political system, we will never regain our lost rights. Over a century of conservative failure should have taught us that.

Q. Under your proposed governmental system, federal courts would be reduced to little more than advisory bodies. What good would such courts serve?

A. Federal courts in a Liberty-Based Society would serve a very important function. By the very nature of that society, the federal government would be limited, therefore the vast majority of its current interventions would not exist. This alone will decrease the opportunity and necessity to appeal to federal courts. Federal court decisions would be enforceable subject only to the ultimate authority of the Sovereign States. The majority of cases brought before federal courts would be decided at the federal level and the courts' decisions would be final. The extreme appeal to nullification and/ or secession would be seldom used, but its *potential* would serve to bridle any impulse of federal courts to attempt to socially engineer America's society via court decisions and court orders. A well-written federal court decision that carefully explains the constitutional logic of its decision will have tremendous persuasive power. The primary purpose of the federal courts would be to ensure that all departments and agencies of the federal government were functioning within the bounds established by the Constitution. As such, federal courts would be the first line of defense against encroachments on our reserved rights.

Q. What you are suggesting, the establishment of a Liberty-Based Society, will be extremely difficult. Why not expend the same amount of effort to elect a conservative president and win control of the Senate? Wouldn't this be a lot quicker and easier than what you are suggesting?

A. The current federal Supreme Court was appointed by "conservative" presidents, and today we have a majority in the Senate. Back when Ronald Reagan was president there was a short period of time when conservatives controlled the Senate. But look at some of the recent decisions of this "conservative" federal court. This court has given the federal seal of approval to reverse discrimination in the form of quotas, it has overturned local laws against pornography, and now it has started down the road to equating same-sex marriage with traditional marriage. If we continue doing what we have always done, we will end up with the same sad results! The time has come to abandon business-as-usual politics and begin the struggle to reclaim our lost liberty. No doubt the party bosses, entrenched incumbents, and special interest groups would prefer that *we the people* remain docile, pacified, and generally distracted by status-quo politics, but I prefer liberty, even though it means years of hard struggle. Liberty—it's worth the struggle.

The Federal Government Failed America on September 11, 2001

The finger-pointing after 9/11 did nothing to determine why our country was so vulnerable to this horrendous terrorist attack. No media opinion maker, no political leader, whether conservative or liberal, asked the right question. The question is not *who* created or allowed this vulnerability—the correct question is *what* caused it. The disaster of 9/11 was a direct result of the fact that the federal government had become too large and the executive branch had become too busy to afford the time and resources necessary to protect the borders of our nation from those who had sworn to destroy us.

From 1900 to 1999 the federal government grew so large that it could with impunity mandate the expenditure of billions of dollars of private income to assure compliance with federally imposed rules and regulations. This politically correct government mandates rules and standards regarding healthcare, medical-records privacy, wetlands conservation, and affirmative action (just to name a few) that are oppressive and complex beyond understanding. Yet this same politically correct government did not have the resources and/or the will to protect our borders from those who wanted to kill us!

Bush II's actions on the day of those infamous attacks demonstrate this disgusting federal failure. Now, what was the president doing the moment those hijacked planes crashed into the Twin Towers, the Pentagon, and a Pennsylvania field? He was holding a photo opportunity in a Florida elementary school! At best, he was engaged in an ongoing political campaign for reelection, and at worst he was engaged in matters that are best handled at the local level, while he was ignoring the primary function of the federal union—protecting the international borders from foreign invaders.

I challenge those super patriots who find my criticism of the president too harsh to find a copy of the Constitution. Read it and find exactly where it directs the federal authorities to be concerned about local schools. Look long and hard, but you will not find the constitutional authority for what President Bush was doing that day. For the last half of the twentieth century, conservatives accepted—indeed many advocated—an increasing role for the federal government in the local educational systems. But in the meantime the borders became an international joke! It was and still is politically correct to advocate federal intrusion into issues that by right belong to *we the people* of the Sovereign States. But on the other hand, it is politically dangerous for federal politicians of either party to demand that the federal government tend to its constitutionally mandated purposes—(1) to protect the borders, (2) to assure domestic tranquility via a free trade zone among our Sovereign States, and (3) to engage in limited but necessary international relations.

If President Bush and his predecessors had expended their energies on accomplishing the federal government's limited and constitutional role, then the attack of September 11, 2001, with all its horrors, would very likely never have happened. Liberals will not admit this because they do not want a constitutionally limited federal government. Neoconservatives will not say it because they too want a big federal government. Of course, behind their argument is the fact that neocons want to be the ones controlling the nation! Thus, we see the sad reality of the failure of the federal government. I wonder . . . if the people onboard those hijacked planes and the people in the Twin Towers and the Pentagon could answer . . . what kind of federal government would they now prefer? Sadly, they can no longer answer—but we can.

CHAPTER 12

The Federal Government's Constitutional Role

According to George Washington, "Government is like fire, a dangerous servant but a fearful master!" The Founding Fathers had a healthy respect for the oppressive nature of government and designed a government that they hoped would be managed by *we the people* in a manner that would assure our continued freedom. The twentieth century has given us numerous examples of the extreme danger posed by governments. In his book *Death by Government,*[1] Prof. Rudolph J. Rummell numbers 174 million deaths caused by governments during *peacetime.* Add to this the relatively small number of government-caused deaths during government-sponsored violence (war) of 36 million[2] and you begin to see the inherent dangers of government. Even "good" governments have within them the seeds of oppression and disaster.

DEMOCRACY—THE GOD THAT FAILED

Democracy is too often cited by well-meaning people as the perfect solution for bad government. Yet democracies are ruled not by angels but by humans and therefore are also subject to becoming oppressive.

A prominent libertarian scholar, Professor Hoppe recognizes not only that political power does not transform political people into selfless saints or all-wise seers, but also that the very structure of incentives that democracy itself establishes brings some of the worst exemplars of mankind to the very top of the political pile. Since political competition is a vehicle for politically talented people to get power, "given that in every society more 'have-nots' of everything worth having exist than 'haves,' the politically talented who have little or no inhibition against taking property and lording it over others, will have clear advantage over those

1. Rudolph J. Rummell, *Death by Government* (New Brunswick, N.J.: Transaction, 1994).
2. Alberto Mingardi, "Ten Books on the State" (www.mises.org, Aug. 30, 2002).

with such scruples." So, far from being a restraint upon political power, democracy "virtually assures that exclusively dangerous men will rise to the pinnacle of government power and that moral behavior and ethical standards will tend to decline and deteriorate all-around."[3]

The above excerpt from a review of Prof. Hans-Hermann Hoppe's book *Democracy: The God that Failed* is worth rereading. It clearly illustrates the irrationality of both liberals' and neoconservatives' faith in the unquestionable virtue of "American big government."

Historically, the greatest assaults on American civil liberties have occurred during times of national crisis. War and economic collapse are the most noteworthy. During America's first major war (the War for Southern Independence), the Lincoln administration ushered in central banking, fiat money via the National Currency Act, the first income tax, the first military conscription, the federal government's first effort to regulate the wartime economy, tripled tariffs, and numerous pork-barrel projects enacted as political payoffs for Lincoln's cronies. And for the first time the United States government paid Old Age Pensions to the politically connected members of the Grand Army of the Republic, i.e., Union veterans.

It should also be remembered that the modern age of total war—war conducted against noncombatants as well as soldiers—was ushered in by the United States government in its genocidal efforts to destroy both its Southern and its Native American enemies.[4] The American "Civil War" destroyed the original political principle of a constitutionally limited federal government, replacing the Jeffersonian model of a democratic Republic of Republics with an all-powerful, centralized federal nation-state. Ambitious and unscrupulous politicians soon recognized the potential of such a system. They knew that government is not impartial. They knew that government is always the extension of a particular group of people. Such a group could be a group of friends, allies, or co-conspirators who agree, either explicitly or implicitly, to rule over their common foe while using "their" government for the purpose of self-aggrandizement. Contemporary scholars have noted the human nature of modern governments that divide the population into friends and foes of the ruling elite:

> The very existence of the state [the government] rests on this dichotomy. This means that, far more than being a third, "impartial" actor, the state is always the expression of a particular group

3. Ibid.
4. Kennedy and Kennedy, *The South Was Right!*, 291-92.

of individuals. . . . No political order can be conceived as universal, but always and only as a form that originates from a concrete partiality. . . . In reality, there are no abstract institutions, but only clusters of men counterpoised as "friends" and "enemies."[5]

Government, even a democratic American government, will tend to repress those who do not control it and reward those who do or who have close connections (a.k.a. special interests) with those who do. Thus in modern America we see and experience the intrusive and oppressive nature of government that the Founding Fathers were trying to avoid. Suddenly the logic of limited federalism, states' rights, local control, and individual responsibility as a model for American government becomes clear. The Founding Fathers would have agreed that the notion of a Liberty-Based Society is not so radical after all.

MOVING TOWARD AN AMERICAN POLICE STATE

Americans are quick to point out how their government is not "evil" like those countless others that during the twentieth century created secret police forces to spy on their citizens. Yet even in America during the twentieth century, we had a Federal Bureau of Investigation that on its own authority violated the privacy rights of numerous Americans as diverse as Martin Luther King, Jr., antiwar activists, the Black Panthers, and KKK leaders.[6] The threat continues to grow even under the "conservative" leadership of Bush II. Attorney General John Ashcroft has proposed to lift restrictions against FBI spying on private citizens as a method to protect us from terrorism. Again we find ourselves in a crisis created by our politicians, who now tell us that the only way to resolve the crisis is for *we the people* to surrender more of our income and our civil liberties to our watchful masters in government, who know best how to protect us.

GOVERNMENT-CREATED MONOPOLIES

Another example of the abuse of federal powers in the last century is the drive to pass antimonopoly laws. Austrian economists have contended that monopolies cannot exist absent the support of government! These economists do recognize that at times various business elements will dominate, but in a free market, where government regulations and laws do not hinder the entrance of competitors, this temporary dominance of one business entity will be just that—temporary. Yet government has used the fear of monopoly to assist special interests and well-connected individuals,

5. Mingardi, "Ten Books on the State."
6. "Keep Checks on Snooping," *USA Today*, Feb. 7, 2002, 14(A).

while providing politicians with another source of personal and political gain. As Thomas J. DiLorenzo wrote:

> In the spirit of the Austrian School, they understood that competition was an ongoing process, and that market dominance was always necessarily temporary in the absence of monopoly-creating government regulation. This view is also consistent with my own research findings that the "trusts" of the late nineteenth century were in fact dropping their prices and expanding output faster than the rest of the economy—they were the most dynamic and competitive of all industries, not monopolists. Perhaps this is why they were targeted by protectionist legislators and subjected to "antitrust" laws.[7]

Government leaders have become adept at cutting deals with certain industries under the pretense of protecting the public from monopolies. But the result is that politicians and their special interest friends enrich themselves at the public's expense. DiLorenzo continues, "This is the now-familiar approach of government officials colluding with industry executives to establish a monopoly that will gouge the consumers, and then sharing the loot with the politicians in the form of franchise fees and taxes on monopoly revenues. This approach is especially pervasive today in the cable TV industry."[8]

The Stigler-Friedland study published in 1962 reviewed the effects of fifteen years (1917-32) of government regulation of utilities. The study demonstrated that under government regulation, prices increased by 46 percent, profits of the government-created utility monopolies increased by 38 percent, and output declined by 23 percent![9] This reduction of output is in line with the shortages that always occur when government imposes price controls. Remember government comes to the consumer with promises of protecting us from unfair businesspeople, but somehow the politicians always end up benefiting from the arrangement while *we the people* end up paying more. Research similar to the Stigler-Friedland study has documented that in cities where government has not established a monopoly cable network—that is, there are competing cable networks—prices are almost 23 percent lower.[10] In Sacramento,

7. Thomas J. DiLorenzo, "The Myth of Natural Monopoly," *The Review of Austrian Economics* 9, no. 2 (1996): 43.

8. Ibid., 48.

9. Ibid., 50.

10. Ibid., 55.

California, the local courts even got into the debate when a jury found that "the Sacramento cable market was not a natural monopoly and that the claim of natural monopoly was a sham used by defendants as a pretext for granting a single cable television franchise . . . to promote the making of cash payments and provision of 'in-kind' services . . . and to obtain increased campaign contributions."[11] The point being demonstrated is how easy it is for government, even local government, to abuse its power, enrich politicians and well-connected special interest groups, and, via its taxing authority, force *we the people* to pay the tab!

THE TYRANNY OF ONEROUS FEDERAL REGULATIONS

The rapid expansion of onerous, confusing, and costly federal regulations is another example of the federal government exceeding its original constitutional authority. Whether we are talking about regulations for wetlands, clean air, worker safety, health records, railroads, stock trading, civil rights, or software, these regulations are so confusing, unstable, and incredibly involved that they eventually require *more* government regulations in an attempt to clarify the original rule!

Regulations are based on the idea that government "experts" are all knowing and that the humans (as opposed to angels?) running government regulatory agencies are possessed of infinite wisdom, ethical standards, and technological know-how. (This must be the case or how else would these bureaucrats be able to substitute their judgment for the judgment of the marketplace?) By their very nature these regulations are not intended to correct a specific problem and then pass away. They are enacted, usually via an administrative procedure, with the intention of remaining on the books forever—thus providing guaranteed employment for federal bureaucrats! But who pays? All costs are eventually passed on to the consumer. Therefore, *we the people* eventually pay via higher prices, or if the regulated business cannot compete, we pay with the loss of jobs when it is forced to close.

Another problem with increasing or changing federal regulation is that it prevents entrepreneurs and businesspeople from making long-range plans. The probability of a long-term investment paying off depends on a reasonably stable economic environment. If after business plans and long-term investment are made the government issues new or different regulations, the original business assumptions may no longer be correct. The probability of the investors making a profit may now be very low. Thus government action tends to

11. Ibid.

drive away long-term capital investment as investors move toward quicker, short-term investments. In plain English, that means fewer real jobs available for America's workers. Walter Williams wrote:

> For most of our nation's history, people could make plans. For the most part, they could expect today's laws to be tomorrow's laws; hence, they could plan for the future. Today, that's not true. A businessman making investment decisions doesn't know what Congress is going to do a year or two down the line making today's investment decisions worthless. As such, it produces the quick-buck mentality—get in and get out.[12]

Again we see how an intrusive and unconstitutional federal government can prevent healthy economic growth while its policies actually encourage quick-return but risky investments such as the dotcoms of the late 1990s. Is this a function envisioned by the Founding Fathers for the federal government?

FEDERALLY MANDATED BILINGUALISM

The federal Office for Civil Rights (OCR) is using its massive powers to force private businesspeople to pay for interpreters for clients who do not speak English! The OCR claims that Title VI of the Civil Rights Act of 1964 gives it this dictatorial power. A review of Title VI will demonstrate that it is silent regarding this new duty that it is imposing on English-speaking Americans—a new duty to provide special assistance to those who come to the country but cannot speak the national language. But it should be recalled that Title VI was passed back in 1964, long before America's liberal/socialist masters discovered and mandated this new duty that *we the people* owe the non-English-speaking world!

The excuse ("excuse"—as in pretended reason for passing an onerous and intrusive law that would have otherwise been rejected by liberty-loving people) for passing Title VI was to "prohibit discrimination on the basis of race, color or national origin in any program or activity that receives federal financial assistance."[13] All healthcare practitioners, even solo practicing physicians, who take Medicare or other federal funds as payment for treating patients come under this rule. The private physician must take steps to assure "that the LEP (Limited English Proficiency) persons have access to the programs and services provided by the physician."[14] This means he must provide

12. Walter Williams, "Threats to Rule of Law in America" (www.jewishworldreview.com, June 5, 2002).

13. "Limited English Proficiency (LEP)" (www.hhs.gov/ocr/lep/appa.html, July 19, 2001), appendix A, 1.

14. Ibid., 2.

an interpreter and the cost of said interpreter shall not be passed on to the non-English-speaking individual. In addition, the OCR guidance material specifically forbids the use of family members as interpreters! Furthermore, "OCR's policy requires the recipient/covered entity to inform the LEP person of the *right* [emphasis mine] to receive free interpreter services."[15] There you have it. Federal liberal/socialist bureaucrats have established a new right that the Founding Fathers so negligently forgot to include in the Bill of Rights! In addition, this new right is "free" as to the non-English-speaking individuals, but we all know who will eventually pay. Because there is no such thing as a free lunch, we know that eventually the cost will be paid by all taxpayers. This is yet another example of how the federal government violates the income and property rights of *we the people.*

CONGRESS AND THE COURTS ABANDON *WE THE PEOPLE*

"No taxation without representation" was a rallying cry for colonial Americans against the tyranny of King George at the beginning of the American Revolution. Until the twentieth century, it was an acknowledged principle of American government that for a law to have legitimacy it must be passed by elected officials following specific constitutional procedures. From the beginning of the twentieth century, this principle has been gradually eroded to the point where today government agents can spy on private individuals (IRS), confiscate privately owned real estate (EPA's "Wetlands Gestapo"), or force private employers to hire according to skin color to avoid costly legal entanglements (EEOC's racism-by-the-numbers gang).

In modern-day America, the land of the free has become a land where federal bureaucrats and unelected agents of the powers that be in Washington, D.C. have virtually unlimited power with few or no constitutional restraints remaining to protect *we the people.*[16] Robert Anthony wrote:

> Can a federal agency official decree that low areas like those on your land are "wetlands" which you cannot develop without a hard-to-get permit? Or declare that, if you try to see a particular doctor of your choice and pay her yourself, the doctor could be penalized under Medicare? Or establish a "model," based on worst-case assumptions, for predicting contamination from regulated waste?
>
> The laying down of law like that should be done by the persons

15. Ibid., 4.

16. Some constitutional rights still exist in principle, but what private citizen or small businessperson can afford the hundreds of thousands of dollars it would cost to fight the massive federal establishment?

designated for that purpose by Article I of the Constitution, the people's representatives in Congress, the branch vested by the Constitution with "all legislative powers herein granted."

But Congress, abetted by the Supreme Court, has promoted the vast exercise of legislative authority by unelected agencies.[17]

Considering how many of our civil liberties are now under the control of a vast and complicated network of federal agencies and bureaucrats, Americans would do well to remember the tenth indictment the Founding Fathers leveled against the tyranny of King George in the Declaration of Independence: "He has erected a multitude of New Officers, and sent hither swarms of Officers to harass our people and eat out their substance."

Occasionally a federal agency's abuse of its rule-making powers will receive notice from a lower court. In *Chamber of Commerce of the United States* v. *OSHA*, a D.C. circuit court chastised OSHA's abuse of its powers by declaring that federal agency's actions to be "high-handed rule-making" and "offensive to our basic notions of democratic government."[18] But as I have already noted, what small business or private individual has the financial resources necessary to fight the federal government? In reality, most of us are forced to meekly submit to each new intrusion of the federal government into the rights reserved to *we the people* of the Sovereign States. We are less free today than were the Founding Fathers when they penned indictment number ten of the American Declaration of Independence! But they were determined to do something about the threat to their liberty. As for us, that remains to be seen. Do we still have the courage and dedication necessary to establish a Liberty-Based Society?

CORPORATE WELFARE: TAKING FROM WORKING PEOPLE AND GIVING TO THE POLITICALLY WELL CONNECTED

According to a 2001 study, the federal government distributes over $87 billion[19] of your income to private business every year! These subsidies go to profitable businesses for projects that either already have or could obtain funding in the usual free market process. Yet the federal government takes your income and distributes it to businesses that are politically well connected.

---

17. Robert A. Anthony, "Unlegislated Compulsion: How Federal Agency Guidelines Threaten Your Liberty" (www.cato.org, Aug. 11, 1998).

18. *Chamber of Commerce of the United States* v. *OSHA*, 636 F2d 464, 470 (DC Cir 1988).

19. Stephen Slivinski, "The Corporate Welfare Budget Bigger Than Ever," Cato Institute Policy Analysis, Oct. 10, 2001, 1.

Many Americans would assume that corporate welfare is the exclusive work of business-loving Republicans. But in the modern federal government, the distribution of other people's money (OPM) has evolved into an art form that guarantees the reelection of incumbents (90 percent or higher) of both parties, liberal and conservative. During Bill Clinton's reign, the president recommended an increase in the corporate welfare tab by approximately 10 percent each year of his presidency.[20]

One would think that "conservatives" would question the legitimacy of this new role for the federal government. They should be the first to point out the inherent inefficiencies in any government intervention in the free market. The Cato Institute has led the fight in bringing this fact to public attention:

> The federal government has a disappointing record of picking winners and losers. The function of private capital markets is to direct investment to industries and firms that offer the highest potential rate of return. The capital markets, in effect, are in the business of selecting corporate winners and losers. Yet the underlying premise of federal business subsidies is that the government can direct the limited pool of capital funds just as effectively as, if not better than, venture capitalists and money managers.[21]

Shortly after Bush II's 2000 election, the director of the Office of Management and Budget criticized the inefficiency of the massive outlay of federal (i.e., your) dollars by noting that the programs supported by OPM "have nothing to show for years and years and years of essentially subsidizing corporate research budgets."[22] Yet even in spite of such criticism, the federal government under President Bush in fiscal year 2001 gave away $87 billion in corporate welfare. How can the so-called "compassionate conservative" justify this unconstitutional role for the federal government? The truth is that he does not even try. It is a given—a fact taken for granted, like the sun rising in the east. Federal politicians are no longer constrained by the outdated verbiage of the Constitution. They do what they like and *we the people* pay the bill.

The Enron debacle is another example of how politicians, both Democrat and Republican, hand out corporate welfare, enrich themselves, and in the process create an unnatural business situation that

20. Ibid., 2.
21. Ibid., 9.
22. Mitch Daniels, as cited in Slivinski, "The Corporate Welfare Budget," 2.

eventually results in consumers losing their jobs, investments, and savings. The Democratic Clinton administration gave over $650 million in loans to Enron-connected companies.[23] A *Chicago Sun-Times* column stated, "Finance staffers have found that Ex-Im, as well as Overseas Private Investment Corp., in a Democratic administration routinely approved loan requests from a supposedly Republican company. Lavish bipartisan political contributions may have helped, as well as a top Enron executive sitting on Ex-Im's Advisory Committee."[24] Ex-Im refers to the Export Import Bank, which used taxpayer-backed funds to support Enron's unrealistic investment-growth strategies. But politicians from both parties got their payback for their support for corporate welfare: Enron contributed to both parties; and another related company called Bechtel gave $820,000 to the GOP and $730,000 to the Democrats.[25]

A review of the table below will give you an idea of the types of companies that, according to federal actions, apparently deserve your income more than you and your family.

Company	$ of OPM Given Away by Federal Government—1991 to 2001[26]
Caterpillar	$24,600,000
Xerox	$19,600,000
Dow Chemical	$18,300,000
Motorola	$16,300,000
BP Amoco	$13,000,000
General Motors	$9,100,000
United Technologies	$9,100,000
Ford Motor Company	$8,700,000
General Electric	$8,200,000

Remember this is not a complete listing but is presented so you and your family will know the general types of companies that are spending your income. Volumes could be written about how your income is misspent by the federal government. For example, arms sales are an important part of our export business. Yet even in this arena, the taxpayer's income is not safe. More than 50 percent of all arms sales are underwritten by the American taxpayer—not foreign governments![27] Again it must be asked—is this a proper role for the federal

23. Robert Novak, "Enron's Corporate Welfare" (www.suntimes.com, Apr. 29, 2002).

24. Ibid.

25. Ibid.

26. Data from Slivinski, "The Corporate Welfare Budget," 12.

27. Slivinski, "The Corporate Welfare Budget," 20.

government? Financing foreign governments' purchase of arms may be a boon for American arms salespeople, but think about the tremendous opportunity cost that *we the people* must endure when our income is confiscated via taxes and "invested" in projects that would not otherwise be able to withstand competitive market forces. Think about the sustainable jobs that would have been created by the free market had *we the people* been allowed to keep our income and dispose of it as we saw fit. Why should free people even be discussing this? It is after all our money—unless we are no longer free but instead have become serfs to Uncle Sam.

According to the Cato Institute study, "If the $87 billion in corporate welfare were eliminated tomorrow, and personal income taxes were lowered by the same amount for the year, taxpayers would receive a tax cut more than twice as large as the rebate checks mailed out in 2001. The budget savings over five years would amount to $435 billion."[28] (Hold that thought—$87 billion. I'll return to ways to use saved taxes when I discuss buying our way out of Social Security in chapter 13.) This is $435 billion that could have been used to develop local businesses, finance investments in new businesses and factories, and create new and better-paying jobs for *we the people*. But the federal government takes citizens' income and uses it to pay off well-connected friends, who in turn will find ways to support those in government who have supported them. This will not be an allowable role for the federal government in a Liberty-Based Society.

THE FEDERAL GOVERNMENT—A FAILURE AND A THREAT TO LIBERTY

Most people are too timid to say it, but it is time that someone stood up and proclaimed that the federal government is more concerned about being politically correct than it is about protecting our borders. It is more concerned about the welfare of illegal aliens than it is about protecting the income of America's working people. It is more concerned about promoting the ideology of nondiscrimination than it is about protecting *we the people* from terrorist attacks.

Some people may think my evaluation is too harsh. Let's look at the facts. According to the last U.S. ambassador to the Sudan, the United States refused to follow up on that nation's offer in the early 1990s to work together to investigate issues dealing with terrorism. The Sudanese offered the Clinton administration information about many of the twenty-two terrorist organizations the U.S. was

28. Ibid., 16.

investigating. Included in this group was Osama bin Laden! According to the former ambassador, "The U.S. lost access to a mine of material on bin Laden and his organization. . . . It was worse than a crime."[29]

In August 2001, one month before the 9/11 attacks, the Federal Bureau of Investigation received a call from a flight instructor who was suspicious about one of his Middle Eastern students. The FBI checked the student's name (Moussaoui) and was informed by the French intelligence service that he might be connected with terrorist organizations. But the local (Minneapolis) FBI office was not able to convince the main FBI office in Washington, D.C. to seek a search warrant. The instructor warned the FBI about the potential danger posed by a fully fueled 747 jet. In addition, this unsung hero continued his efforts to warn federal officials, hoping the government would do something. He called the Federal Aviation Administration (FAA) and informed them about another Middle Eastern student by the name of Hani Hanjour (it is thought that he was the hijacker who flew the plane into the Pentagon). The FAA sent someone to observe Hanjour in the class. The federal official's recommendation was for the school to find someone who speaks Arabic to help Hanjour with his English deficiency problem![30] Recall the discussion about LEP (Limited English Proficiency) and the federal government's crusade to protect the newly discovered "right" of non-English speakers. Too bad the federal government could not be as energetic about protecting the borders and ferreting out alien terrorists in our midst. Note that during this entire episode, in contrast to the federal government's lethargy, a member of the private sector was vigorous in his efforts to protect us. And he is just one example.

Today the federal government subjects air travelers to random searches in an effort to prevent another terrorist hijacking. The federal government is going to great lengths to head off any perception that it is profiling. Under this policy, an eighty-year-old grandmother in a wheelchair is just as likely to be randomly selected for complete search as, say, a nineteen-year-old male from the Middle East. While this may make the advocates of a politically correct America feel good, I doubt that it does anything to discourage terrorists. Think of the absurdity of the government's policy. In all of modern history, how

29. www.drudgereport.com, Nov. 30, 2001.
30. Greg Gordon, "Eagan Flight Trainer Wouldn't Let Unease about Moussaoui Rest" (www.startribune.com, Dec. 21, 2001).

many eighty-year-old grandmothers have been responsible for killing Olympic athletes, or parking a car bomb in the garage of one of the Twin Towers in New York, or setting off a bomb in the marine barracks in Beirut, or kidnapping and murdering journalists such as Daniel Pearl? Strange, but while there were no grandmothers involved in any of these events, there was a common denominator—young Middle Eastern males were involved in all of them! But the politically correct federal government finds it difficult to use profiling as a tool to defend Americans.

Add to this the announcement from the chief of the U.S. Border Patrol out of Houston, Texas that the federal government is responsible for protecting Mexican citizens who illegally cross into the United States. According to this official, *we the people* are responsible for picking up the tab for education benefits, social welfare benefits, and medical care for these illegal aliens.[31] Why is it our fault that Mexico is not a free country? Free markets, stable government, and low taxes would turn Mexico into an economic powerhouse. Yet Mexico's continued attachment to patronage politics and socialist government creates a steady movement of people fleeing decades of government-imposed poverty. The United States provides Mexico's corrupt ruling elites with a safety valve that prevents their little political kingdom from exploding. What would happen if we plugged this valve and then gave the Mexican people an example of the prosperity-generating potential of a Liberty-Based Society? A little tough love would enrich both peoples and perhaps set the stage for a national relationship based on mutual respect. The failure of the federal government to protect the borders is similar to the failure of its domestic policies.

During the Johnson administration, the federal government launched the "war on poverty." By some estimates, Johnson's Great Society spent between one and seven trillion dollars,[32] but poverty still exists, according to government estimates. So add Johnson's war on poverty to the list of federal failures.

Price controls during the gasoline shortages of 1979 are another example of federal failure. As with all good socialists, the Democratic administration under President Carter thought the best way to solve the gas crisis was a big dose of government intervention. Thomas Sowell noted:

---

31. Steve Miller, "Top Agent Says U.S. Must Care for Illegals" (www.washtimes.com, June 27, 2002).

32. Young, "A Retrospective on Johnson's Poverty War."

A minor decline in the amount of gasoline turned into a major crisis at the pump because of that old liberal nostrum, price control. When Ronald Reagan took office in 1981, one of the first things he did was get rid of price controls on oil. Not only did the gasoline lines disappear, oil production increased and prices at the pump fell, despite a liberal chorus of wailing that the price would go up without price controls.[33]

Carter's experience with price controls on oil is similar to Nixon's experience with price controls on healthcare in the early 1970s. Both are examples of federal failures.

THE ROLE OF THE FEDERAL GOVERNMENT IN A LIBERTY-BASED SOCIETY

The preceding pages document the gross failure of the federal government when it ventures (intrudes) into an area in which it has no legitimate constitutional role. The Founding Fathers knew what they were doing when they designed a limited federal government. Liberty is at risk anytime the federal government attempts, even for "good" reasons, to exceed its constitutional role and scope.

Establishing a Liberty-Based Society is the only way to (1) restructure the federal government to one of limited federalism and (2) provide *we the people* with necessary means to assure the federal government will never again stray from its constitutionally limited role. In a Liberty-Based Society, the role of the federal government would be limited to activities such as:

- Defending the nation's borders
- Maintaining a free trading zone among the states
- Foreign relations based on free trade and noninterference
- Serving as the international advocate of liberty by setting the example here at home and by avoiding foreign entanglements
- Maintaining a strong national defense based on armed neutrality

ARMED NEUTRALITY! ARE YOU AN ISOLATIONIST?

The discretionary budget proposed for national defense in 2004 was $399.1 billion. The total discretionary budget is projected to exceed one-half trillion dollars by 2009![34] D. W. Mackenzie pointed

---

33. Thomas Sowell, "Mondale's 'Experience'" (www.jewishworldreview.com, Nov. 5, 2002). Copyright 2002. Used by permission of Thomas Sowell and Creators Syndicate, Inc.

34. "Fiscal 2004 President's Budget, National Defense Topline (Function 050)," DoD News: Fiscal 2004 Department of Defense Budget Release (www.defenselinkmil/news/Feb2003/bo2032003_bt044-03.html).

out, "Military spending rose 45.8% for the second quarter (2003). This is the strongest quarterly increase in military spending since the Korean War."[35] Who will pay for this budget? Remember also that as the baby boomer generation moves toward retirement, as is currently happening, there will be fewer and fewer working Americans left to pay an increasing tax burden. The question must be answered: "How much international policing and 'projection of force' can *we the people* afford?"

If we lived in a perfect world, all governments would be based on the principle of liberty. In such a perfect world, very little military would be required. But the sad reality is that we do not live in a perfect world. Therefore, we will always need a means of national defense. The question is not do we need a strong military capability or even how big of a military do we need. The question is what purpose should the military serve in a Liberty-Based Society?

George Washington in his farewell address warned Americans to avoid foreign entanglements. Gen. Robert E. Lee warned that if the Northern industrial/commercial interests established control of the government, the United States would become "aggressive abroad and despotic at home."[36] In the modern era, the United States is constantly engaged in "nation building" all around the world. *We the people* are constantly reminded by our leaders, both liberal and conservative— especially neoconservatives—that destiny has placed upon us the duty to guarantee the safety, security, and democracy of the world (a new twist on the "white man's burden" concept that was formerly used to justify the British Empire). But should we be playing the role of international policeman? Could it be that our "projection of force" under the banner of nation building is seen by the people of the world as merely a pretext for the enforcement of an American commercial empire? Has any prior empire created international love and respect by the moral persuasion of bloody bayonets? Is nation building creating true friends or blood enemies for America?

The truth of the matter is that most of the world's opinion of the United States ranges from mild dislike to fervent hatred. Why do they hate us? The neoconservatives tell us that they hate us because we are so prosperous. But if prosperity causes them to hate us, why do they not hate Singapore, Hong Kong, Japan, and numerous other prosperous countries?

Free and voluntary exchange between people of different countries, cultures, and religions does not require military force. Foreign trade

---

35. D. W. Mackenzie, "Doubts about Recovery" (www.mises.org, Oct. 8, 2003).
36. Robert E. Lee, as cited in Kennedy and Kennedy, *The South Was Right!*, 41.

does not occur between nations—it occurs voluntarily between people of different nations. If a Middle East country decides that it does not want any of its nationalized oil to go to American companies, what moral right would America have to threaten military force to "open the doors" of trade? In reality, force would not be necessary. If an oil-exporting country refused to deal with American oil companies, that country would still need to sell its oil on the open market. American companies would purchase oil from the North Sea or Russia while others would purchase the Middle East oil. The people in the Middle East do not want their oil resources to remain in the ground. They want to export it in order to obtain financial resources held by other people. This market activity is accomplished by free trade without the need for military intervention. The same principle of free trade between people residing in different countries is true for all forms of trade. Thus the need of a huge military merely to "project force" is limited by free trade. The need of a modern, technologically superior, well-equipped, and trained military in a Liberty-Based Society is purely defensive, i.e., providing deterrence to any potential enemy.

The question then arises, "Do we need military bases around the world?" Why are *we the people* paying an increasingly larger tax burden to protect the people of South Korea, Japan, Europe, or Saudi Arabia? While we are taxing ourselves to protect them, they are not required to shoulder a commensurate tax load and therefore end up with a competitive advantage against American workers in the marketplace.

In the late nineteenth and early twentieth centuries, the United States used gunboat diplomacy to keep Central and South American markets open and to protect private American commercial investments in those countries. Even earlier, Adm. Matthew Calbraith Perry (1794-1858) used American naval power to "open the doors" of the Japanese market for American commercial interests. The American military was used to help put down the Boxer Rebellion in China, which threatened American commercial interests. Of all peoples in the world, the people of the South should be well aware of the Northern industrialist proclivity for using military force to protect its commercial empire. Looking forward, we must question whether or not it is proper for a Liberty-Based Society to send its military forces to far-off corners of the world to protect unwise or risky investments made by American commercial interests in unstable foreign lands. Is it proper for a liberty-loving people who believe in free, voluntary trade to use their overwhelming military power to force commercial relations? The answer is simple: no! Projection of force is acceptable only if it is used as deterrence or to protect our nation from those who have sworn to destroy our liberty.

The Cold War is an example of effective use of deterrence. The United States maintained its position of strength and never allowed the U.S.S.R. to gain military superiority. Weakness is a signal that encourages your enemy to attack. Military strength and technological superiority are requirements for the protection of the nation from those who are ideologically obsessed with the destruction of liberty (as was the case with the evil Communist empire).

Research and development of defense technology should continue. The use of space as the ultimate "high ground" is essential for national defense. Boots on the ground for intelligence gathering are essential in order to know in advance if radical or ideologically driven fanatic nations or groups are planning to attack. Under such circumstances, an overwhelming military response would be appropriate. The world must know we do not lack the resolve to use the most deadly weapons at our disposal to take out anyone who attacks our nation or anyone who harbors such fanatics. In such a response there would be large collateral damage in the aggressor nation, i.e., deaths of otherwise innocent civilians. War is not a game—the best way to win is to never play. The best way to increase the probability of not having a war is to maintain an overwhelming and technologically superior military and show no sign of timidity, i.e., make sure the world knows that if necessary, you will use this force. You must also practice a strict international policy of noninterference.

International noninterference means that if American commercial or banking interests invest in foreign countries, they must be willing to shoulder the responsibility for losses if said countries become unstable or "nationalize" foreign investments. Businesspeople and investors must factor such possible costs into their projections. *The income of the average taxpayer will not be used to underwrite such risky projects.* Let those who hope to reap the rewards bear the risk. The hardworking taxpayer should not be forced to pay for military actions whose real purposes are to protect risky foreign commercial investments. Perhaps it would be more profitable for businesspeople and investors to make those investments in America!

QUESTIONS AND ANSWERS

Q. I'm a conservative and generally agree with what you are saying, but your stand on armed neutrality concerns me. Aren't you really an isolationist?

A. No, I do not advocate that we isolate ourselves from the world—quite the opposite. As an advocate of voluntary exchange, I see us doing business with different peoples all over the world. What I object to is the use of American military force and taxpayers' money to guarantee the security of various business deals American corporations make around the world. A strong military is necessary to deter aggression. An active international intelligence network is needed to find out if extremists or aggressors are planning attacks against our country. In the modern era, space has become the ultimate high ground, and if we do not command it, our potential adversaries will. There is much we can do without projecting ourselves into the political affairs of foreign nations or becoming embroiled in their internal conflicts. This strategy will reduce our profile and remove the image of Americans as interlopers all over the world.

Trade does not need military interventions to be successful. Free commerce and voluntary exchange enrich both parties regardless of whether or not they like or even understand each other. Voluntary exchange brings diverse people together for mutual benefit. What better way to make friends around the world and demonstrate the benefits of liberty?

Q. You said that democracy is a failure. What system would be better than our democratic government?

A. The Founding Father established a republic, not a democracy. Federalists and especially anti-Federalists expressed concern about the potential dangers arising from mass democracy. They mainly worried that it would degenerate into a mobocracy, where the numerical majority would capture the reins of government and use it to loot the numerical minority. Today in America, the top 50 percent of taxpayers pay 96 percent of the taxes, while the bottom 50 percent pay only 4 percent of the cost of government! This is the result of America becoming a mobocracy. This will not be allowed in our Liberty-Based Society. Our society will be more on the order of the original constitutional Republic of Republics.

Q. Who would protect our environment if we did not have the Environmental Protection Agency (EPA) and other federal watchdog agencies?

A. A proper governmental attitude toward property rights (discussed at length in chapter 15) would eliminate the need for most such regulations and enforcement agencies. When the federal government downgraded property rights, more government was required to correct the problems that the intervention created in the first place! But guess what. If you have property downstream from a polluting plant, you already have the right to go to court or some alternate dispute mechanism to obtain relief. You don't need the Federal Clean Water Act. If your property is losing value because of air pollution, then your property rights are being violated and you also have a right to seek a remedy for your loss. You don't need the Federal Clean Air Act. If a company does a good job containing its air and water pollution, but its holding tanks are allowing seepage of contaminants that threaten underground aquifers, then your property rights are in danger and you have a right to seek a remedy. There are rare occasions in which a Liberty-Based Society will want to pass special legislation on the federal level. The mutual benefits of the union will encourage even those states that object to the law to agree to abide by it.

Q. Conservatives have always been in favor of business. Without a strong liberal presence, wouldn't conservatives give away the treasury in the form of corporate welfare?

A. Liberals will not be banished in a Liberty-Based Society. But they will not be allowed to use the government's police power to confiscate other people's money for pet liberal social-engineering projects. As I demonstrated in this chapter, both current political parties have used corporate welfare to their advantage. In a Liberty-Based Society, the potential for misuse will be greatly decreased by the upper limit of a 10 percent taxing authority for all government. Also, our reliance on sound monetary policy will deprive politicians of both parties of indirect taxation, i.e., inflation. Under this system of government, *we the people* will keep our income.

Q. Are you trying to go back to a weak federal government like we had under the Articles of Confederation?

A. The major failure of the government under the Articles of Confederation was that it did not provide for a free trading zone among the states in the union. In our Liberty-Based Society, this free trading zone would be as secure as it currently is, with the addition of the wealth-generating capacity of an unhampered free market. No, I am not advocating a return to a federal government like the one we had under the Articles of Confederation. What I am advocating is a return to a federal government as envisioned by the Founding Fathers when they established the Republic of Republics under the original Constitution and as explained by Thomas Jefferson and James Madison in the Virginia and Kentucky Resolutions of 1798.

Turning Free Men into Slaves

Brother Jonathan was a crafty old Yankee. One day he hitched his team to his wagon, loaded it with supplies, and headed to a small Southern community. When he got there, he encountered a number of citizens sitting outside the local general store.

"Where you going, Brother Jonathan?" one asked the old Yankee.

"I am going down to the swamp bottom to capture those wild hogs and take them to the slaughtering pen—ought to make a handsome profit," he said.

The good ole boys at the store hooted with laughter. They knew those wild hogs were the meanest hogs in the country. They would brag every time one of their dogs would survive a tangle with those dangerous creatures. Those hogs were independent of man and knew how to take care of themselves. The good ole boys shook their heads in disbelief as Brother Jonathan headed toward the swamp bottom. "What a fool," they thought. "No one has ever managed to capture those hogs."

Spring turned into summer and summer turned into late fall. The good ole boys had all but forgotten about Brother Jonathan's absurd plan to capture the wild hogs. But late one cool fall evening, they looked down the road, and to their amazement there came Brother Jonathan with thirty or forty hogs gently grunting as they followed his wagon. "Where you taking those hogs?" they asked in astonishment.

"The hogs don't know it but I am taking them up to the slaughtering pen," Brother Jonathan said, with a note of superiority and self-satisfaction in his voice.

"But how did you manage to get them to blindly follow you?" they asked, still unable to believe their eyes.

"Really it was very simple," Brother Jonathan began. "When I first got down there those hogs avoided me like the plague. But I just began putting out a few ears of corn here and there. At first they just ignored it. But then a few of the younger ones would come up, grab the corn, and rush off back into the brush to eat it. Then before long, the older ones decided to get in on the act. I knew it would not be long before I had them. They were beginning to depend on me to feed them more than they depended on their own natural abilities. Then I quit putting the corn out all over the place and just put it in a pile in the middle of a clearing. It took a while but finally they were all coming to my clearing to eat. Then I began building a fence around the clearing. At first, most of them were skeptical, but the lure of something for nothing got the best of them. Each day I would extend the fence a little more until at last I had the entire clearing fenced except for one small opening that they all had to walk through in order to get my corn. One day when they were all in the fence eating my corn, I closed the gate on the fence. Oh, there was a good bit of squealing at first but by now they had grown so fat and lazy that they would not even attempt to break through my fence. Each day I would drive my wagon around to a different spot of the fence and throw the corn to the hogs. One day I noticed that every one of them were waiting for me and would follow my wagon around and around, me on the outside and them on the inside of the fence. That is when I knew it would be safe to take them to the slaughtering pen without fear of losing a single hog!"

Brother Jonathan knew what all of us "good ole boys" would do well to understand—liberty is the ultimate price we pay when we sacrifice individual self-reliance to gain "something for nothing." This is the essence of the insidious temptation of socialism.

CHAPTER 13

Social Security: It's Time to Pay Up and Get Out

No federal legislation has done more to buy votes for liberal/socialist incumbents than the Social Security Act. No federal legislation has done more to pervert the principle of individual responsibility and liberty than the Social Security Act. The act as it stands at the beginning of the twenty-first century is based upon generations of lies, fraud, and political corruption. Yet despite its faults and anti-liberty nature, we have it, and therefore we must find a way to deal with it.

One of the primary principles of a Liberty-Based Society is that government must not be allowed to consume more than 10 percent of GDP. Therefore, to be true to our principles, we must find a way to remove the onerous Social Security tax burden on present and future generations. But this must be done in a way that will also be fair to those who have for generations been forced to "invest" in this bankrupt "Old Age Pension" system (I include myself in this number). But more important for liberty is the fact that new generations of Americans will at last be able to look forward to the day when they, not an arbitrary government bureaucrat or politician, will be able to invest their income in the manner they freely choose.

SOCIAL SECURITY IS ANTI-LIBERTY
A study conducted by Boston University noted that eighteen-year-olds who begin work at a middle-age pay scale today can expect to pay almost three-quarters of a million dollars of taxes over their working life into the Social Security system. These same workers can expect to draw $140,000 worth of benefits![1] Even the federal government has admitted that the returns on the forced investments into Social Security border on miserly when compared to the same investments in the free market. The Social Security Administration

1. Gregory Bresiger, "The Forgotten Payroll Tax" (www.mises.org, Oct. 16, 2003).

217

estimates that a thirty-year-old average wage earner can expect at the most a 3.4 percent return, but possibly as low as 1.1 percent today. The bad news is that they project that this "high" earning rate will only go down as we progress into the twenty-first century![2]

Liberals/socialists like to portray themselves as champions of the poor, women, and minorities, but when it comes to their unfailing support of Social Security legislation, we see how far reality is from their soulful confessions. The "payout" for Social Security is based on longevity—the longer you live, the more of your "investment" you get back. But is this fair to everyone? Michael Tanner wrote:

> The current Social Security system contains a host of inequities, many of which disadvantage minorities and women. For example, because lifetime Social Security benefits are closely linked to longevity, people with shorter life expectancies can expect to receive less in retirement benefits. At every age and every income level, African Americans have shorter life expectancies than do whites. As a result, an African American who has the same lifetime earnings and pays the same payroll taxes as a white person can expect to receive a lower rate of return. This problem is exacerbated by the fact that African Americans are more likely to begin working earlier than whites and that African American marriages are more likely to end in divorce in less than 10 years. Indeed, no group may be as poorly treated by Social Security as African Americans.[3]

The situation is not much better for some women, especially those who choose to work outside of the home. Because of the Social Security Administration's "dual entitlement rule," a married working woman must choose between the benefits to which her taxes entitle her or to one-half of her husband's benefits. In other words, she may end up never receiving anything for the taxes she paid into the system. Tanner notes, "In addition the loss of up to 50% of a couple's benefits at the husband's death throws every fifth widow into poverty."[4] Now what was that about how much liberals/socialists cared about the poor and disadvantaged?

2. Michael Tanner, "No Second Best: The Unappetizing Alternatives to Social Security Privatizing" (www.cato.org, Jan. 29, 2002), "The Cato Project on Social Security Privatization," SSP No. 4.

3. Ibid., 10.

4. Ibid., 11.

SOCIAL SECURITY IS BASED UPON FRAUD

How could politicians convince freedom-loving Americans to buy into a government-mandated retirement system that on average pays a return of from 3 to 1 percent on our "investment"? Remember that the socialist system of "Old Age Pensions" was brought over to America from Otto von Bismarck's Germany. Remember that in chapter 1 I discussed how FDR foisted this system on an unsuspecting America. Social Security's consequences were never fully understood by the politicians who voted for it, and the little resistance it had dried up when the Republicans learned how to manipulate the Social Security system in order to buy votes in upcoming elections. The federal government's primary goal with Social Security is to keep *we the people* confused and confounded. If we ever learn the truth about the Social Security scam, then we just might decide to cut off the flow of OPM that contemporary elected officials depend on for reelection. Indeed, Gregory Bresiger reported that one government official felt quite confident about keeping us in the dark: "'Continued general support for the Social Security System hinges on continued public ignorance of how the system works,' the official told Baron's Weekly on April 26, 1965. 'I believe that we have nothing to worry about because it is so enormously complex that nobody is going to figure it out.'"[5] Because it was 1965 when the official made such an insulting statement, we can only surmise that he was right—we have been too ignorant to know any better! But the times, they are achanging.

Many Americans go to bed at night secure in notion that their "investments" in Social Security are safe in the federally protected Social Security Trust Fund. I hate to disturb their peaceful dreams of an early retirement, but there is no money in the Trust Fund. Oh my, we've been lied to again—and by "our" federal government no less! See what David M. Walker, former comptroller general of the United States of America, had to say: "'In the case of the Social Security and Medicare Trust Funds,' Walker said, 'the federal government took in taxpayer money, spent it on other items and replaced it with an IOU.'"[6] When Walker was asked what the total bill was, he guessed it to be "tens of trillions of dollars."[7] Bresiger noted, "This is hard to comprehend. So think of it this way: These

5. Bresiger, "The Forgotten Payroll Tax."
6. Gregory Bresiger, "The Discourteous Mr. Walker" (www.mises.org, Sept. 24, 2003).
7. Ibid.

myriad obligations, made by sleazy polls . . . on our behalf, are 'likely to exceed $100,000 in additional burdens for every man, woman and child in America today and these amounts are growing every day.'"[8]

By 2001 the Old Age and Survivors Insurance and the Disability Insurance funds recorded receiving more than one trillion dollars of taxpayer money.[9] However, it is all an accounting transaction that makes Enron look like Sunday-school stuff. The records also show a transfer of all collected funds to the government, to be used for general governmental operations. The only thing in the Trust Fund is federal IOUs backed by its power to confiscate the income of *future* generations of taxpayers.

The Social Security Trust Fund has no real assets; all it has is federal IOUs. Federal politicians took your mandated retirement "investments" into the Social Security system, used the scheme of the Trust Fund IOUs to move your "investments" into the government's general funds, and spent your money just like they spend all OPM! In fact, these politicians are so unscrupulous that they are now spending OPM that belongs to unborn citizens—future generations are being taxed by today's unprincipled politicians, all in the name of "good" government. This is the height of taxation without representation. Some experts put the current Social Security unfunded liability at $9.5 trillion.[10] This is not exactly the type of financially responsible government the Founding Fathers had in mind.

Most people who pay into their private retirement account(s) do so because they want to set aside part of today's income to use when they are no longer employed—hopefully at retirement. As such, we all have real property rights to our retirement investment. It's ours and we can demand it whenever we want to use it. But the fraud of Social Security is so great that most people cannot even contemplate that they have no property rights to the money they invest into the system. Retirees must depend upon the honesty and good faith of the politicians and bureaucrats who control the system! Tanner noted, "Under the current Social Security system, workers have no legal right to their retirement benefits. In two important cases, *Helverign v. Davis* and *Flemming v. Nestor,* the U.S. Supreme Court has ruled that Social Security taxes are simply taxes and convey no property or contractual rights to Social Security benefits."[11]

8. Ibid.
9. June O'Neill, "The Trust Fund, the Surplus, and the Real Social Security Problem" (www.cato.org, Apr. 9, 2003), "Social Security Privatization," SSP No. 26, 2.
10. www.socialsecurity.org/alternative.
11. Tanner, "No Second Best," 11.

If there are no real assets in the Trust Fund, and if *we the people* have no property rights to our income paid into the Social Security system, then why did our benevolent political leaders establish such an entity as the Trust Fund in the first place? June O'Neill answered, "Why then does the Social Security program have a trust fund? It was established by the 1939 amendments and as John Cogan, an economist with the Hoover Institution and a member of the President's Commission to Strengthen Social Security, put it, it was 'a labeling device designed to provide political protection against the charge that the funds were being misspent.'"[12] The Social Security program is indeed a "labeling device," a fig leaf to hide behind and a smokescreen to camouflage political theft of OPM! Do you ever get the feeling that your government has been lying to you?

Pious politicians are quick to tell us that they are taxing us to make sure that honest working people will not be forced into poverty. Indeed, one of the main motivations for passing the original Social Security Act was that it would help to eliminate poverty in America. Both FDR and LBJ promised us that with just a little more OPM spent on such programs, the government (not the private sector) would be able to solve the vexing problem of poverty. What has been the track record of our politicians? As I documented in chapter 5, poverty is actually higher after generations of FDR socialism and years of LBJ's "me-to" socialism. In fact, in 1999, if we had taken just 20 percent of the total Social Security expenditures and given it to the poor, we would have eliminated poverty for those sixty-five and older.[13] Perhaps *we the people* and a free market economy could do a better job eliminating poverty than the federal government. But then again, where would unprincipled politicians gain the revenues so necessary to their reelection? The entire system of Social Security is based upon perpetually defrauding the average hardworking taxpayer. It's time to end the fraud and send the fat-cat politicians back home to try their hand at honest work.

SOCIAL SECURITY—A VOTE-BUYING SCHEME

Organized and unorganized recipients of Social Security today provide liberals/socialists with an easily roused voting bloc. Time and time again we have seen the liberal propaganda ministry (a.k.a. the mainline media) and the high priesthood of liberal/socialist orthodoxy (politically correct academia) frighten the elderly with

12. O'Neill, "The Trust Fund," 3.
13. Ibid., 7.

threats that their Social Security will be cut off if this or that conservative is elected. Liberals/socialists have won numerous elections by playing a combination of the old-age card and the race card. But it would be disingenuous to blame all Social Security voting buying on liberals/socialists. Unprincipled conservative leaders have also been active in the endeavor.

Recall that in chapter 1, "Conservativism: A Century of Failure," I demonstrated that the Republicans initially fought FDR's Social Security plan. After it passed, the Republicans soon learned that they too could garner votes from the elderly by promising more benefits to Social Security recipients. Indeed, when Republicans regained control of Congress in the early 1950s, they made no efforts to roll back FDR's socialist victory! Recall also that the largest increase in Social Security benefits was negotiated by the Republican Nixon administration. This compromise between Democrats and Republicans in Congress allowed incumbents of both parties to go back home and assure elderly voters that they had voted to increase Social Security, resulting in reelection of more than 90 percent of them!

Both parties have voted to overextend Social Security and then as a "vote-getting" maneuver they declare that they have suddenly discovered that the entire Social Security system is on the verge of collapse. The media heralds the dreaded news, targeted at the elderly, who then rise in panic and fear demanding that their political protectors do something before they are reduced en masse to eating dog food. Hearing the heartrending cry from their constituency, the party in power declares a holy crusade to "Save Social Security." After much anxiety, the masterminds and soothsayers in Washington, D.C. hammer out a bipartisan plan, entailing a substantial tax increase on working Americans. Presto, a cure is found, and the elderly voters are beholden anew to their watchful providers in Washington. How many times has this or similar scenarios been played out? A partial listing would include:

1. Democratic president Jimmy Carter saved Social Security by raising taxes in 1970.

2. Republican president Ronald Reagan saved Social Security by raising taxes in the 1980s.

3. Democratic president Bill Clinton saved Social Security by promising that the federal surplus would be used to maintain it in the 1990s. (What surplus?)

Because Social Security is not based on actual monetary reserves, because it is in essence a fraud kept alive by the police power of the federal government, it will perpetually be in need "saving." And this salvation will always come from the pockets of hardworking Americans via increased taxes, decreased benefits to future recipients (the sad truth is that our politicians prefer to shift the burden to future recipients who are not yet born—it's really hard for the unborn to vote against a current incumbent), or borrowing against future taxes. In a word it's a scam—the world's most successful Ponzi scheme!

OPM is the mother's milk of incumbency! Social Security and Medicare have become the best voting-buying schemes in Washington. The pressure on incumbents arises not only from organized and unorganized recipients but also from a well-organized cadre of special interest lobbyists. They provide money for the campaign chests of their "friends" in Congress and also serve as a source of organized grassroots support during elections. While you and I (common working taxpayers) are too busy minding our own business, obeying laws, and creating a decent society at the local level, these lobbyists are busy encouraging "our" elected officials to raise our taxes in order to bring in a fresh new supply of OPM.

For instance, the National Academy on an Aging Society supports the concept that there should be no limit on taxes[14] when it comes to Social Security—just keep raising taxes and keep raising benefits to the recipients. A spokeswoman for the Older Women's League believes that Social Security is such a good and moral thing that taxes have a legitimate place in maintaining it. A spokesman for the National Association of Letter Carriers urged the President's Commission to reject the notion that taxes should not be raised to save Social Security. The Economic Policy Institute advocates not only raising taxes for Social Security but also indexing these new taxes so they would increase as longevity increased![15] Everywhere you look—whether in Washington, D.C. or in the media or academia—you will find liberals/socialists advocating that you should be deprived of more and more of your income in order to keep the scam going. It's time *we the people* took control and put a stop to the fraud called Social Security.

It is dishonorable and grossly unjust for us to saddle young workers with Social Security's enormous tax burden. It is doubly dishonorable to do so at the time most young people are thinking about beginning

14. Tanner, "No Second Best," 2.
15. Ibid., 3.

their families and attempting to accumulate enough discretionary wealth to make a down payment on their first home. What a travesty of liberty—all at the hands of our anti-liberty federal government.

Beginning in 2016, each worker will be forced by the federal government to pay an additional $103 in Social Security taxes to keep the system running on a cash-flow basis. By 2030, each worker will be required to pay another $1,543,[16] and the cost continues to increase. There is no end in sight!

As I demonstrated in chapters 5 and 10, taxes do not have a neutral effect on our economy. The more money the government takes out of private hands, the less the economy grows. The Congressional Budget Office (CBO) estimated that over 500,000 jobs were lost from 1979 to 1982 as a result of tax increases. Another study by two economists (Gary and Aldona Robbins) estimated that 510,000 jobs were lost from 1988 to 1990 as a result of tax increases.[17] Sad as these losses are, they are unseen; therefore, "our" politicians do not have to answer for jobs that never became available. But our politicians' friends and their special interest groups get a new round of OPM. The politicians can brag to the elderly about how compassionate they are, and they are assured of receiving votes from Social Security recipients who now have more "free" benefits. All in all, it's a very clever vote-buying scheme. And who pays? By this time you should know who pays—*we the people* pay.

PREVENTING A WAR BETWEEN THE GENERATIONS

Politicians and special interest groups have set the stage for a virtual civil war between the baby boomer generation of retirees and the post-baby boomer generations who must work to support the boomers' increasing demands on Social Security. Liberals/socialists have managed to divide the generations on this one issue, but it spills over to other issues—to the benefit of the liberal/socialist agenda. Many an otherwise conservative, Bible-believing retiree came to the defense of President Clinton during the Monica Lewinsky affair because Clinton was "a Democrat and Democrats want to protect our Social Security." How many former Sunday-school teachers turned their backs on moral teachings in order to protect the Democrat Clinton because "all the Republicans want to do is take away my Social Security"? Many an elderly, pro-life, devout Christian and devoted church worker will march to the voting booth

16. Ibid.
17. Ibid., 6.

and vote for the Democratic candidate even though that candidate is averse to the retiree's pro-life belief. Fear of losing "my Social Security" determines for whom many of the elderly will vote. Social Security has enabled liberals/socialists to drive a wedge between retired parents and their children, between grandparents and grandchildren, between those approaching eternity and those yet to be born to this world. If we continue down this road, there will come a time when the grandchildren will refuse to be slaves to their grandparents' retirement income.

June O'Neill wrote, "Social Security's actuaries project that the worker-to-beneficiary ratio will fall from its current [2002] level of 3.3 covered workers per retiree to about 2 workers per retiree in 2030, with most of the change occurring after 2010. After 2030 the ratio is expected to continue to decline, albeit at a slower pace, dipping to 1.85 workers per beneficiary by 2075."[18] By 2030 the number of elderly will increase by 80 percent, but the number of workers whose taxes will be needed to support them will have increased by only 16 percent.[19] Added to the increasing number of elderly is the fact that these baby boomers tend to live longer and consume more than our parents' generation. Chris Edwards wrote, "A few decades ago, 70-year-olds consumed one-third less than 30-year-olds, on average. They now consume one-fifth more."[20] If we do not solve the Social Security problem, by the mid-twenty-first century we will end up requiring young workers to pay upward of 25 percent of their wages in taxes for Social Security and Medicare—and this is before the Republican president Bush II offers a prescription drug benefit for Medicare recipients!

HOW DO WE GET OUT OF THIS SOCIAL SECURITY QUAGMIRE?

Since the days of FDR, the majority of working Americans have been forced by the federal government to pay a part of their income into the Social Security system. The resulting drain from paychecks (especially when combined with other state, local, and federal taxes) left little discretionary income for investment in private retirement plans. (Recall what I said in chapter 10 about the effect of taxes on individuals' ability to take care of themselves.) Therefore, it would be unfair simply to announce one day that all Social Security benefits

18. O'Neill, "The Trust Fund," 4.

19. Chris Edwards, "Averting War Between the Generations" (www.cato.org, Nov. 26, 2002).

20. Ibid.

payments would cease. We must find a way that will allow younger workers to buy out of this socialist system while maintaining benefits for those who are too old to amass enough savings and investments to see them through retirement. The first step is to find current federal budget dollars that are being misspent and redirect them to those who are currently on Social Security or who will be eligible within the next ten years.

WHERE'S THE MONEY COMING FROM?

Remember that one of the primary principles of a Liberty-Based Society is limited government—that means all governments must be limited to only those functions that cannot be accomplished by individuals working within a free market. Another principle is that of armed neutrality—a foreign policy that promotes free trade while avoiding foreign entanglements. With these two principles in mind, let us take a look at the federal budget for the fiscal year 2003 and see if we could find some misspent monies that would allow us to take care of those who have had no choice but to pay in and rely upon the ill-fated Social Security system.

That budget had total government expenditures of $2.14 trillion. Of this amount, approximately $365 billion was earmarked for "national defense," another $25 billion for "Homeland Security," and $18 billion for "justice."[21] We can see that of the $2.14 trillion of federal spending, only $408 billion was required for national defense and the general administration of "justice." That leaves approximately $1.732 trillion that the federal government spent on various unconstitutional interventions! George Reisman wrote, "Such spending at Federal level is clearly in excess of 80%, and may well be close to 90%, of total Federal spending. The elimination of this spending would make possible the abolition of the personal and corporate income taxes and the inheritance and capital gains taxes, along with the special taxes to pay for Social Security, Medicare, and Medicaid."[22] Onerous and unconstitutional federal interventions are costing taxpayers billions of dollars each year. These dollars would be better spent buying the nation out of the current Social Security scheme.

What do I mean by federal "interventions"? Take for example the Environmental Protection Agency (EPA). The 2003 federal budget allocated $7.6 billion of your income to this agency. The very nature

21. George Reisman, "What Is Interventionism?" (www.mises.org, Sept. 10, 2003).
22. Ibid.

of this unconstitutional agency allows it to "impose many hundreds of billions, possibly several trillions, of dollars of additional costs on businesses and consumers across the country."[23]

When Pres. George Washington organized his administration under the original Constitution, he had five Cabinet departments. Today the federal government has fifteen Cabinet departments and a whole host of alphabet-soup administrative agencies. The better known of these self-legislating and self-enforcing agencies are: IRS, FRB, FDIC, EPA, FDA, SEC, CFTC, NLRB, FTC, FCC, FERC, NRC, FAA, CAA, INS, OHSA, EEOC, BATF, DEA, NIH, and NASA. (Remember my discussion of the proper role of the federal government in chapter 12. Here we see the results of an unbridled, all-powerful federal government.) In a Liberty-Based Society, your income will be protected from unscrupulous politicians (is there any other kind?) and their friends, the special interest lobbyists. By cutting off federal interventionism, we will do more than just find the dollars needed to buy out of the Social Security scheme. We will make American industry more competitive, thereby increasing the personal wealth of workers and investors. And remember, with the advent of 401Ks, workers and investors are now in many cases the same. Reisman stated in 2003, "I believe that the growing cost of interventionism is what is responsible for the fact that apart from the contribution made by women working more, real income for large numbers of working families in the United States has been stationary or even declining over the last thirty years or more."[24]

It cannot be said enough—in a Liberty-Based Society, *we the people* will be responsible for our own well-being and that of our families. Extended from the family is our natural duty to our community and those in our community who need our help. But this help is given freely out of our personal sense of duty, honor, and moral convictions. In this environment, the free market will produce far greater wealth than we now have and as a result do much more to eliminate poverty. No matter how hard liberals/socialists try, they cannot tax society rich!

Studying this enormous federal budget—just brimming over with OPM—let us see what other monies we might find to use to eliminate our dependency on the fraudulent federal Social Security system. According to Secretary of Defense Donald Rumsfeld, it now costs taxpayers $4 billion a month to "rebuild" Iraq.[25] It may sound

23. Ibid.
24. Ibid.
25. Patrick J. Buchanan, "Approaching Imperial Overstretch" (www.wnd.com, July 21, 2003).

like heresy to the neoconservatives, but I find it a little odd that working people's income should be used to "rebuild" an oil-rich Arab nation! Four billion dollars a month would go a long way in helping to assure that current and near-current Social Security recipients (who were forced by the government to "invest" in this scam) receive their benefits for the remainder of their lives. In addition to Iraq, the government has sent its military to numerous posts worldwide. The cost of maintaining such an international presence is enormous and could be used to fund a Social Security buyout. The United States currently has boots on the ground on bases in South Korea, Japan, Colombia, the Philippines, Germany, Eastern Europe, Bosnia, Kosovo, Afghanistan, and various Arab Gulf States. The current stretch for empire led to an increase of military spending by 45.8 percent in the second quarter of 2003. This is the largest quarterly jump in military spending since the Korean War.[26] Perhaps some of that money could be spent back here in the good ole U.S.A. Is it really the destiny of the American taxpayer to be the financier of international policing?

I my discussion of corporate welfare in chapter 12, I noted that each year the government gave out more than $87 billion of your income to various well-connected corporations. Surely your tax monies would be better spent on buying out of the Social Security scam as opposed to giving it to wealthy corporations. In a Liberty-Based Society, your income is strictly that—yours! It's time we used it to assure the removal of this hideous Social Security scam and make way for the reemergence of liberty.

The potential to buy out of the Social Security system is there—what is missing is the political will to do it! The absence of political will is due to the fact both parties are equally guilty of using Social Security as a vote-buying scheme. Neither party truly wants to remove this socialist system. Therefore, the time has come for *we the people* to take matters into our own hands. We can devise a buyout plan that protects current and near-current recipients and that will eliminate this onerous tax on workers forty-five years or younger. If we do not, we will find ourselves divided into a nation of tax recipients (retired baby boomers) and those young workers who are forced to surrender larger and larger portions of their income to finance this continuing federal scam.

In a Liberty-Based Society, we cannot allow government to take more than 10 percent of GDP in the form of taxes (both direct and

26. Mackenzie, "Doubts about Recovery."

indirect). Therefore, we must find a solution for the federal government's bankrupt Social Security system. The economic upsurge that will occur from a lowering of direct taxation, the elimination of inflation via abandoning fiat currency and unsupported credit, and the removal of onerous federal interventionism will more than repay our efforts. In fact, there is a good chance that our economy will grow so large that federal, state, and local revenues equal to 10 percent of the new GDP will produce a surplus! When that happens, let us all remember whose money it is. The best way to keep government limited is to return any surplus to its rightful owners—*we the people.*

QUESTIONS AND ANSWERS

Q. Do you really think organizations like the AARP (American Association of Retired Persons) will let you win in your effort to buy out of Social Security?

A. They have no choice. Every year the ratio of workers paying into Social Security to the number of beneficiaries keeps getting lower. Soon, very soon, large numbers of baby boomers will begin to retire, but at the same time the numbers of post-baby boomers are much smaller. As this happens, the tax rates of post-baby boomers will have to rise dramatically in order to support baby-boomer retirees. Something tells me that those born after 1965 will not sit quietly as government taxes their income at a time in their life when they are trying to finance their first home purchase or their children's college education. Something must be done, but business-as-usual politicians cannot bring themselves to face this difficult issue.

The AARP and similar leftist organizations are not concerned about their membership as much as they are about the potential detrimental effect our plan would have on their liberal/socialist political power base. I have made and will continue to make it clear that my plan will not cost current or near-current beneficiaries anything. It will assure them of federal payments for the remainder of their lives. For those who will be young enough to opt out of the Social Security system, they will be able to invest (or throw away) their money as they see fit. Certainly they will be able to beat the current 1 or 2 percent return that we can expect on our forced "investment" in this fraudulent system.

Q. Why should young workers be concerned about changing the current Social Security system?

A. As I just noted, baby boomers can expect somewhere between 1 or 2 percent return on their "forced" Social Security investments. For the generations following, that return will eventually go negative. In other words, they will get back less than they pay into the system. That's the way all pyramid or Ponzi schemes work! If young workers are allowed to keep their income, they will be able to build personal wealth in the form of investments, savings, and acquiring and paying off their homes. If we explain our position correctly, it will have an important appeal to the younger generations of workers.

Q. No one has been able to touch Social Security since it was first passed. How will you accomplish your Social Security buyout plan?

A. If we, like our conservative leaders, were to agree to play the political game by the rules as established by our liberal/socialist adversaries, then we too could expect to lose. But we are not playing by their rules—we've changed the game! Our appeal is to all Americans who work for a living, who invest, who save, and who want to increase their independence via increased personal wealth. This cannot be accomplished in the current liberal/socialist-dominated political system. It can only be accomplished in a Liberty-Based Society!

The current liberal/socialist system has obtained power and must maintain its power by granting special favors, entitlements, and unfunded mandates to its clientele. We come to power with a plan to divest special interest groups, such as the Fed and its banking clientele, the military-industrial complex, and corporate welfare and social welfare recipients, of their dependency on other people's money. The federal monies that we will save will be applied to buying out of Social Security. It can be done; the only thing lacking is the political will to do it. With your help we will gain the political power and couple the will with the political power to get the job done!

Q. If we no longer have Social Security, what will happen to those shortsighted individuals who spend all they make today, and in their old age they have nothing?

A. This scenario is reminiscent of the ant and grasshopper story. I think most people are more responsible than you give them credit for, especially if there are no "free" government programs waiting to take care of those who fail to take care of themselves. The absence of Social Security will also strengthen family ties. Individuals will have a vested interest in making sure they do not become a hardship on their families in old age. What is true for the family will extend out to our communities. There will always be private charities available for those in need through no fault of their own, but the indolent and reckless must suffer the consequences of their lifestyle. In family counseling, this is called "tough love."

The Healthcare Tooth Fairy

You find yourself in the middle of a modern emergency room. The ambulance has just brought in Mrs. Smith, an eighty-year-old patient who has fallen in a freestanding dialysis clinic (recently opened and now in competition with the hospital). She has apparently broken her hip. She has no insurance other than Medicare. The probability of a lengthy hospitalization is high, while the probability of her making a recovery is very low. Her hospitalization will run close to $100,000 and a large part will not be covered by Medicare.

Into the room rushes Jane Lutz, M.D. Seven years ago Jane completed her undergraduate work in premed, borrowed upward of $100,000, and entered medical school. After four years she completed her initial medical training and, after borrowing more money, entered a three-year orthopedic residency. She generally works sixty or more hours per week. In addition, on her "free" weekends she "moonlights" to help pay off her educational loan and start her practice. She has just completed a medical malpractice risk management course and is troubled by the instructor's statement that a malpractice lawsuit is more likely for patients who expire in the ER with no family in attendance.

Now enters Bob Downturn, hospital administrator. He is concerned that he has too many ER nursing positions that his director of nursing cannot fill. The hospital is operating at barely the breakeven point, but the director of nursing is demanding higher pay rates in order to fill vacant positions. With Bob is the hospital's chief financial officer, who has an irritating habit of reminding Bob that last month the hospital gave away three-quarters of a million dollars of "free" care. This "free" care is federally mandated and completely uncompensated.

Now Bob gets the good news. The hospital's attorney informs him that the Office of the Inspector General is opening an investigation to determine if the hospital placed incorrect charge codes on patient bills submitted to the federal government.

Given that the American healthcare system is the best in the world when rated for technological innovations, development of new drugs, and medical procedures, and given the reality of limited healthcare resources, you now are given the following instructions: devise a healthcare system that will provide the best care available to the most people at the lowest cost, *and* your system must be fair to everyone involved—patients, physicians, nurses, medical research organizations, hospitals, and society at large.

Your first question should be, "How do I measure *fair?* Is it fair to favor one disease over another? Is it fair to favor those who live in urban areas over those who live in rural areas? Is it fair to force people to surrender their income in order to pay for someone's medical education? Is it fair to use the police power of government to force those who exercise a healthy lifestyle to subsidize those who elect to engage in unhealthy life choices? Is if fair for these decisions to be made by majority vote—thereby compelling the numerical minority to submit to the dictates of the numerical majority?" If you are unable to answer these questions, what solutions could we expect to come from a government bureaucrat?

Lessons Learned: Healthcare resources are limited.

Demands for healthcare resources are unlimited.

There is no such thing as a Healthcare Tooth Fairy.

CHAPTER 14

Healthcare in a Liberty-Based Society

Aspiring politicians are quick to tell us that the healthcare system is broken and in critical need of a political solution. Liberal/socialist special interest groups inform us that 43 million Americans are uninsured[1] and therefore "government must do something" to rectify the problem. Yet while the propaganda ministry of the left (a.k.a. the mainline media) maintains a constant drumbeat of doom and woe, Americans are leading the world in advancements in healthcare technology, pharmaceutical research, and delivery systems. When was the last time you saw Americans leaving this country in search of modern, scientifically based healthcare? No doubt there is a problem in American healthcare, but before we allow liberals/socialists to rush us to judgment, let us make sure we have identified the root cause of the problem and then fix the problem once and for all.

WHAT IS THE PROBLEM AND WHO IS TO BLAME?

Liberal/socialist critics of American healthcare place the blame on "market medicine and its greed-is-good business ethic."[2] They believe that healthcare providers are enjoying "outrageous" profits. But is this the case? The emergency-room example above is typical of modern American healthcare. None of the actors—physician, hospital administrator, or nurses—appears to be enjoying "outrageous" profits! Yet liberals/socialists are quick to blame healthcare providers and insist that America's healthcare "crisis" is a result of the failure of the free market—the result of greedy capitalists extracting unreasonable profits from the sick and dying! Are hospitals enjoying "outrageous" profits?

1. David Himmelstein, Steffie Woolhandler, and Ida Hellander, *Bleeding the Patient* (Philadelphia: Common Courage, 2001), 9.
2. Ibid., 5.

233

According to the American Hospital Association, 58 percent of hospitals lose money treating Medicare patients and 32 percent have a *negative* operating margin.[3] Anyone who has seen a hospital bill lately may want to question whether or not hospitals are operating on small margins. One of the reasons why non-Medicare patients' hospital bills are so large is something called "cost shifting." As we all know, "there is no free lunch." Someone has to pay. When the federal government forced hospitals to treat Medicare patients at below actual cost, the lost revenue was made up by "shifting" it to patients with private insurance coverage. The combination of third-party payers (insurance) and the delivery of care at below actual cost—mandated by the federal government for its Medicare beneficiaries—is one of the primary causes of the rapid rise in the cost of medical care.

As costs were shifted to private insurance, there arose a demand (and reasonably so) from the business community to do something about the skyrocketing cost of employer-provide health-insurance coverage. Enter everyone's favorite villain—managed care or health maintenance organizations. As a result of unrealistic federal mandates on hospitals (requiring them to deliver care for less than it cost to provide—try running your company by such a rule), hospitals were forced to shift the cost to the only party that would pay—private insurance. This shift drove up the cost of healthcare premiums for businesses. At that point, businesses began to demand a way to control these costs. Managed care came in and drove down reimbursements to hospitals but also added a new layer of bureaucracy and costs—not to mention driving a wedge between patients and their physicians. During this whole debacle, Americans paid (1) increased Medicare taxes, (2) increased Medicaid taxes at the state level, and (3) increased private insurance premiums (either directly or through their employers). While this was going on, the federal government was devaluating our money by issuing fiat currency and unsupported credit. If you think this system is crazy, you are right! But who made it crazy? Did physicians or nurses or hospital administrators create this system? It was *liberals/socialists,* and the people who created this dreadful system are now the very same ones who want us to allow *them* to fix it! And make no mistake about it. When liberals/socialists say they want to fix the system, they mean that they want to deprive you of more of your income and liberty!

Liberals/socialists cite the growth in administrative personnel in hospitals as an example of healthcare inefficiency. They cite the fact that from 1970 to 1998, employment in administrative

3. "The State of Hospitals' Financial Health" (www.AHA.org, 2002), 3.

positions in healthcare rose an astounding 2,348 percent.[4] Trust liberals/socialists to create a problem and then be the first to criticize and offer more government to cure that very problem. The growth of government regulations and runaway medical malpractice claims has created a mountain of paperwork for healthcare providers at an enormous additional cost of doing business. Today, paperwork adds thirty minutes to every hour of patient care rendered.[5] The American Hospital Association noted:

> A Medicare patient arriving at the emergency department is required to review and sign eight different forms—just for Medicare alone.
>
> Each time a physician orders a test or a procedure, the physician documents the order in the patient's record. But the government requires additional documentation to prove the necessity for the test or procedure. Although the physician made a clinical judgment, the decision-making process—which resulted in the medical order—must be documented using an establish diagnosis assignment process mandated by the government.
>
> Hospital staff must complete a 30-item Medicare Secondary Payer questionnaire every time a Medicare patient comes to the hospital.[6]

And remember that Medicare is but only one of the numerous "new" regulatory bodies that hospitals and physicians are now accountable to. In the seventy-two months from 1997 to 2002, fifty-nine regulations were issued or modified, all of which hospitals and other healthcare providers were required to comply with[7]—under the threat of civil or criminal prosecution! Yes, something is wrong with the way we are forced to deliver healthcare in America, but let us make sure we correct the problem and not create more problems by blindly following failed socialist planning.

The question comes down to this: "Is there too much profit in healthcare or too much government in healthcare?" In 1998 the federal government temporally solved its healthcare cost problem by telling its agents to delay paying legitimate claims from physicians for services they had already rendered. The federal government even went so far as to tell its agents to route physician calls through voicemail systems.[8] This

4. Himmelstein, Woolhandler, and Hellander, *Bleeding the Patient,* 52.

5. "Patients or Paperwork? The Regulatory Burden Facing America's Hospitals" (www.AHA.org, 2002), 2.

6. Ibid., 4.

7. Ibid., 8.

8. "Medicare Staying Solvent but Doctors Footing Bill," *AMANews* (May/June 1998).

was during a time when the same federal government was paying some "elderly" transportation services more than the physician was receiving for the medical care he rendered to the transported individual! Government interventionism in the free market never improves market efficiencies, while it always distorts the market and generally causes bad investment of scarce resources. The cost of healthcare is not too high because of "price-gouging" physicians and health administrators. It is too high because government has forced healthcare to invest its scarce resources in unproductive paperwork instead of patient care. Think of how much better off patients would be if hospitals could exchange 90 percent of their administrative/clerical staff for direct caregivers. But the federal government has foisted upon us a system that will not allow this to take place. An unhampered free market will drive down prices (in all products, not just healthcare) by encouraging ways to be more productive. Unfortunately, under the current system of "controlled competition," this cannot happen.

WHAT WENT WRONG?

It should be of no surprise that the roots of America's health-care "crisis" go back to the federal government. Today, under third-party payers—health insurance, HMOs, PPOs, managed care—the natural market incentives for efficiency have been removed. When a consumer uses his own money to purchase something for himself, he makes sure the price and quality are the best he can get. This forces the supplier to seek better and less expensive ways to offer his goods and services. The natural result is an improvement in quality and a lowering of price. But what happens when the consumer is using someone else's money to make his purchase? The natural market tendency to seek the best price is distorted. Under this new method, the consumer is no longer as concerned about price or quality. This holds true whether we are purchasing a new car or healthcare services.

Prior to World War II, Americans purchased and paid for healthcare services out of their own pockets. But during the war, the federal government imposed wage and price controls. Employers were having a difficult time attracting labor because, due to these controls, they could not offer higher wages. "If the federal government will not let me offer higher wages," employers reasoned, "then I will offer fringe benefits such as health insurance." As we have seen time and time again, there are always consequences when government injects itself into the marketplace—and most if not all of the destructive consequences are unforeseen. As a result of government actions (wage and price controls),

Americans were introduced to the concept of "free" healthcare, i.e., someone other than the consumer paying the bill. Without realizing it, America was headed down a treacherous road leading to the total distortion of the natural market tendency to drive down price while increasing quality. Thomas Sowell wrote:

> This might make some sense if third-party insurance was cheaper or better than insurance that each individual pays for directly. All the evidence is that it is just the opposite. When third parties pay, use of the insurance—and of the medical resources that it pays for—has skyrocketed beyond anything contemplated at the outset.[9]

Thanks, Uncle Sam; we really needed that!

MORAL HAZARD AND THE COST OF HEALTHCARE

"Moral hazard" is an insurance term used to describe what happens when the existence of an insurance policy increases the probability of something happening. For example, what would you expect to happen if a life-insurance policy agreed to pay in the event of death by suicide? One would expect a significant increase in payouts due to "suicide." A less extreme example would be the increased use of auto insurance to repair minor dents and scratches when the insurance pays "first" dollar. Third-party payers via employer-financed health insurance injected moral hazard into healthcare economics. Because the consumer did not perceive a personal cost, the tendency was to increase the use of medical care regardless of the cost. Basic economics teaches us the effect of increased demand on price. As more people demanded more medical care, the price increased. This pressure gradually grew as more employers offered health insurance to their employees after World War II. By 1965, the vast majority of American workers were covered via third-party payers. In 1965, the federal government got into the act by passing Medicare and Medicaid legislation. Suddenly there was a whole new group of people demanding more and more medical care. Once again, healthcare costs are not a market-created problem but a government-created problem. This is a real problem but one that can be resolved better by *we the people* and *not* by government bureaucrats, crafty politicians, special interest groups, or liberal/socialist activists.

9. Thomas Sowell, "Universal Health Care: Part III" (www.jewishworldreview.com, May 8, 2003). Copyright 2003. Used by permission of Thomas Sowell and Creators Syndicate, Inc.

IS UNIVERSAL HEALTHCARE THE ANSWER?

Liberal/socialist activist groups such as Physicians for a National Health Program are demanding government-controlled medical care via "universal healthcare." Under such a system, everyone would be covered. Coverage would include rehabilitative, long-term, and home care; mental, dental, and occupational care; prescription drugs; medical supplies; and durable medical equipment, as well as preventive and public-health procedures.[10] Universal healthcare would not require a copay or deductible because that "discourages" the poor from availing themselves of care. What would be the "moral hazard" implication of such a plan? But liberals/socialist do not care—after all, if more resources are needed, all they have to do is to raise your taxes. Under universal healthcare, you may be assured that your taxes will skyrocket.

Another problem with universal healthcare (aside from its moral delinquency due to its anti-liberty nature) is that it rewards everyone equally. If you watch your diet, exercise regularly, have regular health exams, and generally avoid an unhealthy/risky lifestyle, you are treated the same as those who elect to follow a risky lifestyle. Liberals/socialists use your healthy lifestyle, with its smaller demands on the healthcare system, to underwrite medical care for those who purposely elect to follow risky/unhealthy lifestyles. Remember, equality is the essence of socialism.

Because socialism, and that is what universal healthcare would be, has no means to measure profit and loss, it cannot gauge how to best allocate scarce healthcare resources. Ludwig von Mises wrote:

> Eliminate economic calculation and you have no means of making a rational choice between the various alternatives.
>
> The paradox of "planning" is that it [a socialist system] cannot plan, because of the absence of economic calculation. What is called a planned economy is no economy at all. It is just a system of groping about in the dark. There is no question of a rational choice of means for the best possible attainment of the ultimate ends sought.[11]

"Groping about" with no evidence of "rational choice" is true for all socialist systems, including modern universal healthcare. Thomas Sowell wrote:

> Under the British government's health service, for example,

10. Himmelstein, Woolhandler, and Hellander, *Bleeding the Patient,* 224.
11. Mises, *Human Action,* 695-96.

more than 10,000 people waited more than 15 months for surgery. These included a woman whose cancer surgery was postponed so many times that it finally had to be cancelled because the cancer had become inoperable. Meanwhile surgery was performed to provide breast implants for a 12-year-old girl. . . .[12]

Probably the first country to have universal health care provided by the government was the Soviet Union. After decades of socialized medicine, what was the end result? In its last years, the Soviet Union was one of the few countries in the world with a declining life span and a rising rate of infant mortality.[13]

Liberal/socialist activists and government bureaucrats cannot devise a "fair" (remember the sidebar—what's fair?) way to allocate scarce healthcare resources. Liberals/socialists substitute scarcity for price. Both socialist scarcity and free market price are ways to allocate limited resources. The question is: "Which way do you prefer?" Socialism never increases wealth; it can only use force to divide what is currently available. This principle is also true for healthcare. Socialism cannot increase the availability of healthcare; it can only use force to divide available healthcare resources. Christopher Mayer wrote:

This is the way to view universal health care coverage. It is an unaffordable luxury. It divides what exists and does not produce anything more. It does not change the fact that such an imposition will create unintended consequences. It does not render the laws of economics obsolete.[14]

Just like Social Security before it, universal healthcare is a politician's plaything designed as another liberal/socialist vote-getting scheme that eventually even conservatives, in a most pragmatic way, will adopt. After all, if they don't, they might lose the next election. Principles be damned!

LIBERTY-BASED SOCIETY'S SOLUTION TO HEALTHCARE

Affordability of healthcare is a function of cost and personal discretionary income. Liberals/socialists attempt to frame the debate around coverage, i.e., the disadvantaged who cannot afford insurance. A more efficient solution would be to cut costs arising from government intrusion. Cost in healthcare can be addressed the same way it

12. Sowell, "Universal Health Care: Part II" (May 7, 2003). Copyright 2003. Used by permission of Thomas Sowell and Creators Syndicate, Inc.
13. Sowell, "Universal Health Care" (May 6, 2003). Copyright 2003. Used by permission of Thomas Sowell and Creators Syndicate, Inc.
14. Christopher Mayer, "Health Care for All" (www.mises.org, June 10, 2003).

will be in other businesses—removing the onerous cost associated with federal interventionism. While this is happening, a rollback of taxes to no more than 10 percent of GDP will greatly improve the competitive nature of American business and instantaneously increase working Americans' income. Add to this the removal of moral hazard of employer-provided health benefits. Workers get the entire dollar value in their paychecks, allowing them to purchase private insurance or establish their own medical savings accounts. The free market will force competing healthcare providers to offer the consumer lower prices and better quality. At the same time, the economy will begin a sustainable expansion, fueled in part by increased savings of American worker—who for the first time will begin to build real personal wealth. The expanding economy will produce new employment opportunities for those who have for so long been marginalized in our distorted market/socialist system. Sowell stated:

> What about the poor when it comes to health care? If this were the real issue, then money could be provided to take care of the poor. But here, as elsewhere, the poor are being used as excuses to fasten a whole system of controls on all of us. The left uses the poor as political human shields.[15]

Another way a Liberty-Based Society will reduce the cost of healthcare is by removing the second largest expense item in a physician's practice—medical malpractice insurance premiums. The current tort system, controlled by a special interest group known as trial lawyers, places enormous costs on healthcare. Very little (less than 5 percent) of this insurance ever reaches patients who actually suffered loss due to medical negligence.

In a Liberty-Based Society, healthcare providers will be free to opt out of the tort system. They and patients will agree via contract that any dispute will be settled by binding arbitration. A system could be devised whereby monies from the providers' medical malpractice insurance will be used to pay medical expenses arising from negligence of the provider. Arbitrators will be independent experts in the field of medicine and their decision will be final. No attorneys will be allowed, but the patient will be provided with a medical arbitration expert to guide him in the presentation of his claim. Decisions made under binding arbitration will be final—no appeals allowed.

15. Sowell, "Universal Health Care: Part III." Copyright 2003. Used by permission of Thomas Sowell and Creators Syndicate, Inc.

BEWARE OF THE NIRVANA FALLACY

Too often when discussing healthcare, we allow liberals/socialists to unfairly frame the debate by appealing to what some have called the "Nirvana Fallacy." Liberals/socialists like to complain about perceived "market failures"—failures that usually arise from federal interventionism—and use such "failures" as proof of the need for government intervention. What they are doing is pointing to what they label as "market failures" and then "compar[ing] allegedly imperfect real markets to imaginary governmental institutions that lack even the smallest imperfection."[16] Typical of liberals/socialists, they use emotional appeals, high-sounding rhetoric, and deceptive logic to hide their real passion, their real agenda—the destruction of individual liberty and the expansion of a socialist society.

No system devised by man for the delivery of healthcare will be perfect. But one thing is certain, no socialist system has ever succeeded in efficiently advancing technology, reducing cost, and allocating scarce resources. On the other hand, no system will give *we the people* a better opportunity to create personal wealth and the financial stability necessary to secure for ourselves a healthy future than an unhampered free market in a Liberty-Based Society. *We the people* can reorder society in such a manner that healthcare prices will be controlled by the natural tendency of the market system, where opportunities abound for healthcare practitioners to answer their professional calling of aiding the sick and injured; where our best and brightest minds can devote their energies to research that will broaden the reach of medical science; and where an expanding economy ensures that citizens will be able to afford the cost of care. This will not happen by government fiat. It will happen when *we the people* take decisive political action, aimed not at treating the symptoms of the healthcare "crisis" but at overthrowing the very cause—a socialized political system that not only burdens healthcare providers with onerous interventions but that has also given us a noncompetitive economy that cannot sustain true economic expansion. The healthcare "crisis" is no different from Social Security, inflation, crime, taxation, and a whole list of other liberal/socialist-inspired maladies that plague our society. The only solution is to remove the current liberal/socialist system and replace it with one based on the principles of liberty. To do less would be to guarantee the continuation of conservative failure and liberal/socialist dominance in the United States.

16. D. W. Mackenzie, "The Market Failure Myth" (www.mises.org, Aug. 29, 2002).

QUESTIONS AND ANSWERS

Q. Something has to be done about the cost of healthcare! Have you been a patient in a hospital lately?

A. You are right. Something must be done, but the question is what. Liberals/socialists who created the economic environment now causing this problem are the first and most vocal in demanding more government to resolve the problem that they created! It really does not matter what social issue you look at, their game plan is always the same. Find a social issue, use the media to whip up emotional support for government intervention, and when the intervention results in additional problems, go back to the media and whip up more emotional support for more government programs to solve these "new" issues.

If hospitals, physicians, and other healthcare providers could spend their resources (and their time is a major resource) on healthcare instead of worrying about complying with endless government rules, regulations, and other paperwork, then the money and time spent "treating" the government could be spent on patients. As I mentioned in this chapter, government red tape adds thirty minutes of paperwork to every hour of provided healthcare. Think of the costs that will be eliminated from your hospital or physician's bill when we do away with these needless regulations.

On the other side—opposite of cost—think about how much more financial resources the average citizen will have when a Liberty-Based Society abolishes all payroll taxes. When government interventions are eliminated and patients have sufficient personal wealth to pay directly for their care, think of the real market efficiencies that will result. When the patient rather than some third party becomes the consumer, healthcare providers will have to improve quality and lower price to lure the consumer into their marketplace. Yes, a Liberty-Based Society can control the cost of healthcare via unhampered market competition and can increase the personal wealth of individuals, allowing them to afford the best care at the best price.

Q. I am a medical doctor. Over the years I have seen how much more I am forced to charge my patients just to cover the increasing cost of frivolous medical malpractice suits. What solution would a Liberty-Based Society offer?

A. As you are well aware, the second most expensive cost of a physician's practice is his medical malpractice insurance. Today, many physicians are calling upon the federal government for tort reform. In effect they are asking the federal government to take over an area of law that has always been the responsibility of the states. This is a most dangerous tactic. A much better option would be to work with us to

establish a Liberty-Based Society. Once our representatives control
your state legislature, they can push through a state constitutional
amendment allowing physicians to opt out the state's tort law as to
medical malpractice (in effect secede from the state's court system!)
and contract with their patients for binding arbitration. The arbitration agreement would use arbitrators who are knowledgeable about
medical malpractice and would also provide a representative to the
patient or family to guide them through the entire process. This
would ensure quick settlement of any dispute and dramatically lower
the cost of practicing medicine. Some may complain that "greedy"
physicians will not pass this savings on to the patients but keep it as a
windfall for themselves. This cannot happen, because in an unhampered free market, price competition will force physicians to lower
their charges in order to keep their patients.

Q. I am a nurse who has spent most of my adult life caring for sick
and injured patients. Today we have a terrible time filling vacancies
in the nursing profession. Most days I leave work depressed because
I could not provide the type of care to my patients that I was taught
to give. Can a Liberty-Based Society do anything about this real crisis in healthcare?

A. As I pointed out in chapter 10, the purchasing power of a nurse's
take-home pay has changed very little over the last twenty years. One
reason you have a nursing shortage is because other industries and
professions that are not as regulated by the government as healthcare
are able to compete for potential nurses with more lucrative positions.
The ability of a Liberty-Based Society to control inflation will be a
major help. In addition, the reduction of paperwork and other needless government regulations will allow nurses and other healthcare
providers to spend more time with direct patient care. An unhampered free market will provide the best resolution to our healthcare
problem, but it will not provide a perfect solution. For instance, some
hospitals are kept in business by federal grants, federal payments, and
local taxes. In an unhampered free market, these hospitals will most
likely go out of business. This will free up healthcare resources to be
spent at more efficient facilities. It is never fun when the company or
hospital for whom you work falls prey to better competitors. But to
keep inefficient hospitals or physician offices open via other people's
money provided by government is to ensure continued bad investment
in them. An unhampered free market will use competition to force
prices down and quality up and it will eliminate inefficiencies in the
healthcare system.

Property Rights and the Defense of Liberty

Why am I so concerned about property rights? The truth is that property rights are key to the defense of liberty and absolutely essential for the expansion of wealth in a society.

Suppose you are in a crowded theater and someone jumps up and shouts, "Fire!" The crowd panics and there is a mad rush for the doors. In fact there was no fire, and when the authorities capture the culprit, he claims that he has a constitutional right of free speech whereas the theater owner has no constitutional right to own a private theater. The culprit is using the same argument that liberals/socialists use in modern America. Liberals/socialists attempt to divide rights into higher and lower orders and then assign property rights to the lower-order group. Government is then free to infringe upon those lower-order rights to a much greater degree than it would have been allowed if our rights had not been divided. But does this culprit have rights higher than the property owner's? An appeal to property rights will quickly resolve the issue.

By falsely shouting "fire," the culprit has denied the theater owner his right to peacefully use his property for commercial purposes. In addition, the culprit has denied others in the audience their property rights, rights they paid for when they purchased their admission tickets. The ticket owners had a right to peacefully enjoy the property represented by the admission ticket. One right, the right of free expression/speech, should not be allowed to overrule another right—even property rights. We must be very skeptical of anyone who claims to have a right to use his special "rights" as a vehicle to deprive us of our rights.

Historical evidence of the importance of property rights can be found in the former Soviet Union. Its constitution did not forbid free speech or expression of religion. But what good was the assumed freedom of speech if people could not own a printing press or rent space in public newspapers (a type of property right)? A promise of free speech is vain and meaningless if an individual is denied all means of expression. Religion in the Soviet Union was suppressed by voiding the property rights that Russian churches had in their buildings. Again, regardless of how many promises might be made in a written constitution, those promises are useless without property rights.

CHAPTER 15

Private Property Rights and Capitalism

Even though private property was not specifically mentioned in the original Constitution, protection of private property is considered its "central purpose."[1] After the first ten amendments were ratified by the states in 1791, private property obtained the protection of the "taking" and "due process" clauses of the Fifth Amendment. The Founding Fathers demonstrated their devotion to private property in their writings during the debate over ratification of the proposed Constitution. Writing in *The Federalist,* Alexander Hamilton urged Americans to support the proposed Constitution because it would provide added safeguards "to liberty and to property." Noah Webster, from New York, also declared that "property is the basis of *power.*"[2] He wrote, "Rights are inseparably connected with the power and dignity of the people, which rest on their property."[3] Colonial Americans were following the lead of earlier English philosophers such as John Locke, who had declared in his *Second Treatise of Government* that property rights were a natural right that preceded the establishment of government. Locke stressed that the protection of property rights was one of the primary purposes for which government existed: "The great and *chief end* therefore, of Mens uniting into Common-wealths, and putting themselves under Government, *is the Preservation of their property.*"[4] Sir William Blackstone, in his *Commentaries on the Laws of England,* had declared that an Englishman's right to his property was an "absolute right, inherent in every Englishman."[5]

1. David M. O'Brien, *Constitutional Law and Politics, Civil Rights and Civil Liberties,* vol. 2, 2nd ed. (New York: W.W. Norton, 1995), 216.
2. Ibid.
3. Ibid., 217.
4. Ibid., 219.
5. Ibid., 217.

PROPERTY RIGHTS—THE DISTINCTION
BETWEEN FREE MEN AND SLAVES

Colonial Americans understood that the right to property is the primary distinction between free men and slaves—a distinction that is too often lost on modern Americans. In 1764 the British Parliament imposed the Sugar Act on the colonies. James Otis, advocate-general for the province of Massachusetts Bay, declared, "The very act of taxing, exercised over those who are not represented, appears to me to be depriving them of one of their most essential rights, as freemen; and if continued, seems to be in effect an entire disenfranchisement of every civil right. For what one civil right is worth a rush, after a man's property is subject to be taken from him at pleasure, without his consent?"[6] The colonial fathers understood the connection between property rights and human rights. The connection was so imperative to individual liberty that they were willing to challenge the Crown when those rights were threatened.

Liberals/socialists challenged the connection between property rights and human rights during the twentieth century. Federal courts began to distinguish between the two, allowing for less judicial protection of property rights. Congress submitted to liberal/socialist pressure and began to pass legislation infringing upon property rights. For example, today the Environmental Protection Agency (EPA) can nullify private property rights[7] via its authority under the Clean Water Act. Similar federal invasions of property rights are occurring in other agencies, such as the IRS and Office of Civil Rights. Under the Civil Rights Act of 1964, private-business owners can be compelled to perform acts of "involuntary servitude" for customers they might otherwise not want to serve. Under the Americans with Disabilities Act (ADA), the federal government dictates to private-business owners the general layout of their businesses and the arrangement of parking spaces. The Equal Employment Opportunities Commission (EEOC) compels business owners to hire by the numbers—as opposed to making the best business decision by hiring the most qualified, regardless of skin color.

Liberals/socialists and many well-meaning "conservatives" will rush to defend these unconstitutional infringements on property rights by declaring that these laws were needed to remedy discrimination. While private discrimination may be reprehensible, it is not

6. James Otis, as cited in "The Stamp Act Crisis: The First Defense of Freedom in America" (www.moraldefense.com).

7. Kennedy and Kennedy, *Why Not Freedom!*, 66-67.

within the purview of the federal government to interfere in a purely social matter. Arbitrary public discrimination, on the other hand, is an entirely different matter. When public monies are used to build a road, for example, it would be anti-liberty to arbitrarily deprive an individual of the right to use the road. "Arbitrarily deprive" is different from legally depriving someone of the use of public roads. Every day, society deprives certain classes of people of driving on public roads—such as the blind or those under age. Jim Crow (racial segregation) laws applied to public facilities would fall under the category of "arbitrary" discrimination.

Denial of the equality of all rights, whether property and human rights, makes all rights to property conditional. In other words, if federal authorities agree that you should be allowed to keep or use your property, then your property is yours to use as you see fit, but if not, then the federal government can place any restraints on the use of your private property it desires. Under this system, a citizen's property is held similar to the conditional standing that a serf had to the lord of the manor.

PROPERTY RIGHTS AND
HUMAN RIGHTS—TOGETHER OR NOT AT ALL

Liberty is like a large ball of wax—you cannot reduce the size of one side of the ball without automatically reducing the entire ball. Human rights and property rights are intertwined and cannot be dissected without doing harm to both. Property rights were recognized by the Founding Fathers as key to all civil rights. Indeed, virtually all of our civil liberties can be defended by an appeal to property rights.

Our first and most fundamental right is the right of self-ownership—which is in fact a property right to ourselves! What is the primary civil disadvantage that a slave suffers? A slave is denied the right of self-ownership. From the self-ownership maxim, we can extend a property right of free men to those things they create. For example, the artist who chisels a work of art from a stone (assuming the stone was in a state of nature in which its ownership was uncontested) has a right to own his masterpiece. The same property right belongs to any creation of labor (including intellectual labor exercised by investors, entrepreneurs, or manual labor) that results in income. The right of free expression is also a property right in action. What use is the promise of free expression if government denies your property right to own or purchase access to means of expression? If man is denied the use of press, or other media, the promise of free expression is vain and insulting. The right to freely assemble is void if government forbids you the use of all meeting spaces. Again, it is your property right that government is limiting, but this is of little solace for a man who wants to get his message out. The same is true of religious freedom. Christians in the former Soviet Union saw all of their churches closed, destroyed, or converted to other use. Their constitution may have promised freedom of religion for Soviet citizens, but by denying their property rights, the government effectually nullified this freedom.

When a government begins to infringe on property, that government is leading its citizens down the precarious road to serfdom. The initial steps may be tentative and appear on surface to be non-threatening, but once the precedent is set that government has the "right" to infringe on "mere" property rights, once that idea is established, the march down the road to serfdom has begun. The danger to liberty is certain, even though our leaders assure us in a most pious manner that the encumbrance of our property rights is for a "good" cause—and rest assured that all government oppressions begin as someone's "good" idea. We must jealously guard our liberty, especially when pious-sounding liberals/socialists approach it. We should watch them with the same alarm a shepherd would wolves approaching his sheep.

Murray N. Rothbard wrote:

> The basic flaw in the liberal separation of "human rights" and "property rights" is that people are treated as ethereal abstractions. If a man has the right to self-ownership, to the control of his life, then in the real world he must also have the right to sustain his life by grappling with and transforming resources; he must be able to own the ground and resources on which he stands and which he must use. In short, to sustain his "human rights"—or his property rights in his own person—he must also have the property right in the material world, in the objects which he produces. Property rights *are* human rights.[8]

CAPITALISM IS NOT A DIRTY WORD

Marxism may be dead as far as the Cold War is concerned, but it and its brother, socialism, are alive and well in modern America. The general hatred espoused by Marxists for property ownership, especially ownership by successful entrepreneurs and businessmen, comes through regularly in classrooms and media in the United States. Liberals/socialists have made a career out of appealing to envy and greed. If someone is successful and rewarded by wealth,

8. Murray N. Rothbard, *For a New Liberty: The Libertarian Manifesto*, 2nd ed. (New York: Collier, 1978), 42-43.

you can be assured that an appeal to envy will be made to justify "taxing" the rich. You will also hear calls to break up a business that has become so successful in supplying consumers with what they want that the business has gained temporary market dominance.

One of the underlying reasons that liberals/socialists hate business success is that it is indisputable evidence that the free market works and their system of government control does not. Liberals/socialists tend to avoid occupations requiring labor or business risk. In general they migrate toward careers as wordsmiths and purveyors of leftist ideas. It is not by chance that most business schools are conservative while the humanities tend to attract those who favor left-of-center— dare we say it—utopian fantasy cults and ideologies. Liberals/socialists tend to live within their own closed society. Recall the journalist in New York the morning after Nixon's unprecedented landslide that carried every state in the union other than Massachusetts who declared that she could not understand how he won, because "I don't know anybody who voted for Nixon!" Liberals/socialists are intolerant of anyone who does not accept their orthodox worldview. The view of Christianity that comes out of Hollywood is an example of this intolerance. Yet these people are now the high priests of contemporary American standards (I refuse to misuse the word "moral" standards).

Liberals/socialists are not necessarily Marxists. Some are but are afraid to admit it, while many are Fabian socialists and some are quasi-National Socialists left over from the defunct American socialist movement of the early 1900s. But most are simply utopian dreamers of the New England school of eternal "isms" and movements who hope to perfect the world through human efforts. Regardless of their pedigree, they all harbor a dislike, distrust, or outright hatred of the free market in general and capitalism in particular. They have an amazing ability to blank out reality by ignoring the absolute failure of international socialism and the destruction brought upon economies that sought to follow the "mixed" market government-control model of economic planning. Liberals/socialists maintain their devotion to government interventionism despite overwhelming proof of its failure. Their faith in government matches if not surpasses the faith of a religious fanatic.

BUT WHAT ABOUT CAPITALIST PRICE GOUGING?

Every time market conditions change, and these changes cause an increase in the price of a commodity, somewhere a liberal/socialist news program will do a documentary on "price gouging." If a new war breaks out in the Middle East, raising concerns about the delivery of crude and a subsequent increase of gasoline prices at the pumps, you can bet your paycheck that soon you will hear calls from the liberal/socialist camp for "price" controls and other government efforts to prevent price gouging. If a hurricane moves up the East Coast, increasing the demand for plywood and subsequently its price, sure as clockwork there will be accusations of price gouging. Yet I have never heard a news program explaining the economic reasons for the sudden increase in price.

Every economy—free market, controlled, or mixed[9]—must have some system to allocate scarce resources. Of course, this means that somehow it must be determined who gets these scarce resources. Well-intentioned liberals/socialists have found it impossible to define "fair," because they have no way to assure that those who get the resources will use them in the most efficient manner.

The free market, on the other hand, assigns value according to the usefulness that people see in an object and their perception (fear or lack of fear) of current or future scarcity of that object.[10] Assume that there is a limited amount of plywood on the East Coast and a hurricane is approaching. A contractor far inland needs plywood for his construction project, but homeowners on the coast need that same shipment to protect their homes. How is the value determined? It is determined by homeowners bidding up the price to the point that the contractor refuses to buy, because he feels sure that once the immediate crisis is over prices will fall. Homeowners value the plywood more and the shipment goes where it was needed the most. This is accomplished without the aid of government controllers, planners, or bureaucrats. In fact, when government injects itself into the process—all in the name of doing "good," mind you, and of course making a few political points with the populace at the same time—the market is distorted and shortages occur.

So how do we justify the increase in oil prices during times of crisis? Llewellyn H. Rockwell, Jr., wrote:

> Of course gas station owners and oil companies want to make a buck. So does everyone else, in good times and bad. They want to charge the highest price possible, consistent with the highest

9. Actually there is no such thing as a "mixed" (part free/part controlled) economy. A "mixed" economy is actually an inefficient and distorted free market economy. Liberals/socialists like to work with "mixed" economies because their government interventions assure eventual "market" failures, which of course will give them yet another opportunity to foist even more government interventions on to the "free" market—not a bad scam from their point of view.

10. Hans Sennholz, "Why Gold?" (www.mises.org, March 6, 2003).

profit. At the same time, consumers want to pay the lowest price possible. It is in the marketplace that these are sorted out in the glorious and peaceful institution of voluntary exchange, where a meeting of minds takes place and society's needs are met.

When the oil price rises, it suggests more supply is needed. More precisely, it sends two signals: to consumers it says conserve, and to producers it says invest. If nothing else changes, and people follow the price signals, the price will end up falling as consumers cut back purchases and producers bring more product to market. Putting price ceiling on oil will short circuit this mechanism, causing producers to offer no more than is currently available (or even less), and consumers to continue buying as much as they always have. Again, if nothing else changes, the result will be shortages, which the government will attempt to rectify through ever more stupid policies.[11]

Price is important, even indispensable, to the free market. It conveys vital information to both those demanding and those supplying a product. Government intervention will not solve the issue of high prices but will only distort price signals to both consumers and producers, which eventually causes poor investment or distribution (inefficiency) in the market. Gene Callahan wrote:

> With prices altered, entrepreneurs are discouraged from pursuing genuine opportunities in some area. For example, farm subsidies will make the search for more efficient methods of farming less urgent. Meanwhile, entrepreneurs pursue other opportunities that, in the unhampered market, would have been considered superfluous—consider the proliferation of lobbyists and tax accountants.[12]

In a Liberty-Based Society, the monies currently misspent (poor investment) on lobbyists and tax accountants will be invested in productive pursuits that will improve the economy's competitive position. An expanding and sustainable economy will provide more jobs and more real wealth to individual workers, and as productivity improves, prices will fall. This cannot happen in a liberal/socialist society where the free market is hampered by innumerable government interventions. Our choice is simple—more of the same under the present liberal/socialist system or a society where the individual

11. Llewellyn H. Rockwell, Jr., "War on Gougers?" (www.mises.org, Feb. 24, 2003).

12. Callahan, *Economics for Real People*, 180.

has the opportunity to increase his personal wealth (property). Not only that, but his property rights will be protected from those envious, deceitful, and/or misguided utopian dreamers who can always come up with new ways to spend other people's money.

QUESTIONS AND ANSWERS

Q. Should the federal government have a role in protecting citizens from the abuses of monopolies?

A. Monopolies cannot exist without the aid of government. For example, government will grant exclusive rights to a selected company to provide cable TV services in a given area, thereby protecting that company from the rigors of competition. In an unhampered free market, visionary companies will outdistance their competition by satisfying consumer demand for lower price and better quality, and for a short while those companies will dominate the market. This is an acceptable market condition as long as government does not limit competition or provide unfair advantage to the dominant company. If the company becomes too aggressive by charging excessive prices or becomes complacent and allows its technology to stagnate, then it will go the way of IBM—brought down by new entries and new technologies in the marketplace. But if government provides "fat" contracts, tax breaks, or other corporate welfare, an unfair advantage results that hinders the entrance of competitors. Thus the dominant company, with government help, can lower quality and increase price without great fear of young competitors threatening its market position.

Q. If you allow property rights to have the same social value as human rights, it would destroy the civil rights protection we worked so hard to enact for women, disabled, and other minorities. How can you justify such a position?

A. In the first place, I do not accept the premise that property rights are inferior rights and infringing upon them will cause no harm to individuals. You are not free if your property is subject to the arbitrary rules of partisan politicians and government bureaucrats, all of whom are working to ensure reelection of incumbents and promotion of the agendas of special interests and those businesses with close connections to the ruling elites in Washington, D.C.

Secondly, "rights" conferred upon a specific group that cannot be exercised without infringing upon preexisting rights of others will ultimately destroy the harmony of society at large. When it comes to the protection of rights, the purpose of the law is to ensure noninterference—individuals or groups will not be allowed to interfere with one's exercise of a given right.

Third, in a Liberty-Based Society individuals have the right to use their private property as they see fit, as long as it does no direct harm to others. If, for example, a black separatist opens a health-food store and does not want to serve "blue-eyed white devils," then he has the right to use his private property as he sees fit—assuming his private enterprise is not located in or on public property. If government forced him to serve someone he did not want to serve, then society, through the police power of government, would be violating his right of self-ownership and would be forcing him to be a slave to those he dislikes.

Finally, the free market will reward and punish businesses. For example; the black separatist very likely will find few customers, even among the black community. Because of his limited customer base, he will not flourish, his prices will of necessity be higher than those of "normal" health-food stores, and eventually he will go out of business. The market will punish his bigotry, but government will not infringe on his right to be a bigot and make bad decisions.

Q. It seems to me that what you describe as a Liberty-Based Society is just a pretext to return to the days of racial segregation and Jim Crow laws. How can you justify such a system?

A. Racial segregation laws were a violation of liberty. Government in a Liberty-Based Society could not pass and or enforce such laws. Remember, one of the primary tenets of government must be non-interference. If government violates individual rights by assigning children to schools according to the color of their skin, then this interferes with the right to freely choose which school to attend. The violation is no less reprehensible if government is doing it to forcefully segregate or integrate public schools. Of course, in a Liberty-Based Society, this issue would be moot because public schools would no longer exist. As I discussed in chapter 9, all education will be provided via the free market. As you can see, one of the major benefits of a Liberty-Based Society is that it limits the role government plays in public affairs.

My argument is with the use of government force to compel social engineering, regardless of the excuse used to screen that force to deprive one group of citizens of their rights. We are moving forward toward the day of individual liberty and economic prosperity and have no time to look backward to the days of Jim Crow segregation. But our opponents do spend a lot of time in the past! They claim to see Jim Crow around every corner and use it as a talisman or magic wand to frighten away those who would consider leaving the liberal/socialist plantation and seeking a better life of liberty and self-reliance.

Avoiding Past Failures

In order to increase the probability of political success, we must avoid several things.

1. We must not pin our hopes on a charismatic leader. George Wallace and Ross Perot are examples of two leaders whose political movements collapsed when the leader was shot or just decided to abandon the effort. We must place our primary effort on promoting the ideology of liberty as opposed to promoting a leader who will "save us" from the evil liberal/ socialist empire.

2. We must not allow our movement to get bogged down in tactical issues even though the issues are good and worthy of success. Success will come to all of our issues once we establish a Liberty-Based Society. We must take a strategic approach and not allow the enemy to tempt us into exhausting our limited resources on peripheral issues. Such issues will take care of themselves once *we the people* of the Sovereign States have control of our destiny.

3. We must make sure all our people have a clear vision of what a Liberty-Based Society will look like and why they should support our candidates, who will be responsible for establishing the political foundations of our free society.

4. Organizations clutter the conservative landscape like so many old cars up on cinder blocks across the countryside. Organizations we have—what we need is a bold vision of a better world and an audacious plan to make it happen. We must stress the importance of organized efforts to promote our vision and our plan for a Liberty-Based Society without becoming entangled in the preening of yet another organization.

5. At all costs we must avoid the failure of not understanding the importance of a "mass" educational effort. Conservatives spend an inordinate amount of time "preaching to the choir" and then we wonder why the mass of voters will not elect our candidates. Our organized effort must be primarily (as in almost completely) directed at winning the hearts and minds of average citizens, people who typically do not get involved in political causes but who do tend to vote conservatively.

6. As individuals and as groups, we must avoid ego issues and infighting. How often have we seen a group of conservative activists split over an issue that is essentially an ego problem, resulting in the destruction of an effective group? Too often during such infighting, I have heard adults declare that not only are they leaving the group but they are determined to get even with their personal nemeses. Regardless of who we are or what we have done for the cause, our personal ego is not more important than the success of our cause. Present and future generations are depending on us to set aside self and work for the establishment of a Liberty-Based Society. They will judge us accordingly.

CHAPTER 16

Political Reality

If we keep doing what we have always done, it should not surprise us when we end up with what we've always had! If you like the welfare state, the best way to keep it is to continue doing what we have been for the past century. If you like inflation, affirmative action, racial quotas, high taxes, government by judges, increased crime, and the general dumbing down of our society, then keep doing what we have always done. It is really very simple. To maintain the status quo, all we have to do is reelect business-as-usual politicians, pin our hopes on contemporary "conservative" leaders, and avoid at all cost any controversy that might endanger their reelection. In a phrase, all we need to do is continue "meeting, eating, and retreating"! But what about those of us who are not satisfied with the status quo and not afraid of being labeled "extremists" when it comes to defending liberty? There is another option for the bold and daring—the movement to establish a Liberty-Based Society.

The logic of political action and how it can be used to restore liberty have been explained in *Why Not Freedom!*[1] and will not be repeated here. Following are seven steps necessary to initiate and carry through a political struggle to establish a Liberty-Based Society. Many may inquire whether it is possible for a small but dedicated group to change the current liberal/socialist society into a Liberty-Based Society. Not only is it possible, but with organized effort, it is highly probable! Note that I said *organized effort,* not another organization. Organizations we have aplenty— what is lacking is a visionary idea for a better society and audacious plans to implement it.

---

1. Kennedy and Kennedy, *Why Not Freedom!,* 257-69, 299-308.

255

FIRST STEP: PROMOTE THE IDEA
OF A LIBERTY-BASED SOCIETY

The first step initially belongs to the author of this book. Books sitting in a warehouse will do nothing for the cause of liberty. The first step after publication will be to spread the word about this book and the possibility of a Liberty-Based Society through book reviews, radio/TV interviews, paid advertisements in pro-liberty journals, and, for the first time, a direct-mail campaign aimed at conservative voters, most of whom will be hearing about this movement for the first time. We no longer will spend all our time "preaching to the choir." As we move to steps two and three, others, hopefully like you, will take on the responsibility for promoting the idea of a Liberty-Based Society.

SECOND STEP: ORGANIZING LIBERTY WORKING GROUPS

Every city and county will eventually have a group of individuals who will be responsible for convincing their friends and neighbors of the need to establish a Liberty-Based Society. These working groups will be responsible for funding direct-mail campaigns in their areas and other activities aimed at converting business-as-usual conservatives into champions of liberty.

THIRD STEP: PREPARE FOR POLITICAL ACTION

Each month the central committee of the Liberty movement (composed of me, my twin brother, and representatives from each state) will send out direct-mail materials on behalf of local working groups. The local working groups will be responsible for contacting individuals who respond to direct-mail solicitations. The idea is to build a grassroots political organization in every city and county. Local working groups will organize local and statewide political-action training sessions to educate supporters on the philosophy of a Liberty-Based Society and provide practical training on effective political activities.

FOURTH STEP: RUN IN GOP PRESIDENTIAL PRIMARY

The logic (brilliance) of contesting the Republican presidential primary is that it gives us a political campaign that is not distorted by the liberal, black, bloc vote.[2] The Republican presidential primary provides us with an opportunity to run in an election that will be decided basically by conservatives. We will not be running against labor unions, NAACP types, and other liberal pressure groups. We

2. Note my complaint is not with "black" but "liberal bloc" voting.

will be taking our message to our people. If we perform step three correctly, we will have an excellent probability of carrying the majority of primaries! The media coverage of such a campaign will make our cause table talk, not only in the South but all across the United States. Remember that the main purpose of these initial political campaigns is to normalize the idea of overturning the present liberal/socialist political system and replacing it with a Liberty-Based model. From this point of view, no matter what the eventual results of this particular election bid might be, we win!

FIFTH STEP: GOP PLATFORM AND
VICE-PRESIDENTIAL NOMINATION

If we work together and perform steps one, two, three, and four correctly, we will win a substantial number of GOP delegates. When we arrive at the national GOP convention, our aim will be to hang the neoconservatives and business-as-usual politicians on the horns of a dilemma—accept our candidate as their nominee for president or at a minimum vice-president and endorse the State Sovereignty Amendment in their platform, or else we will pull out and run a third-party presidential campaign. The third-party presidential campaign will in effect be a plebiscite for Southern independence! The emergence of a modern-day Southern independence movement based on the idea of liberty will be a powerful force that will compel Americans to reconsider the continuation of the current liberal/socialist political system. Although this independence movement will be based in the South, it will extend an active and open invitation to people in all states to join our movement to establish a Liberty-Based Society. Indeed, we hope to see people from numerous non-Southern states flocking to this movement. Our aim must be to establish a Liberty-Based Society—in the present United States if that is the desire of the people, but if not, then we will settle for nothing less than our own Liberty-Based Society in a free and independent South.

SIXTH STEP: STATE AND LOCAL POLITICAL ACTION

Assume that the GOP rejects our demands (not hard to imagine) and that we win a substantial vote in the third-party presidential campaign. We have now normalized the idea of a Liberty-Based Society, and we now have action groups in every city and county. Our next step is to begin contesting local and state elections. Our aim will be to capture control of every governor's office, legislature, and local office, all the way down to constable.

At the same time, Congress will slowly fill with our candidates,

Southerners who are dedicated to adding our State Sovereignty Amendment to the Constitution. As far as the South is concerned, the days of party politics will be over. No longer will *we the people* of the South be taken for granted by the Republican party or ignored by the Democratic party.

At the state level, our elected leaders will constantly embarrass the federal authorities. For example, when Chief Justice Roy Moore of the Alabama Supreme Court challenged the federal government by placing the Ten Commandants in the court building, we all knew what the outcome would be. Now we will conduct similar campaigns but always for the purpose of demonstrating to *we the people* the need to remove ourselves from such an oppressive political system. We move from vain acts to acts of *political civil disobedience.* States will pass and attempt to enforce legitimate non-arbitrary voting qualifications. What will be the federal government's response? We know ahead of time, but we act in order to force the federal government to demonstrate its oppressive nature. Our states will pass laws forbidding racial quotas. We know the response, but we do it anyway. Our aim is to rouse the public and put the federal government on notice that we are no longer willing to play the game by their rules! All manner of public discourse and action (boycotts, petitions, international appeals, etc.) will be organized for the sole purpose of removing the current liberal/socialist political model and replacing it with a Liberty-Based model.

SEVENTH STEP: PASSAGE OF THE STATE SOVEREIGNTY AMENDMENT OR SOUTHERN INDEPENDENCE

All political efforts will be aimed at the restoration of the original constitutional Republic of Republics in the United States. But we must not be overoptimistic. Liberals/socialists and special interest groups have a lot to lose and will do everything they can to prevent the introduction of this amendment, let alone allow their states to ratify it. Therefore, we must face the fact that if non-Southern states will not respect our rights, we must demand our independence. The threat alone may be sufficient. But alas, when freedom is at stake, we must be willing to save our own society, even if our neighbors in other areas of the country are not interested in preserving their liberty.

There is much to do, but every journey begins with the first step. This book is the first step. But eventually, if we are to be successful, we must coordinate our efforts. We must be willing to set aside personal agendas and concentrate on the struggle to establish a Liberty-Based Society. There are many conservative activists who work hard for special interest issues such as preservation of Confederate heritage, pro-life, Second Amendment pro-gun rights, and restoring moral decency to America. While these are all good causes, tactically they consume a large amount of our limited energies while leaving the underlying problem unsolved. I recommend a strategic approach that, once accomplished, will alleviate most of the tactical issues that we now expend valuable time and energy on. Under the present system, liberals/socialists can start more brush fires than we will ever be able to fight. Why not just take their matches away? We have seen the results of a century of conservative failure. It is now time for us to "think out of the box" and adopt a bold strategy that will lead us to victory. Remember Gen. George Patton's favorite saying: "Audacity, audacity, always audacity."

QUESTIONS AND ANSWERS

Q. You say that you do not want to start another organization. How can we establish a Liberty-Based Society without an organization to push our ideas and educate our people?

A. I do not want to start a formal organization. One of the best ways to kill a good idea is to subject it to the strictures of Robert's Rules of Order! What I want to see is an organized effort of men, women, and young people all across the South and many non-Southern states as well. These Liberty working groups will be responsible for financing the mass mailings in their states, congressional districts, counties, or cities. We will form a central committee to handle the direct-mailing campaign and provide the local work groups with names and addresses of people who respond to that campaign. Local groups will be free to meet as they desire and take on other local activities to advance the knowledge of our cause. Once a year we will meet to review our progress and provide an opportunity for working-group members to review our financial records, to assure everyone that all of their money is being used to directly promote the cause. During the year my brother (Donald) and I will be visiting Southern and some non-Southern communities to encourage the work of promoting the cause. There will be ample opportunity for dedicated individuals to contribute their time, talent, and treasure to this movement. But we do not want to become entangled in internal wrangling and attempts to gain control of yet another conservative organization.

Q. I understand that once we have done the groundwork of educating a large number of conservatives about our movement, we will run for the presidential nomination in the Republican primary. How will we decide who our candidate will be?

A. The year before the beginning of the presidential primary, our working groups will meet. A list of all of those who have been actively involved in a working group for at least one year and who express an interest in running will be given out. We will then vote, and the person who wins will be our candidate. Our aim will be to use this effort to normalize the concept of overthrowing the liberal/socialist political system and replacing it with a Liberty-Based Society. If we do our jobs correctly during the years leading up to the GOP presidential primary, we will most assuredly complete the primary with the entire conservative South and many non-Southern states understanding the value of supporting our cause. Remember, this primary is not the end; it is only the beginning of our political revolution.

Q. Why run just in the South? Why not run in every state?

A. We will use the South as our base of support. The number of non-Southern states involved will depend upon their reception of our cause. We must concentrate our efforts in areas where we have spent the most preparatory time and effort.

Q. What makes you think that you, your brother, or some other candidate that will be selected will be able to do better than other conservatives such as Alan Keyes, Phil Gramm, or Pat Buchanan?

A. These other conservatives that you mentioned were attempting to work within the system. Their efforts, while commendable, have not changed the political circumstances, nor do such efforts hold much promise of success in the near or distant future. Our plans are audacious, but at least we recognize that we can never win playing by the rules as established by the current liberal/socialist society. We can win because we will first take our message to *we the people* of the Sovereign States. Our base will be the very people who have suffered the most under the current system. Prior to the initiation of the primary campaign, we will identify thousands of supporters in every Southern state. Our campaign will be unlike anything ever seen in the United States! By the end of the presidential election, there will be no home in the country that has not heard about our struggle to overthrow the liberal/socialist political system and replace it with a Liberty-Based Society. At that point, the struggle will have just begun. In the next phase, we will gain political power in states all across the South, and who knows, perhaps in numerous non-Southern states as well.

Deo Vindice

ADDENDUM I

Monetary Policy and the Free Market
BY JÖRG GUIDO HÜLSMANN

The fundamental issue in banking and monetary policy is whether government can improve the monetary institutions of the unhampered market. All government intervention in this field boils down to schemes that increase the quantity of money beyond what it otherwise would be. The libertarian case for the abolishment of government intervention in money and banking rests on the insight that the latter serves only redistributive purposes.

Monetary policy is concerned with modifications of the quantity of money. Although policymakers might ultimately seek to control interest rates, unemployment or a stock-market index, the attempt to realize any of these goals through monetary policy presupposes the ability to modify the quantity of money.

For example, to reduce short-term interest rates, policymakers must be in a position to produce additional quantities of money and offer them on the so-called money market, lest they could not exercise any downward pressure on rates at all. Hence, the crucial question is: Who should be allowed to produce or destroy money, and which goals should thereby be pursued?

Banking policy is concerned with analogous questions. Rather than dealing with the production of money it deals with the production of money titles, which can be instantly redeemed into money—as opposed to credit titles or IOUs, which can be redeemed into money only at some future point of time. A bank in the sense that is relevant for banking policy is a firm that issues money titles. The latter include bank notes, check books, credit cards, Internet accounts, Smart Cards, etc. Who should be allowed to issue such money titles, for which purposes, and in which quantities? These are the main questions in banking policy.

The Unhampered Production of Money

On the free market, every individual would have the right to invest his labor and his property in the production of money and to sell or give away his product as he himself sees fit. Every money producer would in this sense pursue his own monetary policy just as each shoe manufacturer in selling his products pursues his own "foot fashion policy."

The two main questions of monetary policy are thus answered by the very organizing principle of the market: private property. Each individual is a policymaker, making policy with his own property. And each individual pursues the goals that he would like to pursue.

Historically, very different sorts of commodities (gold, silver, copper, shells, tobacco, cotton, etc.) have been used as money. Yet gold and silver have tended to drive out the other monies from the currency market because of their superior qualities for various monetary functions: they are homogenous, durable, easy to recognize, easy to shape, etc.

Their production is subject to the same laws that rule the production of other commodities. Hence, the "monetary policy" of mine owners and of each mint is strictly oriented toward consumer satisfaction; the quantities produced depending only on consumer demand.

Since paper currencies are the dominant type of money in our age, there has been some speculation about the possibility of a free market in paper money or electronic money. Yet not only is there no historical evidence to support this possibility, but non-commodity monies have at all times and places been creatures of the state.

In modern times, the state has introduced paper money by giving a privileged note-issuing bank (the national Central Bank) the permission to suspend the redemption of its notes. While the historical record does not prove that there could be no non-commodity money on the free market, Austrian economists have argued that money must be a commodity by its nature.

Free-Market Banking

On the free market, every individual would have the right to become a banker. Everybody could offer to store other people's money and issue money titles, which in turn would document the fact that money has been deposited with him and can be redeemed at any time.

Conceivably, bankers would also propose investment schemes that bear a certain resemblance to the business of storing money and issuing money titles. For example, they could offer to issue IOUs for money invested in their bank and try to make these IOUs more attractive by promising to liquidate them on demand at face value. They might even issue them in forms that are virtually identical with the forms in which money titles appear: "bank notes," "smart cards," "credit cards," etc. And this in turn might induce some market participants to accept these IOUs as payment in market exchanges, just as they occasionally accept a mortgage or a stock-market paper as payment.

Some economists think that such investment schemes have been realized in the past and call them "fractional-reserve banking." They also use the term "bank notes" to describe the aforementioned IOUs. Still it is important to be aware of the essential differences that exist between them and money titles. Despite resemblance in appearance and use, money title gives claims to money, while the promise to redeem an IOU gives claims to an effort by the banker. While all money titles can be redeemed at any time, if too many receipt owners desire such liquidation at the same time only a part of these IOUs can be liquidated as promised by the banker.

Identical names and identical outer appearance of both money titles and liquid IOUs are not a mere coincidence. In most historical cases, bankers issuing liquid IOUs took pains to hide the real differences distinguishing their product from genuine money titles. Insofar as such efforts are meant to deceive other market participants, fractional-reserve banking is a fraudulent scheme that violates the principles of the free market and merely serves to enrich some individuals (the bankers and their customers) at the expense of all others.

More on Money and Money Titles

This tendency to conflate money and money titles has never ceased ever since 20th-century government decrees fundamentally transformed the nature of central banks and central bank notes. These decrees have (a) given the national central banks the privilege to deny note redemption to their customers and (b) protected these irredeemable central-bank notes by legal tender laws. For lack of better alternatives in the short run, the central bank notes stayed in circulation. Yet now these notes no longer were money titles since they could not be redeemed against anything else. They had become independent goods: paper money.

Similarly, the central banks were no longer banks at all, but had become money producers. Confusion about this transformation was bound to spread since, physically, both the central bank notes and the central bank itself continued to exist without any change of their appearance—an interesting case of what could be called economic transubstantiation.

This does not mean that money titles ceased to exist. In fact, the government-enacted establishment of paper currencies transformed only the central banks and their products. All other banks continued to issue money titles, with the only difference that the titles they issued referred no longer to the old commodity money, but to the new paper money. Today, the neglect of the fundamental distinction between money and money titles has led to vast speculations about internet money, etc.

Money Production, Banking, and the Government

The great issue in monetary and banking policy is whether free-market banking and the free-market production of money can be improved by schemes relying on coercion. The history of monetary analysis and policy has been the history of debates on the insufficiencies of the unhampered market and on how to remedy them with statist monetary schemes. Virtually all these discussions have revolved around problems of alleged money shortage, and the essence of all institutions designed to overcome these problems is to produce more money than could possibly be produced on the unhampered market.

Mercantilist writers argued that more money meant higher prices and lower interest rates, and that these in turn invigorate commerce and industry. Moreover, taxes can be levied more easily in a monetary than in a barter economy. Thus the mercantilists urged to stimulate imports of gold and silver through tariffs on foreign goods and export subsidies for domestic products. They endorsed fractional-reserve banking to the benefit of the Crown, and they supported special monopoly privileges for "national" or "central" banks.

They had a point: The kings very much profited from increased monetary circulation, which made looting their subjects far easier. However, the French physiocrats and the British classical economists entirely destroyed the rest of the mercantilist scheme. Tariffs and export subsidies cannot permanently increase the domestic money supply, and the amount of money circulating in the economy has no positive impact on trade and industry considered as a whole.

The great contribution of The Currency School to the theory of monetary policy was to show that increasing the quantity of money did not increase the amount of services that money rendered for the nation as a whole. A higher money supply merely leads to higher money prices, but it does not affect aggregate industry and aggregate real output. This is what they had in mind when speaking of money as a "veil" that is superimposed on the physical economy.

Later economists further refined this analysis by giving a more sophisticated account of the impact of money on the real economy. They showed that increases in the money supply bring about two forms of redistribution of income. On the one hand, an increased money supply means that the purchasing power of each money unit is diluted. If this loss of purchasing power is not anticipated, it benefits borrowers at the expense of lenders.

On the other hand, and independently of the anticipations of the market participants, the new money first reaches only some market participants who can now buy more out of an unchanged supply of real goods. All others will buy less at higher prices, since the spending of the additional money units raises the market prices. Hence, while variations of the quantity of money bring no overall improvement for the national economy, they benefit some persons, industries, and regions at the expense of all other market participants.

For a hundred years, the idea that a community could promote its well-being by increasing the money supply beyond what it would be on the unhampered market was discredited among professional economists, even though the influential S. J. Mill undermined this monetary orthodoxy by various concessions.

Then John Maynard Keynes almost single-handedly gave a new life to the old mercantilist policies. The charismatic Keynes was the best-known economist of the best-known economics department of his time. In his writings, public speeches, and private conversations, he used his personal and institutional prestige to promote the idea that multiplying money could achieve more than simply redistribute income in favor of the government and the groups that control it.

Keynesianism has vastly increased government control over the economy. It has given modern states the justification to engage in social engineering on an unheard-of scale and to deeply transform social relations, the geographical allocation of resources, and mass psychology. However, Keynes's greatest legacy is that his ideas keep guiding present-day research in monetary economics.

Today, virtually all publications in academic journals take it for granted that Keynes was right and monetary orthodoxy wrong. Based on the tacit assumption that government can improve money and banking, thus increasing aggregate output, mainstream debates turn around issues of interest for government policymakers. Such issues are, for example, the definition of various monetary aggregates, signaling through the behavior of central-bank officials, various insurance schemes for financial intermediaries, and indicators to predict the impact of monetary policy on prices, interest rates, production, and employment.

There are also free-market economists who discard monetary orthodoxy and try to make the case for a free market in money and banking on mercantilist-Keynesian premises. These economists argue that the supply of money has to be constantly adapted to match the needs of trade or to bring about monetary equilibrium, etc. Yet they think that the institutions needed to ensure this permanent adaptation are most likely to emerge on the unhampered market.

It is difficult to predict which course mainstream thinking in banking and monetary policy will take. For libertarian monetary economists, there are ample and largely unexplored research opportunities relating in particular to the impact of a government-controlled money supply on the economy and on society at large, and to the best ways to abolish government intervention in money and banking.

Bibliography

Anderson, Benjamin. *The Value of Money.* Reprint, Spring Mills, Pa.: Libertarian, 1999.

Austrian Study Guide on Money and Banking, The.

Hayek, Friedrich August. *The Denationalisation of Money.* 2nd ed. London: Institute for Economic Affairs, 1977.

Hazlitt, Henry. *From Bretton Woods to World Inflation.* Chicago: Regnery Gateway, 1984.

Huerta de Soto, Jesús. *Dinero, crédit obancario y ciclos económicos.* Madrid: Unión Editorial, 1998.

Hülsmann, Jörg Guido. *Logik der Währungskonkurrenz.* Essen: Management Akademie Verlag, 1996.

Mises, Ludwig von. *Theory of Money and Credit.* Indianapolis: Liberty Fund, 1980.

Paul, Ron, and Lewis Lehrman. *The Case for Gold.* Washington, D.C.: Cato Institute, 1982.

Rothbard, Murray N. *What Has Government Done to Our Money?* 4th ed. Auburn, Ala.: Ludwig von Mises Institute, 1990.

Salin, Pascal. *La vérité sur la monnaie.* Paris: Odile Jacob, 1990.

Selgin, George. *The Theory of Free Banking.* Totowa, N.J.: Rowman & Littlefield, 1988.

Sennholz, Hans. *Money and Freedom.* Spring Mills, Pa.: Libertarian, 1985.

White, Lawrence H. *The Theory of Monetary Institutions.* Oxford: Blackwell, 1999.

Jörg Guido Hülsmann (jgh@mises.org) is a senior fellow of the Ludwig von Mises Institute. This essay was posted on their site on Oct. 10, 2003.

ADDENDUM II

The Economy Pulls an All-Nighter
BY PAUL CWIK

When economic times are good, people pay very little attention to the work of economists. Only when an economy experiences a downturn do people come to economists asking how this latest disaster happened and how do we get out of it. Unfortunately, the economist tends to speak in a cryptic language using references to things like the NAIRU, the short and long-run Phillips curves, and detrended variables found in stochastic processes.

While the Austrian Business Cycle theory (ABCT) doesn't contain as much jargon as alternative theories of the business cycle, the ABCT is a complex theory that sometimes seems just as confusing and impenetrable to the average reader. In order to overcome this obstacle, perhaps an explanation and an analogy may help. In the course of a business cycle, the ABCT observes that the economy moves through five phases: credit expansion, a malinvestment boom, a crunch, a recession, and a recovery phase.

The Austrian theory states that the initial cause of the business cycle is an artificial injection of credit into the economy. This injection falsifies market signals which induce entrepreneurs to engage in investment projects that are not in alignment with the wishes of the consuming public. These projects are called "malinvestments." While the malinvestments are under construction, there is a boom in the economy. However, this artificial high cannot last forever and sooner or later there is a crunch. The economy either hits a credit crunch (with rising interest rates), a real resource crunch (with rising input prices), or a combination of the two. As the interest rates and prices rise, the malinvestments are liquidated. Much pain is involved in the liquidation process. Only after the malinvestments are cleared from the system will the economy have a solid foundation on which to recover.

To help explain this complex story, an analogy seems to help.

Suppose that, in his 8:00 a.m. class, a student was assigned a paper which is due tomorrow. Of course, he has not yet started working on it. In order to finish the paper on time, he decides to pull an "all-nighter."

As he types along, he starts to feel sleepy. So what does he do? He takes some No-Doze and chases it down with a Jolt Cola ("Twice the Caffeine, and All the Sugar"). This artificial stimulant puts him on an artificial high. Around 2:00 a.m., the effects of the caffeine start to wear off and he has a choice: either take more caffeine or go to bed. Since he is not done with his paper, he chooses to take more caffeine, but this time he has to increase the dosage to get the same effect.

The additional credit in the economy has the same effect as the caffeine in this example. The economy is sent on an artificial boom. The effects of the new credit eventually wear off as the stimulus on real business activity is transformed into increases in prices. The monetary authorities face a choice between further expanding the money supply, or letting the economy "go to sleep." However, an economy doesn't go to sleep, instead it must clear out the effects of the stimulant through the process of liquidation. When the monetary authorities expand the money supply, they must expand it at a rate greater than before to get the same effect.

Now our procrastinating student's roommate comes back from a late night of studying and finds his friend asleep at the keyboard. Knowing that his friend's grade depends on this paper, the roommate wakes him. The student gulps down more caffeine, and gets back to work. However, his mental processes are not at 100% efficiency. He tries to be productive, but his body is reaching its limit. His roommate finds him asleep at the keyboard, yet again, and rouses him. Again the student is jarred back to consciousness. Again our hapless student is not working productively.

When the monetary authority tries to stimulate the economy before the malinvestments are fully liquidated, it is acting in the same manner as the persistent roommate. The economy attempts to get back to previous levels of growth, but because there are many malinvestments that are tied up in nonproductive activities, the economy cannot achieve its potential.

Finally, the student is done with his paper and rushes to his 8:00 a.m. class to hand it in. Now, he can "crash." However, the economy is not so lucky. It is never able to sleep, but it can crash. There comes a point where there are so many resources tied up in malinvestments that a real resource crunch occurs. There are too few resources to complete all the current projects. Despite the monetary authorities' best efforts to "wake up" the economy, it refuses to get back to high levels of growth. It must go through the liquidation process (sleep) before it can again recover on a solid foundation.

Let's say the student is only permitted a few hours sleep before he is awakened again, perhaps by a phone call from his teacher. He is told that he must do revisions. He gets to work on them but, again, the student under performs. So he is awakened again to undertake more revisions. This wake-sleep pattern continues as the student enters into a long decline. This is an interdeterminate stage of the cycle that corresponds very closely to what in economics is considered a secular stagnation of under performance punctuated by bursts of positive signs which only lead to disappointment. The policy authorities try every method to "get the economy going" again (deficit spending, more inflation, protectionism, etc.) but the positive effect, to the extent there is one, is always short term. This seems to correspond to where the US is today.

The lessons from this tale are not only to avoid procrastination and do one's papers early; it also recommends to the monetary authority, that despite the temporary benefits of credit stimulation, the result is a recession. Furthermore, once a malinvestment boom is under way, a recession is a necessary step to return the economy back to a healthy growth rate. Let the student sleep so that he can do better work later!

Paul Cwik (cwik@mises.org) is completing his dissertation as a fellow for the Ludwig von Mises Institute. This essay was posted on their site on Oct. 6, 2003.

ADDENDUM III

The Three Stooges

BY JOSEPH SOBRAN

For the last week we have been reminded by various pundits that the justices of the U.S. Supreme Court are "unpredictable," often surprising the presidents who appointed them. It would be more accurate to put it more narrowly: justices appointed by Republican presidents often issue the most liberal rulings.

Think of Earl Warren and William Brennan (Eisenhower picks); Harry Blackmun (Nixon); John Paul Stevens (Ford); Sandra Day O'Connor and Anthony Kennedy (Reagan); and David Souter (the first Bush). Felix Frankfurter, chosen by Franklin Roosevelt, was the last justice named by a Democrat who turned out to be less liberal than expected.

What gets into these people? Who knows? But they have a strong incentive to move leftward once they get on the bench: glory. The more sweepingly liberal the ruling, the more surely the press will hail it as a "historic" or "landmark" decision—words seldom if ever applied to conservative rulings. The Republican appointee who racks up enough of these "historic" rulings can be assured of flattering profiles in the *New York Times* and the *Washington Post,* cooing that he (or she) has "grown" in the office, "abandoned ideology" (translation: adopted liberalism), and "surprised friend and foe alike" (translation: betrayed friends).

These encomia are to justices what rave reviews are to an actor. They go to the head. They also serve notice to other Republican appointees that the way to get flattering headlines is to disappoint and outrage conservatives. Besides, liberals love it when supposed conservatives do their work for them. In 1973 the Court's liberals, particularly William Brennan and William O. Douglas, realized that they would take less heat if Harry Blackmun, recently named to the Court by Richard Nixon, wrote the majority opinion striking down the abortion laws of all 50 states. So Blackmun served as their

271

willing stooge and reaped praise in the big liberal media for the rest of his life.

O'Connor, Kennedy, and Souter are now the Court's three Republican stooges. Souter is so liberal he hardly counts anymore, but the press still calls O'Connor and Kennedy "moderates," preserving their cover. All three of them came through for the liberals last week. O'Connor and Kennedy wrote the majority opinions in the affirmative action and sodomy cases.

To them the glory goes for this week's *Times* headline gloating that in the just-completed term, "Court Remakes Law." Now "remaking" the law isn't actually part of the Court's job description; the Constitution seems to assume that the Court will merely expound the law and abide by it. But "Court Sticks to Law" would be a dull headline. Definitely not front-page stuff.

For liberals, the Constitution as written is boring old music. They want the Court to play ingenious new variations on it, jazzing it up with penumbras and emanations until it sounds like a totally different work, one they can really dig. In the sodomy case, Kennedy and O'Connor proved themselves virtuosos of the non sequitur. They agreed that sodomy laws "discriminate" against homosexuals as a "class" or "group." Kennedy, ever the metaphysician, added that such laws "demean their existence."

But of course the law in question said nothing about classes or groups; it merely forbade specific sexual acts. You might as well say that laws against theft "discriminate" against burglars as a class (or should we say "demean the existence of the larcenous community"?). By Kennedy's logic, laws forbidding the sodomizing of children discriminate against pedophiles as a class. Where do you draw the line? You can't. Kennedy's and O'Connor's style of thinking makes it impossible to draw any lines except arbitrary ones. They are engaged in what might be called jurisprudence *sans frontieres*. It's not the rule of law, it's empty verbal improvisation.

Substitute *pedophilia* for *sodomy,* and the Kennedy-O'Connor arguments could have served just as well to declare pedophilia laws unconstitutional. In fact such laws could have been condemned for adding another dimension of "discrimination": age. Such nebulous free-association reasoning can lead anywhere, depending on the personal preferences of the justices. I was about to say that I'd hate to live in a country where the law could mean whatever its rulers said it meant, when it occurred to me that I already do.

This essay was posted on www.sobran.com on July 3, 2003.

ADDENDUM IV

The Bipartisan War Machine

BY HUNT TOOLEY

The desperately sad situations in Iraq and Afghanistan, and the dramatic contrast between the promises and the realities of war, have brought into sharp relief the moral and practical calamity of U.S. foreign policy. But while it is tempting to fix blame on only the current managers who occupy the White House, we must also consider the larger picture.

The neoconservative clique and their partners have deepened the commitment to American empire, but Republicans hold no monopoly on building empire in the recent history of our country.

The Bill Clinton regime, now seemingly forgotten except as a kind of Camelot II by the American Left, featured most of the same patterns of imperial conquest and domestic repression, though all of this was marked by Clinton's inimitable style. A different cast of characters achieved the same result with the same methods for the same ends.

For example, the bombing of Serbians to spread democracy, though dwarfed by the latter attack, was in principle little different from the conquest of Iraq. It is vital to remember that the bombing of at least something or someone in Iraq went on practically every day for all the years between the Gulf wars, as did the murderous embargo. Most of this destruction belonged to Clinton.

Indeed, even now much of the bold Democratic (that is to say, social democratic) opposition to the war in Iraq comes from folks who were happy enough to see the war happen, though earlier this year some of those war supporters did add the reservation that our slaughter of Iraqis would be better if we did it in unison with the United Nations.

The hard, antiwar left, was no part of this, but note well that most of the leading Washington Democratic politicos and pundits now coming out as opponents of the Occupation supported both the Serbian war and the war on Iraq.

The greater pattern runs like this, and in some measure it is derived from a system of empire and "democracy" reaching back to the Great Crusade of 1861-1865. We invade some country with some laudable Jacobin slogan on our lips: "make the world safe for democracy," "the four freedoms," "winning the hearts and minds," etc. We demonize the ruler of said country, making him into the "face of evil," so that those in our land who can't quite grasp the meaning of a "crusade for humanity" can latch onto the more prosaic goal of killing a really bad guy. (This is easy enough, since most leaders of modern countries have plenty of skeletons in their closets.)

At the end of the victorious crusade, we "reconstruct" the country, with price tags rising war-by-war. Part of this money goes [to] enhance the power and size of the military establishment policing the occupation. Part of it goes toward rooting out and expropriating of certain chosen, and wealthy, intractable ruling elites and setting up deserving new elites who will be friendly. Part funds the physical reconstruction of the damage done during the war (most of which we did ourselves—some of it at least, gratuitous).

This last part is critical, since it is done by awarding "contracts" to American or other firms to do the work. Most of the contracts are awarded far in advance, and those businesses which receive the contracts will always be among the deserving companies that supported the war in any case. Note well that the United States of America then pays for or organizes the funds for reconstruction of the defeated country. These funds are always based on money taxed or otherwise extracted (through inflation, confiscation, etc.) from private citizens and then handed over to selected firms who support the current administration.

The continuities of this pattern through the alternative Democratic and Republican administrations are absolute, but the alternation provides much scope for Democratic and Republican pundits to be alternately warlike crusaders and rational peace-lovers, depending on how their partisan loyalties match with current political culpability.

All throughout the Clinton years, the Republicans were developing strong anti-empire and even antiwar tendencies. They decried nation building and took steps toward seeing the war machine as an integral part of the problem of big government. During the presidential campaign, Bush tapped into this sense by decrying "national building" and calling for a "humble" foreign policy.

This critique of Clinton's foreign policy didn't stop there. Some on the right began delving into the interest-group analysis along the lines of the old left. A case in point is an important Newsmax story by Carl Limbacher and Caron Grich from 1999, entitled "The Caspian Connection." The story contextualizes the Serbian war by showing the geographic and geopolitical connections of the Balkans and Caspian oil. It is still important to read.

And yet, in the end, it didn't stick. Newsmax.com is a "conservative" news source which follows a kind of Rush Limbaugh trajectory in equating conservatism with whatever the Republican National Committee is cooking up at the moment.

Now that the Bush administration has, seemingly for very different reasons, chosen to invade and occupy two countries which bracket the crucial oil-bearing region, Newsmax.com only runs oil-related stories which bolster the pro-war line, emphasizing competition with the Russians, the need for a "stable" supply of oil, etc. See for example the article from [a] year ago on the Pipeline.

Paleoconservatives and libertarians know this already: though the alternating regimes look different, they tend to follow a series of intertwined policies. Empire is so useful, in both domestic and foreign policy, that no modern administration would be able to resist, even if it wanted to. In fact, since the "teams" are built in advance for precisely this kind of game, there is no way that any new administration would want to.

The Bush White House displays more decorum than the lubricious establishment of la Boca Grande (to borrow from Westbrook Pegler) and the Big Jerk, but its goals and accomplishments are in their essence the same, and its success rate is actually a good deal better. The Dick Cheney strategy differs little from the Madeleine Albright strategy, though each is pleased to point to the failures and missteps of the other.

And the results will be the same: bigger, more intrusive government at home; a world of perpetual war for perpetual peace abroad. The job of a serious believer in liberty is to learn to distinguish between a politically driven attack and a fundamental critique, avoiding the former and focusing as much energy as possible on the latter.

Hunt Tooley (htooley@austincollege.edu) teaches history at Austin College. This essay was posted on www.mises.org on Sept. 17, 2003. He is also the author of "The Hindenburg Program of 1916: A Central Experiment in Wartime Planning" (www.mises.org).

ADDENDUM V

The Roots of the Federal Debt

The issue of government debt and deficits lay dormant through-out the high-revenue 1990s. But with recession and exploding government spending, the issue has become enormously important again. Sadly, just about everyone is missing the central point, which is not that we need budget reform so much as drastic monetary reform.

Federal finance is a shell game of such complexity and trickery that it makes state-level finance, to say nothing of family finance, appear simple by comparison. At the state level, the government takes money from its citizens through taxes. The taxes can be on land, goods, service, or income. The government spends the money it takes in. If the money comes up short the government tries to issue bonds and get people to buy them. Or it raises taxes. If it can't do that, it cuts the budget or seeks a federal subsidy. There are no other options.

State governments fleece taxpayers at every turn, of course, but at least it is hard to disguise. The states embarked on massive new spending in the 1990s before the revenue dried up. States are now struggling to raise new revenue through bond sales and taxes, while avoiding necessary cuts.

When you move from the state to the federal level of government, the fog begins to fall. Right now, for example, we observe the coming together of three trends that would seem to contradict each other. First many Americans are receiving refunds on their taxes as well as unexpected rebates for money already paid into the federal system. Second, government revenue has actually fallen for nearly three years in a row, due not to tax cuts but to lower economic growth. Third, government spending is soaring, with defense and non-defense spending increases breaking all postwar records. Meanwhile, Congress and the president are instituting new mega-spending programs that break all records.

How could all this be happening at the same time? Has government learned how to create something out of nothing? Hardly. The leakage is visible in the federal deficit, which is estimated to exceed the $600 billion mark, and the federal debt, which now stands at $6.7 trillion. And then there's the problem of unfunded liabilities in the system itself, which exceeded $44 trillion.

Of course these numbers, as staggering as they are, are too large to really comprehend. It is not even possible to comprehend the sheer size of the daily increase in the national debt: $1.72 billion. The very meaning of these numbers boggles the mind.

The following question is basic but hardly ever asked: given that this debt cannot be paid, and nobody really believes it can be, how is it that the federal government can continue to borrow so much even as taxes are marginally cut and spending expands at a record pace in the midst of a lackluster economy?

If individuals or corporations—or state governments, for that matter—were this much in debt, they would see the value of their existing debt on the market downgraded. They would no longer be credit worthy. They would default and be bankrupt. The profligacy would come to an end.

How is it that the federal government is able to accumulate all this debt and still market its notes all over the world? The answer to the riddle is understood by the Austrian School: the Fed, the agency of the federal government that enjoys the monopoly privilege to create out of thin air all the money it wants to create. Fed governor Ben Bernanke is right that the Fed is capable of bailing out even the worst debt crisis by merely creating unlimited supplies of dollars. Mises wrote about this as early as 1912, and he saw the grave costs for society.

What are those costs? An inflated money supply distorts the structure of production and leads to serious investment miscalculations. It drives down the value of the dollar on international exchange. It provokes a decline in the purchasing power of each individual unit, thereby gutting savings and discouraging thrift. It redistributes wealth from the productive to the government-connected. As the recent experience of Zimbabwe shows, inflation can literally turn a society and culture upside down.

Even the Fed would regret the consequences of such actions. Why, then, does it continually promise to drive interest rates down to zero if need be? Why do its spokesmen never tire of emphasizing that the whole banking system is insulated from failure?

Your finances are not the first concern of the Fed's primary clients, the large banks and the government that established the central bank. It is short-term thinking at work. In the institution of the central bank, the government has the ultimate tool to permit its profligacy to continue without check and without regard to the future.

If the Fed, the sponsor of the ultimate check-kiting scheme, is so dangerous for society, why doesn't somebody do something about it? For years Congressman Ron Paul of Texas, distinguished counselor to the Mises Institute, has worked to restore the gold standard, because it would mean the abolition of central banking and the instituting of sound money that would keep government in check and stabilize economic growth and inflation.

But he is unusual: a statesman who understands the issue and cares enough about America's future to push a program that would benefit everyone but the banking/government elite. What about everyone else? They either lack the economic education to understand it or just have no real incentive to do the right thing.

We live under what Paul Gottfried calls the managerial state—which is to say a seemingly permanent bureaucratic government subject to little effective democratic control that attempts to plan every aspect of society though it has no real stake in the outcome or its failures. In this respect the modern state is very different from its medieval predecessor in which the king took personal responsibility for the outcome of his decisions.

Under today's system of government, there are few mechanisms in place that operate as an effective check on public looting. The framers of the Constitution didn't imagine institutions such as the central bank, the income tax, and a permanent bureaucratic class, nor did they imagine the explosive growth of the welfare-warfare state that these institutions would underwrite and entrench in public life.

One check on power does remain and it is the one that has been most effective from time immemorial: public opinion. In light of the impending bankruptcy of the federal government at our expense, we might demand to know: where is the outrage? At some point, when it becomes clear that the present level of profligacy cannot continue and we face the consequences as a society, people are going to demand answers.

Ideally, the system would be fixed before a crisis that results in a complete financial meltdown. Given what we know about Washington today, however, the crisis will not be stopped but will result in upheavals of a kind and degree that cannot be known in advance. There are ways around it, of course: put an end to the recklessness and the institutions like the Fed that make it possible.

This essay was posted on www.mises.org on Sept. 19, 2003. It was the introductory editorial to the fall 2003 issue of its quarterly newsletter, the Mises Memo, with news from the Ludwig von Mises Institute. The full issue is available to members of the institute. Join today to receive the Mises Memo and the Free Market and support the institute's work.

What's the Deal with Oil Prices?

BY WILLIAM L. ANDERSON

While they may not be able to solve many of the problems they create, the political classes of this country have proven they are still adept at causing crises—and then blaming others for the results. With gasoline prices rising to their highest levels in years, and then falling again after Labor Day, it was inevitable that the politicians would come out of the woodwork and demand yet another costly investigation of the U.S. oil industry.

According to Reuters, U.S. Energy Secretary Spencer Abraham has ordered the energy department to "investigate" the spike in gas prices. "The nature of this [price] fluctuation struck me as being unusually large as well and in need of greater explanation," Abraham told a Congressional committee.

This is a response to pressure from Congress. According to another report from Reuters:

> Democrats criticized record high U.S. gasoline prices on Friday and demanded that the Bush administration investigate if big oil companies were gouging consumers at the pump.
>
> Democratic Rep. Edward Markey of Massachusetts sent a letter to U.S. Energy Secretary Spencer Abraham on Friday asking for a probe into the skyrocketing of motor fuel costs that occurred just as many Americans took to the roads for a final summer holiday. Markey is a senior member of the House Energy and Commerce Committee.
>
> "If the oil industry is going to tip the driving public upside down to shake their vacation money out of their pockets, then it is time to tip the industry upside down and shake out a few answers," Markey said Friday at a rally at a gas station in Lexington, Massachusetts, near Boston.

Trying to do Markey one better, at least one contender in the

California recall election has decided that the state must do what it can to force down prices, according to Reuters:

> High gasoline prices have become an issue, too, in the California governor recall and election. California Lt. Gov. Cruz Bustamante, who is the leading Democratic candidate for governor, has called for regulating the state's gasoline prices, which are among the highest in the nation.

Of course, at least one Democratic candidate for president, Joe Lieberman (who in 1990 introduced a bill calling for five years in federal prison for anyone who raised gasoline prices without his permission), also demanded some answers from U.S. Energy Secretary Spencer Abraham. Lieberman also asked the Energy Department for an immediate probe into the causes for the price spike just ahead of the Labor Day holiday weekend and its impact on consumers. (Earth to Joe: people paid a few cents more for gasoline: that's the impact.)

"It is imperative that this investigation determine both the underlying causes for these price increases and whether or not industry participants are gouging consumers," Lieberman said in a letter to Abraham.

Actually, for all of the hand-wringing that is coming from the political classes, one does not need to consult Spencer Abraham—or even Abraham, himself, for that matter—to know why gasoline prices have spiked so high recently. The cause is simple and tragic: policies that come from Washington, D.C. and many state governments (such as California). If the politicians really want to know who is responsible for forcing up gasoline prices, all they need to do is look in the mirror. A bit of recent history is in order here. As I wrote in 2001, there are a number of myths about oil companies, and especially about their vaunted "market power." One of the most important things one discovers when researching this industry is that its profitability relative to other U.S. firms has been down for more than two decades.

To put it another way, oil has not been a particularly good investment since the government finally deregulated oil and gasoline prices in 1981. This has been 180 degrees different from the predictions that oil industry critics like Ralph Nader and a number of politicians were making when President Jimmy Carter first began the price deregulation process in 1980.

With that in mind, the "price gouging" accusations made by the above-quoted politicians ring a bit hollow, since if oil companies actually possessed the "market power" that Lieberman and others claim, then oil executives are guilty of a great dereliction of duty towards oil stockholders. If the executives had this "market power" but did not use it to make better-than-average profits, then one would wonder why stockholders even permit these folks to draw salaries.

Yet, it is clear that gasoline prices have increased substantially from even a few weeks ago. While Markey and others claim that oil companies were trying to use the Labor Day holiday to "gouge" consumers, even the anticipated increase in demand would not explain such high price spikes. (Indeed, the holiday premiums rarely are more than a few cents per gallon—and without them there would be almost certain chaos at the gas pumps, as lower-than-market prices would create shortages.)

No, the answers lie not with scheming industry executives or incompetent managers. Politicians and the bureaucrats they empower, on the other hand, have caused major disruptions to oil supplies. Let us count the ways.

a. A new oil refinery has not been built in the United States since the administration of Gerald R. Ford. Environmental laws virtually guarantee that refineries are going to be out of compliance at one time or another, and with avaricious U.S. attorneys anxious to prosecute "environmental criminals," refineries are a losing proposition.

b. The recent East Coast blackout really did disrupt the refining and transportation process, and because the East Coast is a major conduit of oil and gasoline into the interior of this country, a massive shutdown of northeastern refineries is guaranteed to disrupt supplies across the country.

c. The Environmental Protection Agency-enforced regulations set by Congress in the 1990 Clean Air Act Amendments calls for a crazy-quilt set of standards for different areas of the country. When those rules first went headlong into effect in 2000, small pipeline and refinery glitches became major barriers to some cities like Chicago, where special clean air standards kept producers from trucking in gasoline from other parts of the region where gasoline was more plentiful. Chicagoans, according to the polls, believed it was an oil company plot, but their friendly members of Congress who voted for the standards actually were to blame.

d. From high gasoline taxes to a constant stream of condemnation from the political classes, the oil industry as been a favorite whipping boy of politicians since the 1970s. Whether it is blaming oil companies for the war in Iraq or blaming oil companies for global warming, the critics are always out in force demanding new taxes, new regulations, convictions and fines or even outright property seizures.

e. The ongoing political crisis in Venezuela has disrupted the reliability of that nation's oil industry, which has the USA as its largest customer. As long as Hugo Chavez is in power, one can expect that turmoil to continue. Chavez wants to be a "Castro with oil" (as opposed to a Castro with sugar); his policies have angered the dwindling Venezuelan middle class so much that for the most part he has been Castro without oil or sugar.

f. Finally, there is the continuing U.S. occupation of Iraq. Government and industry planners had believed that oil revenues from that country would be enough to pay U.S. firms to "rebuild" the country (that was destroyed by U.S. bombs and other weapons of large-scale destruction). Instead, resistance groups have sabotaged pipelines, refineries, and the oil fields, making the anticipated Iraqi flow very unreliable.

These reasons certainly do not ring with politicians in the way that words like "greed" and "gouging" do, nor are U.S. politicians willing to admit that for the last four decades, they have openly made oil companies Public Enemy Number One—and that such attacks have their deleterious effects.

No, all they can do is to repeat the same tired arguments of the past—and the same lies. Politicians and bureaucrats created the oil crises of the 1970s and it looks as though these folks in the Class of 2003 are trying to outdo their forbears of 30 years ago. Of course, successes of the political classes are gained only at the expense of everyone else. Would that oil company executives were permitted to investigate Congress and the Energy Department. They would find more than a few smoking guns.

William L. Anderson, an adjunct scholar of the Ludwig von Mises Institute, teaches economics at Frostburg State University. This essay was posted on www.mises.org on Sept. 8, 2003.

ADDENDUM VII

Did the Framers Favor Hard Money?
BY H. A. SCOTT TRASK

The Old Republican leader John Randolph, the aristocratic liberal from Virginia, once famously remarked that the framers intended ours to be "a hard-money government." Is it true? Contrary to the efforts of academics and judges to obscure this issue, the framers' intentions in regard to money and banking were quite plain and are easily reconstructed.

On balance, the framers' views can be summarized as follows. On the one hand, they believed in fractional-reserve banking, generally following Adam Smith's currency and banking theories. On the other hand, they were resolutely opposed to government-issued paper money, fiat money, legal tender laws, inconvertible paper currency, and land banks. On the question of a national bank, they were divided, but they all believed in a hard dollar (defining the dollar as a certain weight of silver and/or gold). On a spectrum, their views would be closer to those of Murray Rothbard and Ron Paul than John Maynard Keynes and Alan Greenspan.

To understand the founders' views, one must grasp the meaning of two essential constitutional doctrines—delegation and enumeration. By ratifying the Constitution the states delegated a few defined powers to the federal government, every one of which was enumerated (i.e., written down) in the document. Except by amendment, the federal government has no other powers. The history of the period, the relevant documents, the records of the ratifying conventions, and the test of the Constitution offer overwhelming evidence that these doctrines merely state the prevailing understanding of the period.

If that were not enough, the Tenth Amendment codifies it. "The powers not delegated to the United States by the Constitution, nor prohibited by it to the States, are reserved to the

States respectively, or to the people." Its importance cannot be exaggerated. Jefferson called it the "cornerstone of the Constitution."

What Were "Bills of Credit"?

One must also grasp what the framers meant by "bills of credit." At the time, there was no confusion or uncertainty at all about their character or nature. They were government-issued irredeemable paper money made receivable for taxes—in other words, fiat money. Seven states had issued them just two years before, and the colonies had issued them over and over again throughout the century. They had done so to finance their wars with the French and the Indians, but they had also seized upon them as a means of reviving trade and solving the ever-recurring "shortages of money."

Sometimes the bills were made legal tender, other times not. Massachusetts was the first colony to print paper money in 1690 when it used them to pay the soldiers and discharge the debts incurred during an armed expedition against Quebec. A little later, the colonies created loan offices to lend such bills to citizens on the security of land or real estate. The borrowers were to pay interest, and the bills were made receivable for taxes. Finally, during the early eighteenth century, groups of merchants and others formed private "banks" to print currency and lend it out on interest. These "banks" had no capital, but the Associates promised to accept the paper as lawful money. Some of them had legislative charters, others did not, and still others operated in violation of the law. It is significant that although these were privately issued notes, everyone considered them to be bills of credit too.

The British government did not look with favor upon these experiments with paper currency. In 1741, in order to suppress the private paper-money "banks," Parliament extended the Bubble Act to the colonies. In 1751, they forbade the New England colonies from issuing bills of credit except to pay for administration or meet an emergency, and they forbade them from making them legal tender under any circumstances. In 1764, Parliament extended the prohibition on legal tender paper money to all the colonies. During the War of Independence, both Congress and the states issued bills of credit to finance the war. The depreciating Continentals were bills of credit. In the postwar period, seven states issued bills of credit to pay debts, revive business, and relieve debtors.

The Relevant Financial Sections of the Constitution

a. Loans: "The Congress shall have power . . . to borrow money on the credit of the United States."

b. Coinage: "The Congress shall have power . . . to coin money, regulate the value thereof, and of foreign coin, and fix the standard of weights and measures."

c. Indebtedness: "All debts contracted and engagements entered into before the adoption of this Constitution shall be as valid against the United States under this Constitution as under the Confederation."

d. Restriction on the States: "No state shall coin money; emit bills of credit; make anything but gold and silver a tender in payment of debts."

As one can see, the federal government does not have the authority to print paper money, issue bills of credit, establish a legal tender, or impair contracts; and the states were explicitly forbidden from doing any of these things. Some have argued that the absence of a specific federal prohibition means that Congress can exercise these powers, but the records of the federal convention say otherwise.

A Federal Currency Power?

The committee of detail, which drew up the initial draft of the Constitution, explicitly gave the federal government the power to "emit bills on the credit of the United States." They presented their work to the full convention for consideration on 6 August 1787. The debate was soon joined. Although some delegates spoke in favor of granting the power (including James Madison), the majority were resolutely opposed.

Oliver Ellsworth of Connecticut remarked that since "the mischiefs of the various experiments which had been made were now fresh in the public mind, and had excited the disgust of all the respectable part of America, [it was] a favorable moment to shut and bar the door against paper money. . . . The power may do harm, never good." George Read of Delaware warned that the power "if not struck out, would be as alarming as the mark of the beast in Revelation." John Langdon of New Hampshire said that he would "rather reject the whole plan than retain the three words 'and emit bills.'" The vote was then taken. Nine states voted for striking out the phrase "and emit bills on the credit of the United States." Only two states (New Jersey and Maryland) voted to retain it.

It should be stressed that not all the delegates who favored the power were friends of paper money. George Mason of Virginia confessed to a "mortal hatred to paper money" and Edmund Randolph, also of Virginia, admitted to feeling great "antipathy to paper money." However, with great naïveté, both thought the federal government should have the power for "emergencies."

The heroic Elbridge Gerry of Massachusetts was so alarmed by the prospect of the federal government having this power that he wanted explicit prohibition, but the other delegates thought it unnecessary. Experience soon vindicated Gerry's apprehension and desire for additional safeguards.

During the second war with England, President Madison issued treasury notes to help finance the war. Because these notes were interest-bearing and redeemable in one year, they were not bills of credit, but they were just as inflationary. Murray Rothbard observed that the state banks used these notes as "high-powered money" or "reserves" upon which they could pyramid additional currency and credit; and William Graham Sumner noted they "at once stimulated banking issues in the Middle States." Even worse, at the end of the war, Congress authorized the printing of non-interest-bearing treasury notes of small denomination (as low as $3.00). These were bills of credit in all but name (i.e., government paper currency).

The historian of early American banking, Bray Hammond, leaves no doubt as to the conclusion that any honest historian or constitutional scholar should draw:

> Was it intended that though the states might not issue paper money, establish other legal tender, and impair contracts, the federal government might do so? The question is not to be answered by the Supreme Court's subsequent decision that the federal government does have the power nor by the fact that the federal government has exercised the power. The question is historical and is not answered by jurisprudence or by subsequent practice. Was the power intended? The answer seems clear enough: it is no.

There is an additional question of great importance. Were state bank notes bills of credit, thus falling under the prohibition of the Constitution? The framers thought not, but their knowledge of such notes was based on the experience of only three commercial banks, all of which were specie-payng: the Bank of North America (c. 1781), the Massachusetts Bank (c. 1784), and the Bank of New York

(c. 1784). They clearly did not foresee the multiplication of banks after 1800, the gradual substitution of state bank paper for gold and silver coin as the exclusive circulating medium of the country, and the tricks and threats employed by bankers to escape paying their notes and deposits in hard money.

The question of the constitutionality of bank paper actually came before the Supreme Court in the case of Briscoe vs. Bank of Kentucky (1837). The court ruled by a vote of 6 to 1 that such notes were not bills of credit. They were wrong. In an eloquent and learned dissent, Justice Joseph Story (Mass.) pointed out that state bank notes possessed all the characteristics of the colonial bills of credit.

Although they were not issued by the state government itself, they were issued by state-chartered banks, and it was an established legal principle that what the principal cannot do, its agent cannot do. The convertibility of the notes was mostly nominal, not real. They were accepted for taxes and bonds. The historian Sumner added that they had the effect of driving specie from circulation, creating a currency of inconvertible and depreciated paper, and fueling a business cycle of boom and bust. In short, they had reproduced all the evils of the colonial bills of credit.

Sumner condemned the Court's decision in the strongest terms. "In Briscoe's case the court . . . made the prohibition of bills of credit nugatory. . . . Wild-cat banking was granted standing ground under the Constitution, and the boast that the Constitutional Convention had closed and barred the door against the paper money with which the colonies had been cursed was without foundation." He goes on to point out that these "private" paper-money banks (so beloved by contemporary 'free bankers') "went on their course and carried those States [which authorized it] down to bankruptcy and repudiation." What was worse, fractional-reserve banking "miseducated the people of those States until they thought irredeemable government issues an unhoped-for blessing."

Here was a case where a branch of the federal government had the power to do the right thing but did not do it. To have denied the legal standing of fiduciary media would have been to deprive the state governments of their chief means of funding the construction of public works, and the federal government of its chief source of borrowed funds for war. The Madison administration had financed the War of 1812 by selling bonds for state bank notes and issuing federal treasury notes. Without manufactured paper money to draw

from, both would have had to resort to taxation, which was unpop-
ular and would arouse the attention of the masses. Hence, the Court
ruled to protect what was then the government's chief source of borrowed funds. Surprised?

A Federal Banking Power?

Does the Federal Government have the power to charter a
mixed public/private bank, establish a central bank, or regulate
the currency supply? The question was raised only three years
after the ratification of the Constitution when Secretary of the
Treasury Alexander Hamilton proposed the chartering of a
national bank (mixed private/public ownership) with the power
to discount notes, issue currency, lend money to the government,
and hold and disburse government funds. Hamilton argued that
although the federal government did not have an express warrant
to establish such a bank the power was implied because a national bank would help the federal government borrow money, service the debt, keep the revenue, and pay its creditors. His rule of
interpretation: "If the end be clearly comprehended within any of
the specified powers, and if the measure have an obvious relation
to that end, and is not forbidden . . . it may safely be deemed to
come within the compass of the national authority." This was
ingenious, but it was also subversive.

When Secretary of State Thomas Jefferson heard of the bank
plan, he was greatly alarmed. He saw immediately that the doctrine, if once accepted, would break down the guards on federal
power provided by the Constitution. He wrote, "To take a single
step beyond the boundaries thus specially drawn around the powers of Congress is to take possession of a boundless field of power,
no longer susceptible of definition." He then drove a stake
through Hamilton's argument by citing the records of the federal
convention. "It is known that the very power [to charter a bank]
now proposed as a means was rejected as an end by the
Convention which formed the Constitution. A proposition was
made to them to authorize Congress to open canals, and an
amendatory one to empower them to incorporate. But the whole
was rejected, and one of the reasons for rejection urged in debate
was, that then they would have a power to erect a bank."

In other words, not only did the framers not intend the power,
they thought it was forbidden. Alas, a Federalist-controlled, mercan-
tilist-minded Congress passed Hamilton's charter, and President
Washington signed it into law in early 1791. It is worth noting that

the charter forbade the bank from issuing bank notes less than ten dollars ($200 in today's money). Even the Federalists intended the circulating currency of the country to be composed of gold and silver coin.

During the 1815 debate over chartering a second national bank (the charter for the first bank expired in 1811 and was not renewed by the Republican Congress), supporters raised an additional argument. A national bank was an indispensable means for regulating the currency supply. Opponents responded by arguing that the federal government had no power to regulate the currency. The political economist Condy Raguet pointed out with great force, "Congress has no more authority under it to regulate the currency, excepting that portion of it which consists of coin, than it has to regulate the emission of promissory notes by individuals." The federal compact never "placed the national currency under the regulation of Congress." He was right. Congress has the authority to regulate only the value (i.e., determine the weight and fineness) of gold and silver coin, not that of various kinds of paper currencies.

Two centuries later, our money supply is composed entirely of government-issued fiat currency and bank deposits redeemable in the same currency. The money supply and the banking system are largely controlled by means of federal laws and the existence of a powerful central bank. None of which are authorized by the Constitution. It is yet more evidence that our government is no more constitutional than it is democratic or liberal.

Historian H. A. Scott Trask (htrask@highstream.net) is an adjunct scholar of the Ludwig von Mises Institute. This essay was posted on their site on Sept. 15, 2003.

ADDENDUM VIII

Mises and His School

BY J. G. HÜLSMANN

What is Austrian Economics? A few years ago, at the University of Paris, I gave a course with the title "Introduction to Austrian Economics." It turned out that some of the students who signed up for the course believed it was meant to deal with business conditions in the country that lies between Germany, Switzerland, Italy, Hungary, Slovakia, and the Czech Republic. They were very surprised by the content of my lectures. To be fair, it must be said that one of them stayed on throughout the course. One lady was glad to discover that Austria had brought forth a school of economic thought that up to the present day enjoys a living tradition in the entire world.

Austrian Economics is a body of ideas, and we are here this week to study these ideas. That in itself is already an exciting and instructive activity. After all, the history of ideas is a fascinating subject. However, I take it that most of you have not come to Auburn because you are merely interested in ideas as such. You are interested in ideas that are true—ideas that properly reflect the workings of the real world to which they refer. You are interested in gaining an adequate understanding of the world of social relationships, and in sharpening your judgment in political matters.

If this is what you desire, you have come to the right place. The faculty of our summer university is not a group of bookish scholars that share an antiquarian interest in the history of ideas. Rather, they are intellectuals who not only believe that ideas make a difference in society and politics, but who are firmly convinced that ideas alone reign supreme when it comes to political decision making; and that, therefore, it is of crucial importance for the welfare of our families, regions, nations, and all of mankind that the best available knowledge be applied in matters political.

The reason for the existence of the Mises Institute is that the works of its name patron, Ludwig von Mises, are the best available foundation for an adequate understanding of the issues involved in political decision making. In a word the very point of Austrian Economics, as embodied in the works of Mises, is that it is the foremost political science of our day. It is far more systematic, rigorous, and penetrating than anything else in the field.

This is also the conviction of the faculty assembled here to instruct you during the coming week. This does not mean that we agree among ourselves on each single issue, and neither does it mean that we agree with Mises on all issues. Science is after all very much a work in progress. It does not provide ultimate answers such as revealed religion. It is only a special way, even though a very powerful way, to find guidance for our actions.

In a word, the works of Mises are not something like holy writ for our faculty, and neither should they be for you. But they are a precious starting point for further explorations and critical corrections, and in a rich fountain of inspiration.

Who Was Mises?

Ludwig von Mises was born in 1881 in Lemberg, a provincial capital of what was at the time the second-largest country of Europe: Austria-Hungary. His father was a railroad engineer in Lemberg who had married a lady from a bourgeois family in Vienna, the capital of the country. Both parents were Jews and Mises too received the standard religious education. Let me mention in this context that, although he later became agnostic, he never lost his respect for religious life. In many of his writings and correspondence he also stressed that there was no contradiction whatever between libertarian political views and faith.

When Ludwig was still a small boy, the family moved to Vienna, where his father had obtained employment in the railroad ministry. At the age of eleven, Ludwig entered some sort of an early-age college, where during the next eight years he received a humanistic education. The main subjects taught were Latin (eight hours per week) and Greek (six hours).

Young Ludwig had at that point already developed a vigorous interest in history and politics. He devoured a great number of books on various periods of the history of his country, and it was in these years that he developed the spirit of criticism that is so essential for scientific work and which served him well during the rest of his life. The interest he displayed for the history of his own country, and more specifically for contemporary history, foreshadowed much of his later intellectual development. He was not interested in history merely for its own sake. The point was to learn from the past the lessons necessary to guide action here and now.

When Mises finished school at the age of nineteen, therefore, he signed up as a student at the department of law and government science at the University of Vienna, which in those days was one of the top universities in the entire world. He joined the seminar of Carl Grunberg, an economic historian who studied the evolution of peasant life in Eastern Europe. Grunberg had him write a dissertation on the conditions leading to the liberation of peasants in Galicia, the province in which Mises was born. It was his first academic work and so impressive in the eyes of his professors that it was immediately published as a monograph by the university press.

Mises continued to study the economic condition of the working classes, and under the guidance of Grunberg he learned to understand history as resulting from the interplay of special interests. This bode him well for the rest of his life. In his later works on economic theory, Mises accorded due attention to "the clash of group interests," as he called it, something that distinguished him from many other theorists.

Thus Mises started off as an economic historian, and he very probably would have become a great champion of the so-called Historical School of Economics, which dominated in those days the social-science departments in Germany and Austria. But then something unexpected happened that turned him away from fact gathering, as it was practiced by the Historical School, and toward the study of economic theory. Around Christmas of 1903, Mises had his first exposure to Austrian Economics when he read Carl Menger's Principles of Economics.

He later said that it was this reading that turned him into an economist. For the rest of his life, Mises would say that books are the best university. This one book certainly made a huge difference in his life.

Menger convinced Mises that historical research, important though it was, did not cover all layers of social reality. There was an entire universe of things that played a crucial role in human conduct, but which could not be grasped by empirical field studies or archival work. Scarcity, value, intentions, choice, error, and uncertainty were such things. They could only be grasped through an intellectual process of reflection or meditation, and knowledge about these things was not "history," but "theory."

After reading Menger, Mises turned back to the great classic works of economic science, to Hume, Smith, Say, and Ricardo. And he came to see that theory was not merely necessary for a full understanding of human behavior, but also that theory alone provided a firm guidance in all practical matters, in particular, in political decision making.

The Historical School could not offer such guidance. One of its critics, writing in Mises's day, said that the method of this school verged on the absurd. "They go into workers' apartments, measure the surface, and then claim that they are too small" (Ludwig Pohle). But by which standards were the apartments too small? And even if one came to agree that the living conditions of workers were not very good by some absolute standard, it was not at all clear which political consequences this entailed. For the crucial question was whether government interventions could improve these conditions at all. Historical enquiry could not answer this question, theory could.

Hence, Mises became a theoretician—in fact, the foremost economic theoretician of the 20th century—not for the sake of intellectual pleasure derived from playing with constructions of his own making. He had no talent to be some sort of an early game theorist or general-equilibrium model builder. He became a theoretician because Menger had shown that theory could describe a part of reality that was not covered by any other type of knowledge. In short, it was Mises's quest for greater realism and his interest in practical questions that led him to study and develop pure theory in the way Carl Menger had done it before him.

When Mises became interested in Menger's work, Menger himself had already retired from the University of Vienna. He had left the field to his two most important disciples, both of whom taught at this university from 1905 onwards. Their names were Eugen von Bohm-Bawerk and Friedrich von Wieser.

Wieser's work was inspired at least as much by the Englishman Jevons as it was based on Menger's Principles. Like Jevons, indeed, much like present-day theoreticians, Wieser made in his theories ample use of fictions. The central element of his economic thought was the concept of "natural value." This type of value had nothing to do with the wealth of any concrete acting person, and it was objective in the sense that it was the same for all persons.

Yet although his analysis of value was much less realistic than Menger's, Wieser felt no inhibitions to derive sweeping political conclusions from his constructions. The fact that real-life economies were necessarily different from economies in which natural value reigned did in his eyes not count against his theory; it counted against the real world. He saw in his brainchild of natural value an economic ideal and recommended that economic policy should make sure that all factors of production be treated according to their natural values. According to Wieser, this might be achieved in a perfect communist state. But it might also be achieved through heavy government intervention in the market economy.

In his early years, Mises was very sympathetic to Wieser's policy stance, but he was not at all impressed with his lack of realism. Rather than attending any one of Wieser's classes, Mises attended the classes of the man who seemed to represent most faithfully the Mengerian legacy, and who was also in Carl Menger's own judgment his most important follower.

Starting in the fall of 1905, Eugen von Bohm-Bawerk conducted a graduate seminar at the University of Vienna. He had just retired from his position as a Minister of Finance and dedicated the last years of his life (he died in 1914) to research and writing, and also to some debating in the Austrian House of Lords. Mises graduated in early 1906, but he continued to attend Bohm-Bawerk's seminar until the very end. It was here that he received his final polish as an economics student and, most importantly, it was here that he formed his ideas about what a professor should be like.

At the same time, Mises did the research on his first great theoretical treatise in the Mengerian spirit, *The Theory of Money and Credit*. Let me mention in passing that Mises could work on the project only in the evening and night hours. He never found a full paid university position in Vienna, and therefore had to earn a living with other activities. In 1909, he accepted a job at the local chamber of commerce and remained an employee until he left Vienna in 1934, when he finally did obtain a university chair—in Geneva, Switzerland.

After some five years of hard work in his spare time, then, Mises published his treatise on money in 1912. Some sixteen other books would follow in the coming years and decades. But the money book belonged to the four truly great books that he had written and which every student of Austrian Economics should read. The other three great books have the titles *Socialism* (first published in 1922), *Human Action* (1940/1949), and *Theory and History* (1956).

Money

In *The Theory of Money and Credit,* Mises demonstrated that Carl Menger's value theory could also be applied to the case of money. Menger himself, as well as Bohm-Bawerk, had left money out of their considerations. Following the classical economists—Hume, Smith, Say, Ricardo, Mill—they had assumed that, ultimately, money does not have an impact on the wealth of nations; real factors alone determine productivity and incomes.

Critics of the Austrian School had argued that this neglect was a rather serious shortcoming. Money was in fact quite unlike all the other goods when it came to the relationship between value and price. In the case of other goods, the price resulted from the inter-action of the subjective values of different individuals. Value was the cause of price. But in the case of money, there was no such one-sided casual determination. The value of money certainly had some impact on the formation of money prices, but money prices were themselves causes of the value of money. A unit of money with a higher purchasing power was after all more valuable, *ceteris paribus,* than a unit with a lower purchasing power. But if this was true, there seemed to be an inescapable circle: the value of money—some sort of a chicken-egg problem.

The first Austrian to take up the challenge was Friedrich von Wieser, but unfortunately he again came up with a theoretical con-struct based by and large on fiction. The challenge had remained unanswered.

It was in this situation that Mises stepped in and provided a truly Mengerian "realist" solution. He showed that the use of money was determined by marginal value, just as the use of any other good. The key to his demonstration was the regression the-orem. Mises argued that the circle in the explanation of money prices was only apparent. It was not the case that marginal value determined the formation of money prices, and that these very same money prices in some sort of a feedback process determined the values from which they had sprung. Rather there was a time component in the chain of causation. Market participants relied in their present value judgments on the money prices of the past, not on the money prices that in the present resulted from those present value judgments.

But what about those past money prices? How did they come into existence? Through the same process. They resulted from value judgments that relied on money prices existing even further back in time. The same explanation could be applied to all money prices existing in times past. Each time one had to go back to somewhat older prices.

But was this not an infinite regression—and thus a nonexplanation? Mises argued this was not the case. If one went back far enough, one would reach the point at which money emerged from some pre-existing commodity that had not been used in indirect exchange. At this point, money prices would result from values that were based on the nonmonetary uses of these commodities.

Mises's regression theorem has remained one of the core elements of Austrian price theory, and more recently it has found an important new application in the field of currency competition. Indeed, the regression theorem tells us that it is impossible to launch a new paper money in the way one would launch any other new product on the market. Nobody would have any idea about the purchasing power of such a new paper money, precisely because it is new, and thus the market participants could not evaluate it.

Mises made other important contributions in his *Theory of Money and Credit*. He delivered a thorough analysis of the redistribution effects that go hand in hand with changes in the money supply. Additional quantities of money reach certain individuals first and allow them to bid up prices and thus to buy commodities that would otherwise have been bought by other market participants. It follows that money is never neutral. It has a profound impact on the allocation of resources through time and space.

But the single best-known contribution of The Theory of Money and Credit *is probably its business-cycle theory, which Mises called the circulation-credit theory of the business cycle and which is today usually called the Austrian theory of the business cycle. Mises argued that the business cycle results from fractional-reserve banking. Under a fractional-reserve banking system, bankers can create money substitutes* ex nihilo *and give these substitutes to their customers in the form of fiduciary credit or circulation credit.*

When this happens, the new supply of fiduciary credit reduces interest rates below the equilibrium level. This in turn distorts entrepreneurial calculations. At the lower interest rate, more investment projects appear to be profitable than would otherwise have been the case. But this impression is fallacious because the quantities of real resources have not increased. It is not possible to complete any additional investment projects. If entrepreneurs, deluded by the increased availability of fiduciary credit, launch new investment projects, they squander resources and set the economy on a crash course. It is physically impossible to complete all the projects that have been started, because there are just not enough real resources. Sooner or later a decision must be made where to put the available resources; all other projects must be abandoned. This is what happens in the bust phase of the business cycle [emphasis added].

Let me draw your attention to the implications of this theory for the interpretation of the boom phase and the so-called bust phase of the business cycle. In the popular mind, the boom is the period of growth—certainly an exuberant growth, but growth nevertheless. And the bust is a period of stagnation and destruction.

By contrast, in the light of Mises's business-cycle theory, one understands that the apparent improvement of things in the boom is just that—an illusion. What really happens is that scarce resources are wasted and society as a whole is therefore objectively impoverished. The illusion springs from the fact that the wasting goes hand in hand with a simultaneous redistribution process (remember: money is not neutral). Some members of society do improve their lot during the boom, and because public attention is on these happy fates, the general impoverishment goes unnoticed.

Similarly, the bust or—as it is sometimes called—the crisis is not, as in the popular perception, the beginning of all trouble. Rather, it is the beginning of a new sanity. The outbreak of the crisis occurs at the very moment when entrepreneurial fantasies meet the hard rock of economic reality, and finally cease. Entrepreneurs now abandon projects that cannot be continued with the available resources, and they watch out for new projects that are better adapted to present conditions. There is some stagnation in a crisis, but from the point of view of the Austrian business-cycle theory, stagnation is certainly better than a continued boom, because after all it does not waste resources.

Socialism

The next major contribution that needs to be mentioned is Mises's critique of socialism. The first champions of socialism had depicted their ideal society as some sort of a small self-contained egalitarian community. Then the classical economists pointed out that living in autarky is not very productive. The socialist projects would therefore tend to be islands of misery in a capitalist world; and it was very unlikely that many people would be attracted by such prospects.

The socialist intellectuals could not help but accept this critique, but now they came up with a new idea. They claimed that central planning, the characteristic feature of socialism, was more productive than the anarchy of the market. It made no sense to establish socialism in little islands. What was needed was worldwide central planning, or at any rate central planning on as large a scale as possible. This was the state of the debate at the end of World War I, when Mises set out to critically examine the socialist tenets.

In one of the greatest economics articles ever written, Mises once and for all destroyed the claim that central planning would make production in society more efficient than the division of labor in a market economy. The article had the title *"Die Wirtschaftsrechnung imsozialistischen Gemeinwesen"* ["Economic Calculation in the Socialist Commonwealth"].

What is a rational allocation of resources? The allocation of a resource unit is rational when this unit is used in a project that is more important than any other project in which it could also have been employed. Hence, the rationality or non-rationality of a resource use is to be decided on the basis of a comparison between alternative uses of that resource.

Now Mises raised the crucial question: What is the standard of comparison, in terms of on which criterion can or should we compare investment alternatives? Mises pointed out that a market economy could use the profitability criterion. For all investments, entrepreneurs can estimate the selling proceeds as well as the cost expenditure in terms of money prices. And then they can compare the ratios that spring from these estimates.

Let us notice that entrepreneurs are of course not somehow compelled to only look on profitability when they make their decisions. The point is that they can look at the profitability criterion and that in the light of this criterion all investment alternatives in a market economy are indeed comparable.

Now what about a socialist economy? Mises argued that monetary calculation is here out of the question. For money prices can only come into existence in market exchanges, and market exchanges presuppose the existence of at least two owners. But in socialism there is only one owner of all means of production—the very definition of socialism—and thus there are no prices for factors of production. It follows that it is impossible, in a socialist regime, to calculate a profit rate for any investment project and to compare the profitability of different alternative investments.

The central planning agency of a socialist society is therefore deprived of the very means of economic rationalism. It is confronted by a huge array of heterogeneous resources, but it cannot compare the conceivable alternative uses of these resources in terms of a common unit. For example, one cannot tell whether 1,000,000 gallons of milk are somehow more (or less) than the 1,000 cows that produce this milk, just as it is impossible to say whether a castle park is more (or less) than the 100 gardeners that brought it in shape. All these things are heterogeneous and cannot therefore be compared quantitatively—the problem of adding up apples and oranges. For the same reason it is also impossible to tell whether using the cows to produce the milk is more efficient than using the gardeners to bring the garden in shape.

Only if all of these things are exchanged against money can we make such quantitative comparisons, namely, by comparing their money prices. It follows that while capitalism is a truly rational economic system, socialism is like a huge ship without a compass. Far from overcoming the alleged "anarchy of production," socialism actually produces more chaos than would have existed without the imposition of central planning. Socialism, as Mises would say, is planned chaos.

Epistemology

You might think that, with his business-cycle theory and his critique of socialism, Mises had stirred up more than enough trouble for a lifetime. But I can only encourage all of you to read his books, in particular the four great books, very carefully. Each of them is a rich mine of insights and arguments. Tonight we cannot do more than go through some of the highlights.

Let me therefore move on to another one of these highlights: Mises's clarification of the epistemology of economics. Mises stated that economic science is a particular branch of a more general science—praxeology, the science of human action. The laws of this science are valid a priori, that is, they cannot possibly be refuted or verified by any facts that we gather through our senses. They can only be verified or refuted by discursive reasoning, which in turn is based on our reflective knowledge of what human action is.

Let me give you just one example. Consider first the most basic phenomenon that lies at the heart of all modern economic theories: human choice. There is absolutely no doubt that human beings can make choices and do make choices, and that, if it were not so, it would be pointless to engage in economic science at all (and several other disciplines such as ethics and law would of course be pointless as well). No school of economics disputes this fact, neither the monetarists, nor the supply-siders, nor the Walrasians, nor the game theorists, nor the Keynesians (old, new, post, and whatever sort of Keynesianism we will get yet).

Now ask yourselves how we come to know about the existence of choice. Do we actually observe choices with our eyes? Do we hear choices? Do we smell them? Clearly, this is not the case. But this means that the most basic phenomenon of economic science is known to us, not by facts we gather through our senses, but through an act of reflection on our own actions. And the knowledge that we gain this way does therefore not depend on information we gather from our senses, and thus it cannot be refuted or verified by any such information. It can only be verified or refuted by a more exact reflection on the structural features of our actions.

This is why Mises is right in his claim that economic science is valid a priori. And all other economists, who believe that economics is empirical in the very same sense in which for example the natural sciences are empirical, are wrong.

Most mainstream economists have never given any serious thought to the epistemology of their science. They just repeat the slogans of a few academic high priests, who endlessly profess the litany of positivism, the doctrine according to which all scientific knowledge comes from observed facts or other sense-based methods of fact gathering. These words might sound harsh to some of you, but it is no exaggeration to say that positivism, despite all beneficial effects it might have had at some point in the past, has today become a quasi-religious creed. We can be sure that Auguste Comte, the founding father of positivism, now marvels in his grave, because that is exactly what he had in mind: replacing Christianity with his brain-child.

This bad new religion does not make good weather for the Austrians. Today mainstream economists disdain Mises and his followers for shunning empirical work and engaging in the armchair gymnastics of a priori theorizing. Many mainstream economists cannot pronounce the words "a priori theorizing" without grinding their teeth.

Milton Friedman once characterized a priori theorizing as a deadly undertaking. If two Austrians disagree, according to Friedman, there is only one solution left for them: they have to shoot it out. Now, I can assure you that in the ten years or so during which I have had the opportunity to observe the Austrians at a fairly close distance, it never ever came to a shooting; all the while we constantly disagreed with Mises, Rothbard, and amongst ourselves. The Mises Institute is located in Alabama, a state blessed with very liberal gun laws. There is no problem whatever to go to one of our nice local gun shops, buy a decent weapon, and so prepared go to the Mises Summer University or to the Austrian Scholar's Conference to apply Friedman's precept. But nobody has ever done this. I therefore think it is high time now that Friedman finally accepts the historical record as an empirical refutation of his hypothesis. But I doubt he will.

When two Austrians disagree, they do not shoot it out; rather, each of them tries to come up with a better argument next time, but usually the disagreements remain. Things are not at all different in mainstream economics. It is a grave error to believe that empirical field studies provide something like a final verdict on a contested question. The empirical record shows that disagreements between positivists remain in the face of even the most impressive findings.

If anything, therefore, Friedman's horror scenario applies with equal right to the positivist camp. If two positivists disagree and refuse to accept each other's empirical studies as the final word, there remains only one solution: the trigger. But of course this is as nonsensical as it is in the case of disagreements between Austrians. Science is process; it is never something like a final state of rest. Disagreements are not only avoidable; they are also necessary and even beneficial to spur scientific progress.

So much for Friedman's errors. But even many Austrian fellow travelers feel uncomfortable about Mises's views on what economics is all about. They encourage students of Austrian Economics to leave the ivory tower and apply the theory in empirical work.

This recommendation also rests on a serious misunderstanding. Carl Menger, Ludwig von Mises, Murray Rothbard, Hans Hoppe, and many other excellent Austrians engage in a priori theorizing not because they shun empirical work, but precisely because a priori theorizing is the only way to adequately describe certain features of the real world, without which it would be impossible to fully understand human behavior and to give a scientific underpinning to political decision making.

If anything, we need not less exercise in pure theory, but much more of it. It is true that not everybody is born to be a theorist and that applied historical case studies have a great pedagogical value. But the future of our science, and thus the future of our civilization, will depend on the number of young intellectuals willing to learn pure theory in the realist tradition of Menger and Mises, and to develop this tradition to the best of their abilities.

Realism

This brings us to a final issue. As I just said, it is important that we develop praxeology in the realist tradition of Menger and Mises. Austrians should not become more like the mainstream, based on the false hope that thereby our ideas will become more palatable to academics. Turning Austrian Economics into just another branch of the mainstream will at best flatter the little egos of the protagonists. Austrians should become and be all that they can be as the bearers of realist economic theory. But they can do this only if they are willing to immerse themselves in the tradition of Austrian realism.

This tradition is most vividly present in the works of the main line of Austrian theorists: Menger, Bohm-Bawerk, Mises, Rothbard, and today in the works of Hans-Hermann Hoppe and the other senior fellows of the Mises Institute, as well as in the works of a few others, such as Jesús Huerta de Soto, Pascal Salin, and George Reisman. It is less present in the works of Friedrich von Wieser, Friedrich von Hayek, and those who, following in their footsteps, place too much emphasis on the use of fictitious constructions, for example, on the equilibrium construct and on processes of equilibration.

The quest for greater realism in the social sciences—this is the core mission of Misesian scholarship in our times. At its heart this is a quest for the full truth, and even though we cannot expect to ever gain a full picture of anything here on earth, we will try to get as close as we can in the coming week. If Misesians remain faithful to their mission it will not fail to yield a rich harvest. For not only the truth, but the mere honest quest for realism has a great power of attraction.

It has brought the Austrians important converts from the mainstream. For example, at the beginning of the twentieth century, Ludwig von Mises himself defected from the mainstream of his time—the Historical School. In the 1970s, Hans-Hermann Hoppe, who is among us tonight, defected from the mainstream philosophy of the Frankfurt School; and in the 1980s, Jeffrey Herbener, also here tonight, defected from neoclassical economics.

Today the Austrian School is a vibrant and growing movement of economists, historians, philosophers, and other social scientists united in their love for the search of truth and in their courage to say the truth even if it does not fit the political or academic fashions of our day. There is no better place and no better occasion to become acquainted with this movement than the Summer

University here at the Mises Institute, and I hope you will make
good use of it.

J. G. Hülsmann is a senior fellow of the Ludwig von Mises Institute. This was the
opening lecture to the Mises Summer University, delivered Aug. 3, 2003. It was posted on www.mises.org on Aug. 6, 2003.

ADDENDUM IX

Sins of Businessmen, Crimes of Politicians
BY GEORGE REISMAN

People who are ignorant of the writings of Ludwig von Mises are unaware of the role of credit expansion in creating recessions and depressions. Not knowing the actual cause of such calamities, they turn to false and often absurd explanations, such as the doctrine of a general overproduction, and end up blaming increased production and supply, which is the very essence of greater prosperity, as the cause of impoverishment—allegedly we are poor because we are rich.

Another popular and equally false explanation of the present recession is the fraud and dishonesty of businessmen. To be sure, there are many dishonest businessmen. It would be surprising if there were not. We live in an age in which principles of any kind are widely regarded with contempt. And at least since 1937, when the Supreme Court of the United States abandoned the protection of economic freedom, our government has been free to do almost anything it likes in the economic realm. It is no longer restrained by such principles as having to respect property rights and the freedom of contract. The result has been that the government has gained almost total power both to break and to make businessmen, i.e., either to destroy or enrich them, as it may choose.

This state of affairs compels businessmen, especially large, successful businessmen, to pay regular extortion money to politicians and government officials. They have to pay bribes, in the form of "campaign contributions" and "donations," to various pressure-group organizations in order not to be harmed or altogether destroyed. And because there are now so few restraints on the government in the economic realm, and because few businessmen know anything of moral and political philosophy beyond the doctrines of pragmatism, relativism, and assorted brands of statism that they may have absorbed in today's so-called education system, the line is easily crossed between bribes that are mere extortion money, paid to avoid being harmed by the government, and bribes that are paid to use the government's apparatus of compulsion and coercion, as Mises called it, in one's own favor—for example, to gain government subsidies or to harm one's competitors, by such means as instigating antitrust proceedings or other regulatory actions against them. Thus, a heavily interventionist economy necessarily seethes with corruption and immorality.

Now add credit expansion to this mix, and an environment is created in which almost every business venture is given the appearance of prosperity, while the underlying reality is one of the massive diversion of capital into malinvestments. It should not be surprising that in many cases efforts are made to sustain the appearance of prosperity by means ranging from questionable to blatantly fraudulent, and that such efforts are encouraged by the conviction that given only a little more time, the apparent general prosperity will make those efforts good and permanently conceal their nature.

But even in this environment, a vital distinction remains between businessmen, on the one side, and politicians and government officials, on the other. And that is that the activity of businessmen qua businessmen, that is, as producers of goods and services for sale in the market, is inherently positive. It is the creation of wealth that sustains and promotes human life and well-being. Indeed, it is the saving and investment and profit motive and competition of businessmen that are responsible for practically all of the wonderful technological advances of the last two hundred years or more, and for the ability of practically everyone in the capitalist countries to afford them.

Acts of dishonesty and fraud have no more essential connection to business activity than they do to the practice of medicine or the performance of music or to any of the arts or sciences. Just as the existence of dishonest physicians, musicians, artists, or scientists has no actual bearing on the nature of those activities as such, so too the existence of dishonest businessmen has no actual bearing on the nature of business activity as such.

In sharpest contrast, the activity of politicians and government officials is always inherently negative—it is always destructive or threatens destruction. This is because the foundation of all law and government activity is physical force or the threat of physical force. This is expressed in the ancient Latin dictum "nulla lege sine poena," which means "no law without punishment." That is, there is no such thing as a law, administrative ruling, edict, decree, or government order of any kind that is not backed by the threat to use physical force to compel obedience to it. In the absence of the government's ability to use physical force to compel obedience, its declarations would be without effect. They could simply be disregarded at will.

The only legitimate use of this negative power is to negate the negative constituted by the private use of physical force, that is, to prohibit and punish such acts as murder, assault, robbery, rape, kidnapping, and fraud. To that strictly limited extent, i.e., the banning of physical force from human relationships, the government can make it possible for the positive activity of the private citizens to then proceed unhindered and achieve all the beneficial effects it is ultimately capable of achieving. However, insofar as the government steps beyond this narrowly circumscribed, strictly delimited domain of legitimate activity, it acts as a destroyer in the same manner as private criminals [emphasis added].

Given the extent and scope of the transgressions of the government today, one must say that while there may be many businessmen engaged in activities ranging from various sharp practices to outright fraud, the government and the politicians who determine its activities are routinely, day in and day out, engaged in massive theft, which is what the income and estate taxes clearly are, and in their massive violations of individual rights, which are inherent across the board in the government's using or threatening to use physical force against individuals who have not themselves resorted to force.

Far more often than businessmen commit fraud, the government and the politicians commit or are accessories to the commission of such criminal acts as extortion, theft, and unjust imprisonment. This last occurs not only when people are incarcerated for crimes they did not commit, which happens as the result of carelessness, and worse, more often than one might think, but when they are incarcerated for acts they did perform, but which are not genuine crimes, such as the commission of so-called victimless crimes and "economic crimes."

And when it imposes a draft, the government is engaged in kidnapping and enslavement on a massive scale, in that it forcibly compels people to be where and do what it wants them to do rather than be where and do what they choose to do. The same characterization may arguably be said to apply in a milder form to public education and compulsory school attendance laws, under which parents are given the choice of surrendering their children's minds or going to jail.

Fortunately, in this country and the other countries whose legal systems are still within the Anglo-Saxon legal tradition, the government and the politicians have not yet gotten around to the commission of murder, though the politicians of many other countries certainly have.

So much for the comparison of the misdeeds of businessmen with the misdeeds of government and politicians. The fact that it is nevertheless the misdeeds of the businessmen that are featured, indeed, blared forth, while the far greater and more fundamental misdeeds of politicians and government officials are for the most part ignored, is the result of the anti-capitalistic political philosophy and economic theories that guide the great majority of today's intellectuals, including, of course, the great majority of today's editorial writers and reporters.

This will not change until there is a new generation of intellectuals, who will have read and studied the ideas of Ludwig von Mises and Ayn Rand, and their predecessors and successors, that is, until there is a radical change in the content of education.

George Reisman is professor of economics at Pepperdine University's Graziadio School of Business and Management in Los Angeles. This essay was posted on www.mises.org on Sept. 23, 2003.

ADDENDUM X

The Problem of Corporate Greed
BY BRAD EDMONDS

The prospect of "corporate greed" terrifies everyone in government, everyone in leftist mass media, and most men on the street. Unethical corporate behavior is blamed for water pollution, air pollution, major bankruptcies, low wages, global warming, product-safety problems, skin cancer, and cultural ennui.

What free-marketeers don't always make explicit is that the government and media Chicken Littles are right in part: Corporations are indeed out to make a profit. Of this point, we must first observe the first lesson of business economics, as taught by the classical school markets in the 18th century.

However greedy or altruistic a business person happens to be, the institutions of the market channel his or her motivation to a social end. Business must serve society in order to thrive, so, from the point of view of its economic effects, the moral merit of the motive for engaging in commerce has no necessary bearing on the services that commerce provides to society. The insight is as profoundly important, as well as neglected, now as ever.

But what about the executives who will cut corners, even to the point of breaking the law, to expand their own salaries and power? Here the Chicken Littles are correct about the problem, but they're wrong about the solution.

Government has been trying to solve the problem of corporate greed for decades. Product-safety regulations, for example, attempt to force manufacturers to produce goods with no safety risks. Meeting these regulations has obvious costs: Most products get more expensive, such as when some vehicles (but not others) must have doors of a certain strength, high-mounted rear brake lights, and more; and other products disappear from the market entirely, such as zippy microcars sold in Europe and Japan that would be perfect for American college students and big-city dwellers but which don't meet American roof-strength and emissions regulations.

Less obvious costs are the opportunity costs of increasing regulations. Consumer choice suffers: Many of us were wearing seat belts before the law required it, and would prefer our vehicles without government-mandated airbags that inflate forcefully enough to break wrists even when they're not needed. And the government departments that produce the regulations absorb money without producing any wealth, thereby decelerating the real production of wealth in the private economy.

When government sets out to solve the problem of corporate greed, it does the same thing every time: It creates laws and regulations, and these invariably add costs, limit choices, and result in half-witted, one-size-fits-all solutions that fail to solve the problem for at least a whole bunch of us. Worse, many government mandates only worsen the problems they're intended to solve (see the Department of Education for one example).

And government regulations often contain the seeds of their own failure. Pollution regulations, for example, indicate how much pollution manufacturers are allowed to toss into the environment. This guarantees certain levels of pollution, since it will be cost-effective for manufacturers to pollute very near the allowed levels; the regulations usually provide no incentive for producers to pollute far below those levels. And the levels themselves often are set through wrangling and negotiations among politicians who desire to curry the favor of the very industries they're regulating. Some of the regulations are set by the EPA itself, but their regulations are often written on the advice of bad scientific research (that's the kind of thing that happens when an agency is not held accountable).

Given that government is not the solution, is it also the case that government is part of the problem with corporate greed? Of course the answer is yes—government at all levels implicitly encourages corporate greed and sloth in many ways. Enron was given loans and grants by the government at the same time that executives where working within regulations to successfully hide Enron's losses on subsidiaries' balance sheets.

American steel producers continue to be inefficient while government props up their profit margins at consumer expense through tariffs on imported steel. (This issue will be a reelection problem for Bush as industries that use steel are threatening to oppose Bush in 2004 if tariffs are not lifted, while the steel industry will oppose him otherwise.) Indeed, through the promise of favorable legislation in exchange for campaign contributions and votes—as well as the threat of unfavorable legislation without them—Congress effectively extorts American business. Don't expect ethical behavior from anyone you threaten that way.

What's the alternative? Don't regulate at all. What happens when a business produces an unsafe product? The news gets out immediately (the press already loves to do this), corporations can be sued in both public and private courts (they already are), and corporations go out of business (which they already do). Sales—whether of products or services—keep corporations alive. A bad public image does terrible damage to any business, and lawyers and the media are continually poised to strike. After all, lawyers get rich, and reporters get promotions, when they are the first to expose corporate error.

The same goes for financial solvency: Without the SEC and its henchmen, corporations would be free to cook books however they want and disclose only what they want. The result would be warier investors. "Investors," whoever they are (investment banks, mutual funds, Warren Buffett), don't want to lose their money any more than you do. It doesn't take an SEC to inspire investors to ask difficult questions of the corporations who want their money. Corporations who refuse to disclose what investors want to know, or who produce financial reports that aren't persuasive, would find it impossible to attract funds for growth.

Pollution is a stickier problem. To solve the other problems of corporate greed, the government needs only to erase its regulations. To solve the pollution problem, the government has to give away all the land it owns. Once all property is private, property owners will defend their own interests against polluters. Rather than the government of the State of New York petitioning Washington for help against acid-rain producers in Illinois, with the government in Washington then regulating the industry in Illinois (with the industry in Illinois lobbying congressmen not to regulate too stiffly), individual property owners in New York would be in a better position to sue polluters in other states.

Right now, typical lawsuits involve the government of one state suing polluters in another state not over the issue of whether the polluters are polluting—this is never in much doubt—but over whether polluters are meeting federal regulations such as the Clean Air Act. It can be immensely difficult to establish whether someone's meeting miles of regulations written in bureaucratese. Having the government as middleman in the whole process sometimes produces comedy (or, it would be comedy if it didn't cost you and me tens of millions of dollars per event): The State of New York sued the EPA over acid rain in 1997.

Corporate executives are just like anybody else. Some percentage of them will take advantage of opportunities the government (and only the government) can provide to make life worse for the competition and the customer and better for themselves. Without government regulation, written and enforced by people who have no real stake in the outcome, the market would agree to pursue problem resolutions its own way, with every participant participating because he does have a stake in the outcome.

When every corporation is held to the high standards imposed by a free market, and when every corporation operates without the safety nets imposed by government, we'll all be pleased with how honest CEOs suddenly become, and how quickly and relatively costlessly the few bad apples are exposed and driven out.

After all, through lawsuits and bankruptcy, the market provides natural disincentives to wrongdoing, while at the same time it provides natural incentives through the profit motive for businesses to provide reliable, safe, stylish products at a reasonable price in the first place. It's too bad that kind of discipline can never be applied to government.

Brad Edmonds is a banker in Alabama. This essay was posted on www.mises.org on Nov. 14, 2003.

ADDENDUM XI

The Origin of Money and Its Value
BY ROBERT P. MURPHY

The importance of the Austrian school of economics is nowhere better demonstrated than in the area of monetary theory. It is in this realm that the simplifying assumptions of mainstream economic theory wreak the most havoc. In contrast, the commonsensical, "verbal logic" of the Austrians is entirely adequate to understand the nature of money and its valuation by human actors.

Menger on the Origin of Money

The Austrian school has offered the most comprehensive explanation of the historical origin of money. Everyone recognizes the benefits of a universally accepted medium of exchange. But how could such a money come into existence? After all, self-interested individuals would be very reluctant to surrender real goods and services in exchange for intrinsically worthless pieces of paper or even relatively useless metal discs. It's true, once everyone else accepts money in exchange, then any individual is also willing to do so. But how could human beings reach such a position in the first place?

One possible explanation is that a powerful ruler realized, either on his own or through wise counselors, that instituting money would benefit his people. So he then ordered everyone to accept some particular thing as money.

There are several problems with this theory. First, as Menger pointed out, we have no historical record of such an important event, even though money was used in all ancient civilizations. Second, there's the unlikelihood that someone could have invented the idea of money without ever experiencing it. And third, even if we did stipulate that a ruler could have discovered the idea of money while living in a state of barter, it would not be sufficient for him to simply designate the money good. He would also have to specify the precise exchange ratios between the newly defined

315

money and all other goods. Otherwise, the people under his rule could evade his order to use the newfangled "money" by charging ridiculously high prices in terms of that good.

Menger's theory avoids all of these difficulties. According to Menger, money emerged spontaneously through the self-interested actions of individuals. No single person sat back and conceived of a universal medium of exchange, and no government compulsion was necessary to effect the transition from a condition of barter to a money economy.

In order to understand how this could have occurred, Menger pointed out that even in a state of barter, goods would have different degrees of saleableness or saleability. (Closely related terms would be marketability or liquidity.) The more saleable a good, the more easily its owner could exchange it for other goods at an "economic price." For example, someone selling wheat is in a much stronger position than someone selling astronomical instruments. The former commodity is more saleable than the latter.

Notice that Menger is not claiming that the owner of a telescope will be unable to sell it. If the seller sets his asking price (in terms of other goods) low enough, someone will buy it. The point is that the seller of a telescope will only be able to receive its true "economic price" if he devotes a long time to searching for buyers. The seller of wheat, in contrast, would not have to look very hard to find the best deal that he is likely to get for his wares.

Already we have left the world of standard microeconomics. In typical models, we can determine the equilibrium relative prices for various real goods. For example, we might find that one telescope trades against 1,000 units of wheat. But Menger's insight is that this fact does not really mean that someone going to market with a telescope can instantly walk away with 1,000 units of wheat.

Moreover, it is simply not the case that the owner of a telescope is in the same position as the owner of 1,000 units of wheat when each enters the market. Because the telescope is much less saleable, its owner will be at a disadvantage when trying to acquire his desired goods from the other sellers.

Because of this, owners of relatively less saleable goods will exchange their products not only for those goods that they directly wish to consume, but also for goods that they do not directly value so long as the goods received are more saleable than the goods given up. In short, astute traders will begin to engage in indirect exchange. For example, the owner of a telescope who desires fish does not need to wait until he finds a fisherman who wants to look at the stars. Instead, the owner of the telescope can sell it to any person who wants to stargaze, so long as the goods offered for it would be more likely to tempt fishermen than the telescope.

Over time, Menger argued, the most saleable goods were desired by more and more traders because of this advantage. But as more people accepted these goods in exchange, the more saleable they became. Eventually, certain goods outstripped all others in this respect, and became universally accepted in exchange by the sellers of all other goods. At this point, money had emerged on the market.

The Contribution of Mises

Even though Menger had provided a satisfactory account for the origin of money, this process explanation alone was not a true economic theory of money. (After all, to explain the exchange value of cows, economists don't provide a story of the origin of cows.) It took Ludwig von Mises in his 1912 *The Theory of Money and Credit* to provide a coherent explanation of the pricing of money units in terms of standard subjectivist value theory.

In contrast to Mises's approach, which as we shall see was characteristically based on the individual and his subjective valuations, most economists at that time clung to two separate theories. On the one hand, relative prices were explained using the tools of marginal utility analysis. But then, in order to explain the nominal money prices of goods, economists resorted to some version of the quantity theory, relying on aggregate variables and in particular, the equation $MV = PQ$.

Economists were certainly aware of this awkward position. But many felt that a marginal utility explanation of money demand would simply be a circular argument: We need to explain why money has a certain exchange value on the market. It won't do (so these economists thought) to merely explain this by saying people have a marginal utility for money because of its purchasing power. After all, that's what we're trying to explain in the first place—why can people buy things with money?

Mises eluded this apparent circularity by his regression theorem. In the first place, yes, people trade away real goods for units of money, because they have a higher marginal utility for the money units than for the other commodities given away. It's also true that the economist cannot stop there; he must explain why people have a marginal utility for money. (This is not the case for other goods. The economist explains the exchange value for a Picasso by saying that the buyer derives utility from the painting, and at that point the explanation stops.)

People value units of money because of their expected purchasing power; money will allow people to receive real goods and services in the future, and hence people are willing to give up real goods and services now in order to attain cash balances. This expected future purchasing power of money explains its current purchasing power.

But haven't we just run into the same problem of an alleged circularity? Aren't we merely explaining the purchasing power of money by reference to the purchasing power of money?

No, Mises pointed out, because of the time element. People today expect money to have a certain purchasing power tomorrow, because of their memory of its purchasing power yesterday. We then push the problem back one step. People yesterday anticipated today's purchasing power, because they remembered that money could be exchanged for other goods and services two days ago. And so on.

So far, Mises's explanation still seems dubious; it appears to involve an infinite regress. But this is not the case, because of Menger's explanation of the origin of money. We can trace the purchasing power of money back through time, until we reach the point at which people first emerged from a state of barter. And at that point, the purchasing power of the money commodity can be explained in just the same way that the exchange value of any commodity is explained. People valued gold for its own sake before it became a money, and thus satisfactory theory of the current market value of gold must trace back its development until the point when gold was not a medium of exchange.*

The two great Austrian theorists Carl Menger and Ludwig von Mises provided explanations for both the historical origin of money and its market price. Their explanations were characteristically Austrian in that they respected the principles of methodological individualism and subjectivism. Their theories represented not only a substantial improvement over their rivals, but to this day form the foundation for the economist who wishes to successfully analyze money.

---

*Notice that fiat moneys have always emerged through their initial ties to commodity moneys. For example, we can trace back the purchasing power of U.S. dollar bills until the point when the notes were redeemable in gold or silver, and at that point we need merely explain the purchasing power of gold and silver.

Robert P. Murphy has been a summer fellow at the Ludwig von Mises Institute and now teaches economics at Hillsdale College. This essay was posted on www.mises.org on Sept. 29, 2003.

ADDENDUM XII

The Worst Scandal in Our History
BY JAMES RONALD KENNEDY AND
WALTER DONALD KENNEDY

The fraudulent methods used to enact the Fourteenth Amendment were the subject of a two-page editorial in the September 27, 1957 (republished January 26, 1970), issue of *U.S. News and World Report*. David Lawrence, editor, openly admitted that "no such amendment was ever legally ratified."

The editorial noted that the Fourteenth Amendment was the legal excuse used by the Supreme Court in its various "desegregation decisions." As we have already noted: It is these Reconstruction acts that have been repeatedly used by the Northern-controlled liberal government to impose and re-impose various forms of Reconstruction upon the Southern people.

David Lawrence noted that to achieve its purpose the Northern Congress:

1. Expelled the South from Congress (an open and flagrant violation of Section V of the U.S. Constitution).

2. Illegally used military forces to occupy peaceful states (remember, the war was over and new civil state governments had been established and their representatives and senators sent to Congress).

3. Disfranchised a large portion of the population (i.e., those who had supported the Confederate government—a violation of the constitutional prohibition against the enactment of *ex post facto* law).

4. Declared that no Southern state could have its seats back unless such state ratified the Fourteenth Amendment (i.e., forced ratification).

5. Counted as ratifying the Fourteenth Amendment the states of Ohio and New Jersey, both of which had rescinded their ratifications. In addition, the Oregon legislature rescinded its ratification

three months later due to the "illegal and revolutionary" methods used by the proponents of enactment.

According to David Lawrence, the history of the Fourteenth Amendment "is a disgrace to free government," but he reminds us, "it is never too late to correct injustice."

This addendum was originally published in Kennedy and Kennedy, *The South Was Right!*, 375-76. Here we see that a major American news journal took an editorial stand in support of the claim that the federal government used fraudulent methods to enact the Fourteenth Amendment. Of course, the Yankee mythmakers have done a great job in making sure that these facts are kept out of public sight.

ADDENDUM XIII

Secession

BY WALTER DONALD KENNEDY

A Northern View

*The secession of a state from the Union depends on the will of the people of
that state. The people alone . . . hold the power to alter their constitution.*
—William Rawle[1]

Secession, poke salad, and crackling bread, in modern America,
are viewed with the same skeptical eye. Anyone advocating even the
study of the *right* of secession is viewed as an eccentric at best or a
radical neo-Confederate at worst. Yet there was a time in the early
days of this republic when the right of secession of an American
state was fully embraced by the vast majority of Americans. Although
secession, poke salad, and crackling bread are associated with the
South, only the latter two, delights of Southern cuisine, can be said
to be fully Southern. In modern America, secession is inextricably
linked with the Southern Confederacy, yet a study of the right of
secession will show us more about what our Founding Fathers of
1776 wrought and less about the Confederacy and the "Civil War."

A casual perusal of the early constitutions of Northern states
demonstrates that these early Americans viewed their states as sovereign entities within a federation of states. For example, consider how
the state of New Hampshire describes her political existence: "The
people of this state have the sole and exclusive right to governing
themselves as a free, sovereign, and independent state."[2] Four years
after the adoption of the federal Constitution, New Hampshire bold-
ly proclaims to the world her sovereign right to rule herself. The people of New Hampshire go even further by declaring that they have

---

1. William Rawle, *A View of the Constitution* (1825; reprint, ed. Walter D. Kennedy
and James R. Kennedy, Simsboro, La.: Old South Books, 1993), 238.
2. New Hampshire State Constitution, 1792, Article VII.

the right to "establish a new government" at their own volition: "Whenever the ends of government are perverted, or public redress are ineffectual, the people may, and of right ought to, reform the old, or establish a new government. The doctrine of non-resistance against arbitrary power, and oppression, is absurd, slavish, and destructive of the good and happiness of mankind."[3] Thus, according to the people of New Hampshire in 1792, nonresistance to arbitrary power is "absurd." That which was true in 1792 was equally true in 1861 and remains true today—that is, it is absurd to think that a free people would offer nonresistance to arbitrary power.

Other Northern states were equally opposed to the arbitrary abuse of power by the central government. Twelve years before New Hampshire's declaration of state sovereignty, Massachusetts proclaimed: "The people of this commonwealth have the sole and exclusive right of governing themselves, as a free, sovereign and independent State."[4]

These are two representative samples of the people of Northern states affirming their belief in state sovereignty and real states' rights. Even after the adoption of the federal Constitution, the people of Northern states maintained the view that each state was a free and independent commonwealth within the federal union. Thus, when in 1825 Mr. William Rawle of Philadelphia published his textbook on the United States Constitution, which included information on how and under what circumstances a state could secede from the union, no national outcry was heard. Mr. Rawle, a Northerner, abolitionist, and friend of both Pres. George Washington and Benjamin Franklin, was merely restating a recognized fact in early American history. Lincoln and the Radical Republicans conveniently forgot this fact thirty-five years later.

One year after its publication, Mr. Rawle's textbook was reviewed by the eminent Boston journal, *North American Review.* Surely, if secession is un-American, seditious, or treasonous, the good folks in Boston would be more than happy to share that knowledge with the rest of the nation. Yet in a review of over 1,900 words, this textbook, which advocates the right of secession by a state within the federal union, was blessed by the *North American Review* with the following comment: "For those, who are desirous of studying the noblest monument to human wisdom, the Constitution of the United States, we recommend the treatise of Mr. Rawle as a safe and intelligent

---

3. Ibid., Article X.
4. Massachusetts State Constitution, 1780.

guide."[5] Note that these Yankees not only failed to write one negative word about Mr. Rawle asserting the right of secession, but they
go further by stating that Rawle's textbook is a "safe and intelligent
guide." This textbook was the same one used at the United States
Military Academy at West Point, both as a textbook and a reference
book for the study of the United States Constitution.

From the first chapter to the last chapter of his textbook, Mr. Rawle
advocates the view that the states were the prime movers in the formation of the federal government. That is, the states existed before the
formation of the federal government and were the sole source of any
power the federal government possessed. Commenting upon the very
first paragraph of the Constitution (Article I, Section I), Rawle states:
"The first paragraph evinces that it [the federal government] is a limited, and not a general government. The term 'all legislative powers
hereby granted,' remind both the congress and the people of the existence of some limitation." The very act of "granting" demonstrates the
action of a superior (the people of the Sovereign States) to an inferi-
or (the federal government). This is just one of many examples of Mr.
Rawle's defense of a strict construction view of the Constitution.

The chapter titled "Of the Union" forms the grand finale of Mr.
Rawle's book. It is in this chapter that Mr. Rawle takes off his gloves
and, without reservation or equivocation, states that secession is the
natural right of a free people. As Mr. Rawle states, "to deny this right
would be inconsistent with the principle on which all our political
systems are founded, which is, that the people have in all cases, a
right to determine how they will be governed."[6] Here, Mr. Rawle is
directing his readers back to the Declaration of Independence. In
1776 the Founding Fathers asserted that the right of freemen to live
under a government of their choice was an unalienable right. It is
granted to man from God and therefore, no government, no king,
no battle won or battle lost could negate that which God had granted. True, a tyrant or a tyrannical system could deny a people the
right to life and free government, but tyrants do not destroy those
principles that are "unalienable." Anyone in the past, present, or
future who declares his opposition to this American principle of government—that is, *government by the consent of the governed*—is making
the ultimate *un*-American statement.

The constitutions of early Northern states and the words of Mr.
William Rawle of Pennsylvania stand in sharp contrast to the view of

5. *North American Review* 22 (1826; reprint, New York: AMS Press, 1965): 450.
6. Rawle, *A View of the Constitution*, 235.

the Radical Republicans in 1861. Also, the Chicken Littles of today who run and hide anytime the issue of the right of secession is broached should be seen for what they have become—true chickens. The South was right in 1861 and, as the Declaration of Independence so clearly states, she is *still* right! To deny this right is, as Mr. Rawle so correctly noted, "inconsistent with the principle on which all our political systems are founded."

If true American freedom is ever to be revived, we cannot play the part of Chicken Little nor keep company with those who insist the sky is falling every time the subject of the right of secession, i.e., "government by the consent of the governed," is broached. Chicken Little is fit only to live in Colonel Sanders' chicken house. A chicken house is not a fit place for freedom-loving people. As for me, I choose freedom—*real* American freedom. The freedom Mr. Rawle, a Northerner, wrote about is the same freedom that Northern states codified in their constitutions, the freedom won for us by our colonial forefathers and defended for us by our Confederate forefathers. I will not be afraid or ashamed of the right of secession, because it is the very cornerstone of *real* American freedom.

A Southern View

If the bond of union be the voluntary consent of the people, the government may be pronounced to be free; where constraint and fear onstitute that bond, the government is no longer the government of the people, and consequently they are enslaved.

—St. George Tucker[7]

As I explained in the first part of this review of the issue of secession, the right of government by the consent of the governed is not just a Southern idea. The Declaration of Independence, the early constitutions of Northern states, and a noted Northern constitutional authority confirm the right for freemen to alter or abolish their government. Therefore, with great authority I can state that the right of secession, which is a function of freemen acting to "alter or abolish" the government they live under, is a central theme of *American* political philosophy. For the first few decades of these United States, the concept of state sovereignty bolstered the idea of secession as a right of the people of an American state. Although viewed as an almost

7. St. George Tucker, as cited in Clyde N. Wilson, ed., *A View of the Constitution of the United States, with Selected Writings* (1803; reprint, Indianapolis: Liberty Press, 1999), 27.

exclusively Southern idea today, as has been demonstrated, the right of secession of an American state from the union is very American.

If Mr. Rawle is viewed as the representative of Northern advocates of the right of secession, Mr. St. George Tucker of Virginia should be viewed as Rawle's Southern counterpart. Tucker's *View of the Constitution of the United States,* published as part of his edition of Blackstone's famed *Commentaries on the Laws of England,* was released in 1803, making Tucker one of the first commentators on the federal Constitution.

Tucker's distinguished military career during the War for Independence established him as an American patriot. After independence, he continued his patriotic service as a delegate to the Annapolis Convention, which was responsible for the calling forth of the Philadelphia Constitutional Convention. During this time Tucker taught law at William and Mary College and served as a judge on Virginia's highest court. As a distinguished patriot, jurist, and author, Tucker's advocacy of the right of secession cannot be disregarded. His theory of state's rights has given much grief to those who advance the bankrupt notion that secession was the brainchild of rabid Southern slaveholders. Tucker of Virginia, like Rawle of Pennsylvania, was a strong opponent of the institution of slavery. Tucker evens goes beyond Rawle by advocating ending discrimination against free people of color. More than one hundred and fifty years before the modern Civil Rights movement, we see a Southern abolitionist pointing out areas of American life that he views as restricting the liberty of Americans. Yet this man is a proponent of the right of secession, i.e., government by the consent of the governed.

According to Tucker, the glue that binds a union of *free* men together is the free choice, i.e., consent, of those people who are being governed. Free men have the right to consent to the government they live under; un-free men (slaves) do not have that choice. According to Tucker (see above citation), with the removal of consent, freedom is destroyed and slavery becomes the condition of a once free people. Now reconsider what Lincoln did to these (once free) United States of America. According to Tucker, by destroying consent and replacing it with coercion (the point of a bloody bayonet), Lincoln reduced *every* American, regardless of color, from freedom to slavery. As Tucker notes, when "constraint and fear" hold a union together, the people "are enslaved." This should be a sobering thought for all Americans, including the Chicken Littles who run and hide at the mention of the right of secession.

By their very definition, free governments are bound by the will of freemen. A union that tramples upon the will of freemen cannot be said to be a "free" government any longer. In these United States, the will of the people has been linked to and voiced by the people of the Sovereign States. The signing of the Declaration of Independence, the adoption of the first government under the Articles of Confederation, the secession from the Articles of Confederation, and the accession to the union under the federal Constitution were all actions of freemen done by the authority of "we the people" of the Sovereign States. Given the history of secession in early America, is it any wonder that Tucker states: "It then becomes not only the right, but the duty of the states respectively, to throw off such government, and to provide new guards for their future security. To deny this, would be to deny to sovereign and independent states, the power which, as colonies, and dependent territories, they have mutually agreed they had a right to exercise, and did actually exercise."[8]

Both Rawle and Tucker agree that free government is destroyed when and if the right of government by the consent of the governed is denied. Thomas Jefferson, the primary author of the Declaration of Independence, and James Madison, the Father of the Constitution, agree with Mr. Rawle and Mr. Tucker's view of state sovereignty. In the Kentucky Resolutions of 1798, Jefferson states: "That the several states composing the United States of America, are not united on the principle of unlimited submission to their general government . . . That to this compact [union] each state acceded as a state . . . That the government created by this compact was not made the exclusive or final judge of the extent of the powers delegated to itself." Likewise, James Madison, in the Virginia Resolutions of 1798, states: "In case of a deliberate, palpable, and dangerous exercise of other powers not granted by the said compact [Constitution], the States, who are the parties thereto, have the right, and are duty bound, to interpose for arresting the progress of the evil, and liberties appertaining to them."

At this point two things should become clear. First, secession is not a Southern idea or scheme, and second, the right of secession and secession itself are not un-American or unpatriotic. The *unalienable* right to "alter or abolish" the government we live under is enshrined in the most basic and fundamental document of American history, the Declaration of Independence. Until men such as Joseph Story, Daniel Webster, and Abraham Lincoln came along, state sovereignty,

8. Ibid., 86.

state's rights, and secession were viewed as American rights. Lincoln, his sycophants, and Appomattox changed the view of state sovereignty and, as a consequence, turned these United States upside down.

Secession: A Modern View

> *The first thing I have at heart is American* liberty;
> *the second thing is American union.*
>
> —Patrick Henry[9]

Patrick Henry understood something many Americans today have trouble understanding, that is, form without substance is meaningless. "The first thing I have at heart is American *liberty.*" With this statement Mr. Henry points out that the true meaning of being an American comes from the blessings of liberty. Putting it bluntly, as Americans, we embrace the idea that in our system of government, "liberty trumps everything." If liberty comes first, what comes second? According to Mr. Henry, "the second thing is American *union.*" Ah, the contrast between Mr. Henry's and Mr. Lincoln's views of the federal union could not be more pronounced. Mr. Lincoln's view proclaims that any American liberty may be sacrificed in order to preserve the union. Mr. Henry's view places liberty first and the federal union second.

Today, the United States of America reflects Lincoln's model and rejects Patrick Henry's model of American union. This is more than just a historical fact or a footnote to American political philosophy. For all Americans there are real and deleterious consequences from the imposition of Lincoln's view of government over Henry's. Today, the federal government, unrestrained by any power other than itself, has become an "autocratic" government. America's citizens cannot resist federal edicts without facing the dire prospect of federal prison. This is the natural consequence of placing the American union *first* and American liberty *second.*

As an example of just how intrusive and belligerent the federal government has become vis-à-vis a citizen's private property, consider the federal government's "glancing geese" wetlands policy. According to Washington bureaucrats, if a flock of geese glances down upon your property, spies a body of water, and *thinks* about landing on that property, your land then falls under the control of the federal government. You may not improve, change, or otherwise use your property without

9. Patrick Henry, as cited in William Wirt Henry, ed., *Patrick Henry: Life, Correspondence, and Speeches*, vol. 3 (1891; reprint, Harrisonburg, Va.: Sprinkle Publications, 1993), 449.

first obtaining *federal* permission. I can bear witness to the fact that these rules also hold true for beavers and their dam projects!

If the abuse of federal power were limited only to the use and ownership of private lands, that would be enough to ignite a firestorm from patriots like Henry, Washington, Jefferson, and Madison. But as the old adage states, "power corrupts and absolute power corrupts absolutely." Without the check and balance of true federalism, that is, a system of balance between the state and federal governments where the abuses of the federal government can be challenged and defeated by *we the people* of the Sovereign States, all American liberty is in danger.

Today, the average American worker will have to work four to six months just to earn enough money to pay his yearly taxes; his children are the property of the federal government's courts and will be bused to and placed in schools as the federal government deems necessary; common laws of decency, which protect his family from all forms of pornography including sodomy, are being overturned by federal courts; and God, the Bible, and the Ten Commandments are being ejected from his state by the federal government. Is there anyone so simpleminded who would think that Henry, Jefferson, and Madison would agree with and submit to this type of federal government? According to Jefferson, Madison, Tucker, and Rawle, among many other patriots, one of the prime rights of a state is the authority to judge for itself how long it would remain in the federal union. Do the Chicken Littles, who run and hide at the mention of the right of secession, honestly believe that Judge Roy Moore's Ten Commandments would have been removed from the Alabama Supreme Court Building if the people of these United States believed in the right of secession?

Yet, because of the destruction of state's rights, that is, the right of secession, our freedom today is nothing more than a grant to us from the federal government. Unlike our ancestors who believed that our freedom was a grant from God, today's Americans are apt to naively accept the idea that our rights and freedom are a *grant* from the government. If the federal government is to be the guardian of our freedom, then "who shall guard the guards?"

The right of secession is *the* guardian of our freedom from federal abuse. At this point every American needs to voice the words placed upon the Confederate battle flag of Company F, Fifth South Carolina Volunteer Infantry, Kings Mountain: "Like our Ancestors, We shall be Free." Once *real* state's rights have been restored, like our ancestors, we will be free!

Recommended Reading

Bastiat, Frederic. *The Law.* 1850. Reprint, Irvington-on-Hudson, N.Y.: Foundation for Economic Education, 1979.

Bradford, M. E. *Original Intentions: On the Making and Ratification of the United States Constitution.* Athens: University of Georgia Press, 1993.

Callahan, Gene. *Economics for Real People: An Introduction to the Austrian School.* Auburn, Ala.: Ludwig von Mises Institute, 2002.

DeRosa, Marshall L. *The Confederate States Constitution of 1861.* Columbia: University of Missouri Press, 1991.

———. *The Ninth Amendment and the Politics of Creative Jurisprudence.* New Brunswick, N.J.: Transaction, 1996.

DiLorenzo, Thomas J. *The Real Lincoln.* New York: Three Rivers, 2003.

Gordon, David, ed. *Secession, State and Liberty.* New Brunswick, N.J.: Transaction, 1998.

Kennedy, James Ronald, and Walter Donald Kennedy. *The South Was Right!* Gretna, La.: Pelican, 1994.

———. *Was Jefferson Davis Right?* Gretna, La.: Pelican, 1998.

———. *Why Not Freedom! America's Revolt Against Big Government.* Gretna, La.: Pelican, 1995.

Kennedy, Walter D. *Myths of American Slavery.* Gretna, La.: Pelican, 2003.

Mises, Ludwig von. *Human Action: A Treatise on Economics.* 1949. Reprint, Auburn, Ala.: Ludwig von Mises Institute, 1998.

Quirk, William J., and R. Randall Bridwell. *Judicial Dictatorship.* New Brunswick, N.J.: Transaction, 1995.

Rockwell, Llewellyn H., ed. *The Economics of Liberty.* Auburn, Ala.: Ludwig von Mises Institute, 1990.

———. *The Gold Standard: Perspectives in the Austrian School.* Auburn, Ala.: Ludwig von Mises Institute, 1992.

Rothbard, Murray N. *America's Great Depression.* 5th ed. Auburn, Ala.: Ludwig von Mises Institute, 2000.

———. *The Case Against the Fed.* Auburn, Ala.: Ludwig von Mises Institute, 1994.

———. *The Case for a 100 Percent Gold Dollar.* 1962. Reprint, Auburn, Ala.: Ludwig von Mises Institute, 2001.

————. *For a New Liberty: The Libertarian Manifesto.* 2nd ed. New York: Collier Books, 1978.

————. *What Has Government Done to Our Money?* Auburn, Ala.: Ludwig von Mises Institute, 1963.

Wilson, Clyde. *The Essential Calhoun.* New Brunswick, N.J.: Transaction, 1992.

————. *From Union to Empire: Essays in the Jeffersonian Tradition.* Columbia, S.C.: Foundation for American Education, 2003.

Bibliography

BOOKS

Bastiat, Frederic. *The Law.* 1850. Reprint, Irvington-on-Hudson, N.Y.: Foundation for Economic Education, 1979.

Bresiger, Gregory. *The Revolution of 1935: The Secret History of Social Security.* Auburn, Ala.: Ludwig von Mises Institute, 2002.

Callahan, Gene. *Economics for Real People: An Introduction to the Austrian School.* Auburn, Ala.: Ludwig von Mises Institute, 2002.

Friedman, Milton. *Free to Choose.* New York: Harcourt Brace Jovanovich, 1979.

Hall, Kermit L., ed. *The Oxford Companion to the Supreme Court of the United States.* New York: Oxford University Press, 1992.

Himmelstein, David, Steffie Woolhandler, and Ida Hellander. *Bleeding the Patient.* Philadelphia: Common Courage, 2001.

Kennedy, James Ronald, and Walter Donald Kennedy. *The South Was Right!* Gretna, La.: Pelican, 1994.

———. *Was Jefferson Davis Right?* Gretna, La.: Pelican, 1998.

———. *Why Not Freedom! America's Revolt Against Big Government.* Gretna, La.: Pelican, 1995.

Kennedy, Walter D. *Myths of American Slavery.* Gretna, La.: Pelican, 2003.

McDonald, Forrest. *A Constitutional History of the United States.* Malabar, Fla.: Kriger, 1982.

McWhiney, Grady. *Cracker Culture: Celtic Ways in the Old South.* Tuscaloosa: University of Alabama Press, 1988.

Mises, Ludwig von. *Human Action: A Treatise on Economics.* 1949. Reprint, Auburn, Ala.: Ludwig von Mises Institute, 1998.

Murray, Charles. *Losing Ground: American Social Policy 1950-1980.* New York: BasicBooks, 1984.

O'Brien, David M. *Constitutional Law and Politics, Civil Rights and Civil Liberties.* Vol. 2, 2nd ed. New York: W. W. Norton, 1995.

Olasky, Marvin. *The Tragedy of American Compassion.* Washington, D.C.: Regnery, 1992.

Quirk, William J., and R. Randall Bridwell. *Judicial Dictatorship.* New Brunswick, N.J.: Transaction, 1995.

Rockwell, Llewellyn H., ed. *The Economics of Liberty.* Auburn, Ala.: Ludwig von Mises Institute, 1990.

Rothbard, Murray N. *America's Great Depression.* 5th ed. Auburn, Ala.: Ludwig von Mises Institute, 2000.

———. *The Case Against the Fed.* Auburn, Ala.: Ludwig von Mises Institute, 1994.

———. *The Case for a 100 Percent Gold Dollar.* 1962. Reprint, Auburn, Ala.: Ludwig von Mises Institute, 2001.

———. *Education Free and Compulsory.* Auburn, Ala.: Ludwig von Mises Institute, 1999.

———. *For a New Liberty: The Libertarian Manifesto.* 2nd ed. New York: Collier Books, 1978.

———. *What Has Government Done to Our Money?* Auburn, Ala.: Ludwig von Mises Institute, 1963.

Rummell, Rudolph J. *Death by Government.* New Brunswick, N.J.: Transaction, 1994.

ARTICLES FROM INTERNET SITES

Adams, Charles. "Taxes in America." www.mises.org/freemarket_detail.asp?control=297&sortorder-articledate, June 12, 2003.

Anthony, Robert A. "Unlegislated Compulsion: How Federal Agency Guidelines Threaten Your Liberty." www.cato.org, May 12, 2002.

Bresiger, Gregory. "The Disastrous Deal of 1972." www.mises.org, May 12, 2002.

———. "The Discourteous Mr. Walker." www.mises.org, Sept. 24, 2003.

———. "The Forgotten Payroll Tax." www.mises.org, Oct. 16, 2003.

Bureau of Economic Analysis. www.bea.gov/bea/regional/spi/drill.cfm, Aug. 12, 2003.

Corrigan, Sean. "Say's Law for Our Time." www.mises.org, Sept. 5, 2002.

de Rugy, Veronique. "The Latest IRS Scare Campaign." www.cato.org, Apr. 12, 2002.

DiLorenzo, Thomas J. "Regulation and the Stock Market." *Mises Daily Articles.* www.mises.org, Aug. 20, 2002.

www.drudgereport.com, Nov. 30.

Edwards, Chris. "Averting War Between the Generations." www.cato.org, Dec. 12, 2002.

———. "Top Ten Civil Liberties Abuses of the Income Tax." www.cato.org, May 12, 2003.

"Facts & Figures." www.cato.org/research/fiscal_policy/2002/factsfigs.html, May 12, 2003.

"Fiscal 2004 President's Budget, National Defense Topline (Function

050)." DoD News: Fiscal 2004 Department of Defense Budget Release. www.defenselinkmil/news/Feb2003/bo2032003_bt044-03.html, May 12, 2003.

Galles, Gary. "Less for Our 'Labor' Day?" www.mises.org, Sept. 2, 2002.

Hanke, Steve H. "A Hayekian Hangover." www.cato.org, July 12, 2002.

"Limited English Proficient (LEP)." Appendix A, Office for Civil Rights. www.hhs.gov/ocr/lep/appa.html, May 12, 2002.

MacKenzie, D. W. "Doubts about Recovery." www.mises.org, Oct. 8, 2003.

Mayer, Christopher. "Health Care for All." www.mises.org, June 10, 2003.

———. "The Imaginary Evils of Deflation." www.mises.org, Sept. 11, 2002.

Mingardi, Alberto. "Ten Books on the State." www.mises.org, Aug. 30, 2002.

Nastas, George, and Stephen Moore. "A Consumer's Guide to Taxes: How Much Do You Really Pay in Taxes?" Cato Institute Briefing Paper No. 15. www.cato.org, May 12, 1997.

O'Neill, June. "The Trust Fund, the Surplus, and the Real Social Security Problem." *The Cato Project on Social Security Privatization,* SSP No. 26, 2. www.cato.org, May 12, 2003.

"Patients or Paperwork? The Regulatory Burden Facing America's Hospitals." www.AHA.org, May 12, 2003.

Reisman, George. "The Stock Market, Profits, and Credit Expansion." www.mises.org, Aug. 2, 2002.

———. "What Is Interventionism?" www.mises.org, Sept. 10, 2003.

Rockwell, Llewellyn H., Jr. "Freedom Is Not 'Public Policy.'" www.mises.org, June 20, 2002.

———. "Is the Gold Standard History?" www.mises.org, Sept. 27, 2003.

———. "The Mises Institute: The Next 20 Years." www.mises.org, Oct. 20, 2002.

———. "War on Gougers?" www.mises.org, Feb. 24, 2003.

Samples, John, Christopher Yablonski, and Ivan G. Osorio. "More Government for All: How Taxpayers Subsidize Anti-Tax Advocacy." Cato Institute Policy Analysis No. 407. www.cato.org, May 12, 2002.

Sennholz, Hans F. "The Fed Is Culpable." www.mises.org, Nov. 12, 2002.

———. "Why Gold?" www.mises.org, March 6, 2003.

Shostak, Frank. "Can More Yen Save Japan?" www.mises.org, Sept. 25, 2002.

————. "The Supply-Side Gold Standard: A Critique." www.mises.org, June 27, 2002.

Slivinski, Stephen. "The Corporate Welfare Budget Bigger Than Ever." Cato Institute Policy Analysis. www.cato.org, May 12, 2002.

"Socialism vs. Market Exchange." *Mises Daily Articles*. www.mises.org, Aug. 15, 2002.

Stansel, Dean. "The Hidden Burden of Taxation: How the Government Reduces Take-Home Pay." Cato Institute Policy Analysis No. 302. www.cato.org, Apr. 15, 1998.

Tanner, Michael. "No Second Best: The Unappetizing Alternatives to Social Security Privatizing." *The Cato Project on Social Security Privatization*, SSP No. 4. www.cato.org, May 12, 2002.

————. "The Stamp Act Crisis: The First Defense of Freedom in America." The Center for the Advancement of Capitalism. www.moraldefense.com, May 12, 2002.

————. "The State of Hospitals' Financial Health." www.AHA.org, May 12, 2002.

"Total Federal Revenues, 1900-2003 (Percent of GDP)." www.cato.com, May 12, 2002.

Tucker, Jeffrey. "The Spoils of Victory." www.mises.org, Nov. 18, 2002.

Vassallo, Philip. "Empowering Parents Through School Choice." www.cato.org/dailys/10/20/00, May 12, 2002.

"Why the Fed Should Not Lower Rates." www.mises.org, Aug. 21, 2002.

Young, Adam. "A Retrospective on Johnson's Poverty War." www.mises.org, Dec. 31, 2002.

COLUMNS FROM INTERNET SITES

Buchanan, Patrick J. "Approaching Imperial Overstretch." www.wnd.com, July 21, 2003.

Malkin, Michelle. "Next: Get Rid of Racial Boxes." www.jewishworldreviw.com, Jan. 17, 2003.

Novak, Robert. "Enron's Corporate Welfare." www.suntimes.com, Apr. 29, 2002.

O'Reilly, Bill. "Racism in Public Education." www.worldnetdaily.com, May 30, 2001.

Schlafly, Phyllis. "Foreign Language Ballots Are a Bad Idea." www.eagleforum.org, Aug. 28, 2002.

Sobran, Joseph. "Why Wolves Rule." www.sobran.com/columns/, July 25, 2002.

Sowell, Thomas. "Abstract People." www.jewishworldreview.com/cols/sowell1asp, Jan. 28, 2002.

———. "Death Sentences." www.jewishworldreview.com, July 1, 2002.

———. "'Friends' of Blacks." www.jewishworldreview.com, Sept. 4, 2002.

———. "Hard Times for Envy." www.jewishworldreview.com, Jan. 20, 2003.

———. "India Unbound." www.jewishworldreview.com, July 12, 2001.

———. "Mondale's 'Experience.'" www.jewishworldreview.com, Nov. 5, 2002.

———. "Universal Health Care." www.jewishworldreview.com, May 6-8, 2003.

Williams, Walter. "American Contempt for Rule of Law." www.jewishworldreview.com/cols/williams1.asp, July 5, 2001.

———. "The Cost of Academic Integrity." www.jewishworldreview.com, Feb. 20, 2002.

———. "An Evil Racist Plot . . . " www.jewishworldreview.com, Jan. 31, 2001.

———. "Family Secrets." www.jewishworldreview.com, Nov. 20, 2002.

———. "A New Racist Strategy." www.jewishworldreview.com, Feb. 28, 2002.

———. "The Politics of Envy." www.jewishworldreview.com, Nov. 6, 2002.

———. "Threats to Rule of Law in America." www.jewishworldreview.com, June 5, 2002.

NEWSPAPERS

Chicago Sun-Times, Apr. 29, 2002.

Miami Herald, Dec. 1, 2000.

New Orleans Times-Picayune, Aug. 28, 2002.

New York Times, March 30, 1861.

Nurseweek, May 28, 2001.

Star Tribune, Dec. 21, 2001.

USA Today, Feb. 7, 2002.

USA Today Snapshots, March 13, 2003.

Wall Street Journal, March 1, May 12, and July 10, 1995; July 8 and Sept. 16, 1997; May 11 and Aug. 31, 1998; Dec. 18, 2001; March 1 and June 6, 2002; May 2 and Dec. 15, 2003.

Washington Times, June 27, 2002.

JOURNALS

National Review (May 20, 2002).

The Review of Austrian Economics 9, no. 2 (1996).

Southern Mercury 1, no. 3 and 5 (2003).

COURT CASES

Albemarle Paper Company v. *Moody,* 422 US 405 (1975).

Chamber of Commerce of the United States v. *OSHA,* 636 F2d 464, 470 (D.C. Cir 1988).

Griggs v. *Duke Power Company,* 401 US 424 (1971).

Miranda v. *Arizona,* 384 US 436 (1966).

MISCELLANEOUS

The Free Market 18, no. 4 (Apr. 2000).

AMA News (May/June 1998).

Index